Metaverse

by Ian Khan

Metaverse For Dummies®

Published by: **John Wiley & Sons, Inc.,** 111 River Street, Hoboken, NJ 07030-5774, www.wiley.com

Copyright © 2023 by John Wiley & Sons, Inc., Hoboken, New Jersey

Published simultaneously in Canada

For general information on our other products and services, please contact our Customer Care Department within the U.S. at 877-762-2974, outside the U.S. at 317-572-3993, or fax 317-572-4002. For technical support, please visit https://hub.wiley.com/community/support/dummies.

Wiley publishes in a variety of print and electronic formats and by print-on-demand. Some material included with standard print versions of this book may not be included in e-books or in print-on-demand. If this book refers to media such as a CD or DVD that is not included in the version you purchased, you may download this material at http://booksupport.wiley.com. For more information about Wiley products, visit www.wiley.com.

Library of Congress Control Number: 2022951804

ISBN 978-1-119-93387-8 (pbk); ISBN 978-1-119-93388-5 (ebk); ISBN 978-1-119-93389-2 (ebk)

SKY10043225_022023

Contents at a Glance

Table of Contents

PART 2: ENGAGING IN HOBBIES AND PERSONAL INTERESTS

Introduction

Metaverse For Dummies shows how the metaverse functions as just one part of a rapidly growing digital economy.

Thanks to the availability of the Internet, the emergence and consumption of new ideas and technologies take very little time. Take a minute and think about the early days of the Internet. It took at least a decade before the World Wide Web, as we know it, was being used commercially across the world.

Now consider the release and growth of smartphones, starting from the iPhone and others. Smartphones grew exponentially and, within a span of fewer than five years, were being used widely across the world.

The metaverse is now emerging and developing in an already developed marketplace where the essential building blocks are already available. These include high-speed microprocessors and memory, breakneck Internet speeds, high-definition graphics, and others. In this era, the metaverse is likely to develop much faster than we saw other technologies grow.

World-renowned futurist and pioneer Alvin Toffler said that "Technology feeds on itself," meaning that technologies give rise to other technologies, and at a faster pace. This is true for any innovative solution that emerges today and is accepted by the masses. The metaverse is such a thing.

This book is your guide to cool places to explore the metaverse, early metaverse successes, and emerging metaverse platforms — from what it is to what it can do to where it can go.

A countless number of my friends and acquaintances have been excited to see this book released. There is a lot of excitement about the first such reference manual being written about a complex and emerging technology that is impacting millions of people right now.

One thing I can guarantee as the author is that the metaverse domain will continue to change and meander through the needs of the era we live in. More investments into developing the metaverse will likely happen, more jobs will be created into niche faculties of the metaverse, new career paths for eager technology professionals will emerge in the metaverse and related industries, and more value creation through the metaverse is at the horizon of this exciting era. You, as a reader, are part of this exciting era, and I look forward to taking you on an insider journey to the metaverse through this book.

About This Book

This book covers the essentials and beyond to get you up to speed with the metaverse. Throughout *Metaverse For Dummies*, I describe how people are putting the metaverse to use in their personal and professional lives. I also describe what the future may hold for how individuals and businesses use this highly emerging technology.

Here are some advantages of find out about the metaverse from *Metaverse For Dummies:*

>> This book massively simplifies concepts that are usually complex.

>> I've written in an easy-to-understand way, with careful focus on keeping things simple.

>> The book covers many areas of the metaverse and, as such, forms a great comprehensive reference.

>> This book covers the personal *and* business side of the metaverse.

This book is an ideal starting point to see how you can get the most from your metaverse experience. The metaverse is changing daily, and new information, vendors, and platforms are constantly emerging. Staying on top of the metaverse means reading and learning constantly.

Within this book, you may note that some web addresses break across two lines of text. If you're reading this book in print and want to visit one of these web pages, simply key in the web address exactly as it's noted in the text, pretending as though the line break doesn't exist. If you're reading this as an e-book, you've got it easy — just click the web address to be taken directly to the web page.

Foolish Assumptions

In this book, I assume that you have very little knowledge about the metaverse. You also understand that, today, most people can't avoid technology touching their lives in some way or another. Your experience as a reader could be very little or extensive. You may use apps on your phone and tablet, or you may manage complex server farms. One thing is for sure: Your curiosity about the metaverse has brought you to this book, and you're in the right place.

Here are some other assumptions I make about you:

>> You may not have a background in technology, but you're familiar with the Internet and social media.

>> You're curious about technology in general and the metaverse in particular.

>> You want to either explore how you can use the metaverse for personal use or use it to enhance your career or business.

>> You may be an entrepreneur or leader who enjoys experimenting with and potentially championing new ideas within your organization or industry.

Icons Used in This Book

Throughout this book, icons in the margins highlight certain types of valuable information that call out for your attention. Here are the icons you'll encounter and a brief description of each.

TIP

The Tip icon marks tips and shortcuts that you can use to make your experience in the metaverse easier.

REMEMBER

The Remember icon marks information that's especially important to know. To siphon off the most important information in each chapter, just skim through these icons.

TECHNICAL STUFF

The Technical Stuff icon marks information of a highly technical nature that you can skip over if you're short on time.

WARNING

The Warning icon tells you to watch out! It marks important information that may save you headaches as you explore the metaverse.

FUTURECAST

The Futurecast icon highlights paragraphs where I put my "futurist cap" on and describe how the metaverse may be put to work in the real world. My ideas are based on my experience as a professional technology futurist, emerging technology consultant, educator, and creator of the Future Readiness Score, to name a few.

Beyond the Book

In addition to what you're reading right now, this book comes with a free access-anywhere Cheat Sheet that includes tips to help you prepare for the metaverse. To get this Cheat Sheet, simply go to www.dummies.com and type **Metaverse For Dummies Cheat Sheet** in the Search box.

Where to Go from Here

This book is not linear. You can turn to any chapter and read it from beginning to end, or you can read specific parts of chapters that answer questions you have today.

Here are some good places to start:

» Chapter 1 is where it all begins! This chapter paints a picture of what the metaverse is. It's a great place to start, regardless of your background and expertise.

» Chapter 6 lays out all current virtual reality (VR) headset models and what's available in the market. The chapter is not a buyer's guide — I don't rate the headsets — but it provides an overview of what's popular as of this writing.

» Chapter 12 is a great resource to understand the future of work and the role of the metaverse therein. It's a good place to start if you're curious about the future of work and you have some basic understanding of the metaverse.

1
Getting Started with the Metaverse

Chapter **1**

Making Sense of the Metaverse

This chapter introduces you to the history and development of the metaverse — from its early beginnings within personal computing to its evolution into a $2-trillion-plus industry in the next decade. Knowing where the metaverse started will be useful when connecting the dots between vendors, big tech, gaming, and other stakeholders. It'll also help you think more clearly about incorporating the metaverse into your organization's product strategy and in your personal life.

GOING "META" WITH TERMINOLOGY

The word *meta* has many connotations and meanings. Ancient Romans used *meta* to indicate a column or post, or a group of columns or posts, that marked the turns on a racetrack. The term also has meanings specific to chemistry and art. English uses the prefix *meta–* to indicate something that describes itself or another thing in an encompassing or more abstract way. If you work in marketing, web design, or another related field, for example, you may recognize the term *metadata,* which describes header and identifying information in a digital asset (such as a JPG image in which the metadata tells you when and where the picture was taken) or data packets or a web page identifier tag in web design.

The word *meta* may mean many things, but in the context of this book, the *metaverse* refers to virtual reality–based online worlds. Some of these worlds are gaming environments or online games, and others function more as online virtual places where you can do other activities such as meet people, learn new things, or simply hang out. And the types of virtual worlds you can find in the metaverse continue to expand and are likely to continue to evolve. This book covers many of these worlds and shows how they work.

In technology and pop culture, the word *meta* has been used to signify a positive change toward the future. Facebook CEO Mark Zuckerberg was so motivated by the possibility of the metaverse that he renamed Facebook *Meta.* So, if you come across the company name Meta, it's the former Facebook I'm referring to. Meta has its own metaverse world called Horizon Worlds, which I talk about throughout this book.

For the sake of the book, though, *metaverse* is the collection of the virtual worlds, and *Meta* is the company run by Zuckerberg.

Getting How the Metaverse Started

Much of how the metaverse works and what it feels like to use it is built on knowledge first gained by the gaming industry. Graphics technology, for example, affects how quickly images appear and move onscreen. The better your graphics card, the more colorful, detailed, and interactive the display can be without compromising a computer's performance. Computer game creators knew that what worked to power a Windows dialog box could also be used to power more picturesque and interactive gameplay. So, they used the same hardware advancements that helped the Windows operating system run smoothly and in color to enrich the visual experience of the games they developed without overheating their players' computers.

Similarly, virtual reality (VR) went mainstream in the 2010s. As VR headsets became more affordable and consumer-grade hardware began to make entry into the marketplace, gaming providers started designing games that would work with VR headsets and provide gamers with new experiences.

Metaverse-based VR worlds have taken a new direction. Part 2 of this book covers more about gaming in the metaverse. New metaverse worlds and providers are emerging, however, focused not only on gaming but also on other activities.

In this book, I take a deep look at existing and emerging metaverse worlds and how they're growing. I also look at how technology vendors are opening up these platforms for non-gamers, hobbyists, professionals, and others. There is also a push by other industries, such as high-end fashion, that are entering the metaverse. Part 3 of this book shows how businesses leverage the metaverse as an independent marketing channel either on its own or to complement existing "real-life" channels. In Part 4 of this book, you see how the metaverse can shape the future of collaboration and communication.

REMEMBER

The metaverse has its roots in gaming, but its potential applications reach far beyond gaming. This book covers the impact of the metaverse on health care, entertainment, professional services, and a number of other industries and professions.

Anticipating What's Ahead for the Metaverse

In terms of development, the metaverse today is where the Internet was in the early 1990s. The early Internet was shaped by new ideas, technologies, and ways of doing things. With the right investments, adoption, and usage, the Internet grew into the Internet we know today (for better or for worse, depending on who you ask!).

Similarly, the metaverse today provides an interesting place for many activities, but many of them are still in the early days of development, such as gaming, art exhibitions, group activities, hobby clubs, and others that have just started to develop and gain traction. The investment and attention put into building the metaverse over the next five to ten years will determine what the metaverse ultimately becomes and the value it creates.

The metaverse can help the real world by:

>> Serving as an opportunity to create economic value

>> Creating jobs and new professional opportunities

>> Creating new experiences

>> Connecting people and building communities

>> Adding value

Chapter 19 provides ten case studies that show how the metaverse is being used in the real world.

Bringing the Metaverse into Your Personal Life

What is the role of the metaverse in your personal life? Imagine you're spending time with your friends and family, your loved ones, and you aren't at work. Your role is different from when you're at work. What role can the metaverse play in this case?

In order to answer this question, you need to understand what you do in your personal life that's different from what you do at work. Today, with the emergence of technologies, smartphones, tablets, and ubiquitous Internet connectivity, the gap between the workplace and personal lives has slightly diminished. Today, with remote work and work from home, boundaries between being at work and being at home are sometimes blurry.

That said, you can use the metaverse as an avenue for learning, entertainment, and other aspects of life that have nothing or little to do with being at work. Here are some examples of how you may use the metaverse at home and in your personal life.

Finding entertainment in the metaverse

The metaverse is a conduit to a whole new world of entertainment. You can play online games, some of which are based on a network play and some in which you join a specific metaverse world and start engaging with others. You can also watch some of your favorite musicians and artists perform in the metaverse, attend concerts and performances, and attend major sports events. These avenues for entertainment are just the start. Turn to Part 2 for more about entertainment in the metaverse.

Getting fit with the metaverse

Special accessories can make metaverse fitness more engaging, so not surprisingly, the fitness industry is embracing the metaverse. You can join a fitness class or a specific group-fitness activity in the metaverse. Chapter 15 covers some of the fast-growing health and fitness areas in the metaverse and how you can get the most from them.

Learning in the metaverse

The metaverse is making learning more engaging. Maybe you have younger children who need to learn about a specific topic, or maybe you'd like to learn something new yourself.

If so, get your VR glasses and join a learning experience curated by a museum in the metaverse, or visit a far-off land such as New Zealand, which is promoting itself in the metaverse. You can find many options for learning about new things in the metaverse, and as organizations, providers, and other entities enter the metaverse, learning will catch up quickly.

From enabling remote learning to helping students experience learning in a 3D format, the future of education is likely going to be very experiential through the metaverse. Imagine being able to walk with virtual dinosaurs or fly with bees as they pollinate different flowers — everything is possible in VR!

To find out what learning can mean in the metaverse, check out Chapter 14.

Socializing in the metaverse

Fifty years ago, people met in social gatherings. In the 2000s, people met online in chat rooms. Now you can meet people in the metaverse when you engage in group activities, such as developing personal interests, hobbies, and professional networking. The next section, "Finding hobbies in the metaverse," and Chapter 9 cover finding hobbies in the metaverse.

As with social media, you may find that some of your friends are exclusively metaverse friends, and others may become friends you communicate with through other means — text, email, phone, social media, and so on. You may even choose to meet in real life.

Take precautions when taking your conversations in the metaverse into actual, physical life on planet Earth. Meet in a public places with other people around, in order to create a personal safety net. Turn to Chapter 3 for more on staying safe in the metaverse.

Finding hobbies in the metaverse

Hobbyists will find the metaverse interesting when they're able to find people with similar interests in the metaverse and ready to share their expertise, time, and enthusiasm for their hobbies.

As more and more people connect to each other in the metaverse, hobbyists will be able to create groups, forums, and perhaps new metaverse worlds focused on specific hobbies.

Think about meeting your journal writing group in the metaverse or attending the next LEGO Builders Club meeting in the metaverse. Anything is possible! Right now is a very early time in the development of the metaverse, and as a result, we have a lot to look forward to in terms of hobbyists leveraging it to its full extent.

See Chapter 9 for more about finding hobbies in the metaverse.

Using the Metaverse for Work

From small businesses and entrepreneurs to large enterprises, the metaverse can find its place in every nook and cranny of the work world and be a useful tool to perform a specific task. The metaverse can serve as a channel of engagement, to build a customer base, sell products, and even provide customer service.

In the public sector, governments can use the metaverse to change government experience and reduce friction between citizens' services and how governments deliver those services. Turn to Chapter 10 for some examples of how this is already happening and how some private and public sector entities are jumping on board to create better governance and value for citizens.

At a business level, a number of activities are emerging in the metaverse. In Chapter 4, I look at non-fungible tokens (NFTs), the retail industry, the emerging metaverse real estate, and perhaps the application of the metaverse for specific professionals.

If you were around when the Internet started growing exponentially, around the year 2000 and after, many new things were happening on the Internet, including

"Internet banking," where you could actually log in to your bank and check your balances (amazing!). Today, accessing a bank online or with an app is a feature most consumers expect. There was also a time when early Internet users were introduced to the ability to order something online and get it delivered by mail. Believe it or not, most people hesitated to buy anything online, but some experimented with it. Today e-commerce is a multi-trillion-dollar industry, and most people order things with an app without giving it a second thought.

TECHNICAL
STUFF

It's way too early for most people to even fathom how the metaverse will affect the workplace, but there are people who specialize in foresight and forecasting who can shed light on what the future may look like for work. Here are some ways the metaverse may be used for work:

>> **Customer service reps:** New careers will emerge that will need people to do specific jobs in the metaverse. Most of these could be customer service, customer relations, and meeting people.

>> **Metaverse designers:** Complex environments in the metaverse require a lot of brain work and creativity. Your skills will be needed if you can program, design, or imagine new worlds and ideas.

>> **Virtual offices:** We've heard about virtual offices in the real world, but virtual offices in the metaverse will host specialists who are experts in things such as NFTs and metaverse design.

>> **Teachers and instructors:** Are you a teacher or an instructor and do you want to build a following in the metaverse? The other avatars you see in the metaverse are people, too, and many of them may fall into your target audience. Future teachers will hold classes and teach new skills in the metaverse — everything from Spanish to how to create new 3D art.

>> **Meetings:** Many companies have started using the metaverse on an experimental basis to see its suitability for collaboration. This means hosting some meetings and creating employee collaboration opportunities in the metaverse.

If you're curious to see more about how the metaverse might affect your work experience, head over to Chapter 12.

Visiting a Metaverse World

So, how do you enter the metaverse or connect with one of the many VR worlds? The next few sections walk you through entering the metaverse for the first time.

Among the emerging metaverse worlds you can visit, some focus on gaming, some focus on meeting people, while others are trying to create new shopping and event experiences in the metaverse.

Accessing the metaverse

Accessing a metaverse world requires computer hardware and access devices such as a VR headset, that have enough capacity and computing power to be able to properly display graphics and provide an optimal metaverse experience.

For a typical metaverse world, you can use a browser such as Microsoft Edge, Google Chrome, or Firefox. Any of these browsers will be able to open the main page of the metaverse world you're trying to access.

This section provides the URLs (web addresses) to some of the most common metaverse worlds, some of which I cover in later chapters. To visit any of these metaverse worlds, type the URL exactly as shown into your browser address bar and press Enter.

Following is a general list of interesting places in the metaverse. These are popular metaverse VR worlds that can be accessed through a web browser in most cases, although some may ask you to exclusively have a VR headset.

WARNING

Enter the URL into your web browser exactly as written in the following table. Depending on your browser settings, you may or may not get a warning that the website is unsafe. Proceed with caution if you do get this warning, or just don't go to the website, if you prefer. Things are constantly changing online.

Metaverse	URL
Bloktopia	www.bloktopia.com
Decentraland	https://decentraland.org
Horizon Worlds	www.oculus.com/horizon-worlds
Illuvium	http://illuvium.com
Roblox	www.roblox.com
The Sandbox	www.sandbox.game
Somnium Space	www.somniumspace.com
Voxels	www.voxels.com

There are hundreds of metaverse worlds you can visit online. The preceding list is a small representation of the popular metaverses. Chapter 2 describes in detail what each of these metaverse worlds offers.

Choosing a metaverse world to visit

When you're choosing which metaverse world to visit, consider what you want from your metaverse experience. Some metaverse worlds focus on gaming, and others may focus on activities such as visiting a museum in the metaverse or even attending a metaverse concept.

Think of visiting a metaverse world similar to browsing an online social network. Many social networks are available to choose from — Facebook, Twitter, Snapchat, TikTok, and others. Not all platforms are relevant for every person. Some people prefer to use Facebook to stay in touch with their friends or engage in a specific type of activity, such as hobbies, attending art and entertainment events, and more. Others prefer Twitter because it offers information in a different format with a different type of audience mix. When you choose which metaverse world to visit, consider matching your interests with what the metaverse offers.

Save time by knowing which metaverse world you want to visit and why before taking all the steps to join or create an account for it. Joining a metaverse platform takes effort and can be time-consuming — from creating an account or connecting your wallet to customizing your avatar. Browsing a metaverse platform and finding your place within the metaverse also takes time. Researching the suitability of a metaverse platform with your interests saves time in the long run. For an overview of metaverse platforms, turn to Chapter 2.

Setting up a metaverse profile

Every metaverse world requires users to create a profile. Like any other website or platform online that requires users to create a username and set a password, the metaverse is very similar. A common factor among all metaverse worlds here is the requirement to create a username and select a secure password.

To ensure the greatest possible security, use a different password for each of your metaverse world profiles. And of course, be sure that all your metaverse (and other) passwords are unique from the passwords you use for your email or banking website.

In some cases, you may also be able to use your Microsoft, Google, or Facebook account to log in without creating an account. This happens because of an agreement between these entities or single sign-on (SSO) or the fact that the metaverse is connected to one of these vendors. For example, to access Horizon Worlds, you need to use your Meta (previously Facebook) login, rather than create a new username and password. Horizon Worlds is part of Meta and doesn't require you to create a new username and password.

After you've created your username and password, you'll be able to further customize your profile with information such as your age and date of birth. You'll also select security questions and their answers and then create your first avatar, or the virtual you, for that metaverse.

Creating an avatar

An *avatar* in the metaverse can be defined as your visual representation within a metaverse. You may choose to represent yourself as a human figure, an animal, a cartoon character, or a superhero, or choose from hundreds of other options. You may also be able to customize your appearances such as changing your hair color, your height, eye color, and other aspects of your appearance.

You can also decorate your avatar or your virtual self using different clothes available on various metaverse worlds. Some leading fashion brands also offer digital clothes in which you can dress your avatar. Many fashion brands are also tapping into the metaverse and selling digital clothes for avatars. The world of avatars is undergoing exciting changes as it expands and connects with the world of fashion.

At this time, there's no way to use the same avatar across different metaverse worlds. For example, you can't use your metaverse avatar from Roblox on Horizon Worlds, or from the NVIDIA Omniverse on Decentraland and others. We're currently in the early development stages of the metaverse, though, so this may change.

TIP

You can always continue participating in your metaverse with a default avatar and come back to customize it later. No need to feel rushed!

Personalizing your experience

Experiences in the metaverse depend on a number of factors, including the metaverse world you're visiting. Each metaverse world offers its own experience. Horizon Worlds, for example, may offer proprietary games and activities, while Roblox may offer a completely different experience offering the ability to create your own games within a unique 3D graphic interface. As you participate in the metaverse world of your choice, personalizing your experience will be about choosing some parameters and options for your avatars.

Funding your metaverse account

Good news: You can buy things in the metaverse! As of this writing, what you can buy is mostly digital goods, digital art, digital clothes, and accessories for your metaverse avatar and other digital wares.

In order to purchase something in the metaverse, you need to fund your wallet on that specific metaverse. A full chapter on mastering money in the metaverse is coming up in Chapter 4, where I cover the essentials of money in the metaverse, funding your wallet, and buying and selling in the metaverse.

Funding your metaverse account will get you started with the world of cryptocurrencies. In Chapter 4, I go through the process of funding your metaverse account, also called a *wallet*, with a tiny amount of cryptocurrency, and converting that into a metaverse proprietary cryptocurrency. Different metaverses are accepting different cryptocurrencies. Some have created their own cryptocurrencies, which can be converted from U.S. dollars, British pounds, Canadian dollars, and other commonly used currencies.

There is a limit on which currency can be converted into cryptocurrency and ultimately used to fund your metaverse wallet. The reason for this is that cryptocurrency is currently not recognized by all monetary agencies worldwide and your bank may not allow you to convert your local currency into crypto. If this happens, don't be disappointed. You can still participate in many metaverses but your ability to buy digital goods may be limited.

Funding your metaverse account is a very simple and straightforward process. Funding the account will give you the ability to have a wallet through which you can purchase a digital product in the metaverse.

This book doesn't recommend or suggest you buy any product or service in the metaverse. The only reason I cover this subject is because of the crucial aspect of creating safe and secure buying and selling experiences in the metaverse, and to help you as a first-time metaverse participant to know the exact process of funding buying and selling. Your safety is my prime concern.

EVERYONE WANTS TO RULE THE METAVERSE

As the metaverse evolves, many new private- and public-sector entities are trying hard to lead the push to the metaverse. Meta has completely changed its organization focus and has renamed the company to reflect the seriousness of its focus on the metaverse. Governments are not behind. The government of the United Arab Emirates and the city of Dubai are making many first things in the metaverse happen. These include the world's first government office in the metaverse, the world's first wedding in the metaverse, and other trailblazing efforts.

In the end, the metaverse will become what people choose to put into it. It will offer the ability to communicate better if people create new and better ways to communicate in the metaverse. It will help with engagement if people create highly engaging experiences on it. With every technology, there is an adoption curve, and the metaverse will have one as well. The progression from early adopters to mass adoption takes time, as people lay the foundation of a metaverse that has appeal for the masses.

Cool places to visit in the metaverse

There are many cool places to visit in the metaverse. The following places are part of some of the metaverse worlds listed earlier, so you may need to log in to a metaverse to visit or experience these:

>> **Musee Dezentral, the world's first metaverse museum:**
    https://musee-dezentral.com/museum

>> **Metamall, the world's first metaverse mall:** https://metamalls.io

>> **MetaVegas, Las Vegas in the metaverse:** https://dreamlandxr.com/metavegas

>> **Metaverse Fashion Week:** https://metaversefashionweek.com/

TIP

Throughout this book, I mention many metaverses and provide links that you can access either with a computer browser or through VR headsets. Although you don't need to purchase a VR headset to experience the metaverse, having one will generally offer you a better experience.

IN THIS CHAPTER

» Exploring the experiences provided by popular metaverse platforms

» Anticipating how the metaverse may evolve

Chapter **2**

Investigating Metaverse Platforms

This chapter covers the most popular metaverse providers (as of this writing) and their metaverse platforms. Content in this chapter will change as new metaverse providers emerge, and metaverse worlds fade in and out of popularity. I suggest becoming curious about the metaverse and periodically checking your favorite tech websites and media platforms for the latest on what's changing in the metaverse. The upcoming sidebar, "Keeping up with the metaverse," lists some of my favorite tech websites that keep me well informed.

KEEPING UP WITH THE METAVERSE

TIP

The metaverse is growing at the speed of, well, the metaverse. Here are some of my favorite tech websites that help me keep a finger on new developments:

- **CoinDesk:** www.coindesk.com

- **Cointelegraph:** https://cointelegraph.com

- **Decrypt:** https://decrypt.co

(continued)

(continued)

- **Mashable:** https://mashable.com

- **TechCrunch:** https://techcrunch.com

- **TechRadar:** www.techradar.com

- **TNW:** https://thenextweb.com

- **VentureBeat:** https://venturebeat.com

- **The Verge:** www.theverge.com

- **Wired:** www.wired.com

Differentiating between Metaverse Platforms

The term *metaverse* refers to a general category of 3D worlds, mostly accessible with virtual reality (VR) headsets, that you visit and interact with in real time. Metaverse providers such as Decentraland, Horizon Worlds, The Sandbox, and many others have already created 3D worlds offering communities, entertainment, and a host of activities you can participate in with other users. In recent days, the metaverse has seen a high level of interest as cryptocurrencies and non-fungible tokens (NFTs) are being used for added experience delivery on most platforms. In this chapter, I cover the metaverse platforms that exist today, how they differ from each other, and the types of experiences available on a select few of them.

TECHNICAL STUFF

At the time of writing this book, more than 150 companies are building metaverse platforms.

When you browse the Internet, you look for websites that suit what you want to accomplish. Today the Internet is a place the majority of us visit to connect with friends, buy or sell goods or services, listen to music or watch a movie. You could be using the Internet to learn something new, attend classes, or book flights for your next vacation. Depending on what you need, you probably visit a host of different websites that get you where you want to go or help you accomplish your goals.

The metaverse is new and yet similar to the Internet. As with the Internet, when you "browse the metaverse," you choose the metaverse world that best suits the activity, or *experience*, you want to immerse yourself in. You may want to meet friends in your hobby group, learn something new, or enjoy a live concert by your favorite artist. The metaverse offers a wide range of activities and yet not all metaverse worlds are the same or identical.

The following sections describe the types of metaverse worlds currently available. The section "Future metaverse variations" considers what interacting with the metaverse could be like in the future.

Metaverse

Metaverse is a general term that describes a virtual 3D world where users can engage in activities. Just as we use the term *email* or *Internet* to define a general category of online tools, in a similar, way the metaverse is a very general category of a specific 3D world that has many levels of interactivity. *Metaverse* is used as a blanket term for various platforms and communities currently available and being developed within the framework of the metaverse. Specific communities and platforms provide different types of abilities to users, just like different social media platforms provide different experiences.

REMEMBER

The *metaverse* is the collection of all the different metaverse platforms that have been created. These platforms are of different shapes and forms, have different visual elements, and may offer different types of functionalities for their participants. The metaverse is ultimately a three-dimensional medium of communication or a channel. Within this channel, there are many elements. The most defining one is an artificially created 3D environment. Providers have created various 3D environments that are referred to as *metaverse platforms.* These platforms offer different levels of interactivity and experience. Some offer the ability to meet other users on the platform and engage in a game, while others offer the ability to collaborate on 3D design and industrial applications. The metaverse is just evolving and is at a very initial stage. There is a lot to look forward to!

Private and public metaverses

In the future, private and public versions of the metaverse will exist. I'm defining a *public metaverse* as a metaverse where anyone can register for an account and join the activities or engagement therein. Metaverse platforms that are available today and that I cover throughout this book are part of a public metaverse.

FUTURECAST

In addition to a public metaverse, the future may see *private metaverses* that house platforms for a specific member-based community. Participation in a private metaverse is likely to be enabled by an invite-only platform or accessible because the users are part of a group or have certain rights or privileges. For example, a professional group, university, or corporation may create its own metaverse platform to be used by its members or employees only.

Future metaverse variations

Future metaverse platforms can possibly have other variations as well. This could include a hybrid metaverse platform where members can create or belong to communities accessible on the public metaverse by members only, usually based on credentials or other criteria. These metaverse platforms may be hosted on private networks rather than public ones. Similar to a private cloud versus a public cloud environment, future metaverse platforms are likely to be niche-focused, private, and customizable.

As adoption of the metaverse grows, imagine being able to join platforms that are extremely selective when it comes to providing access — for example, a private metaverse for membership-based groups and communities where access to the masses is not a core mandate. Think about an alumni group, a niche skill member group, a high-performance athletic group, or a high-net-worth entrepreneur group, all of whom may create private metaverse platforms. Everyone can be part of the metaverse!

REMEMBER

Some of these concepts are extremely future-focused and may not even officially exist. People are creating new ground in the metaverse, and many terms and definitions will start to appear in the mainstream in the next few months and years.

Horizon Worlds

Horizon Worlds (shown in Figure 2-1) is a metaverse world created by Meta. It features entertainment, gaming, live shows, and celebrity appearances. As a product of Meta, Horizon Worlds naturally appeals to a wide range of users.

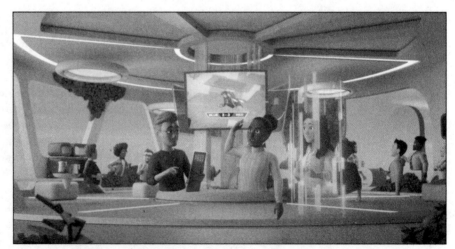

FIGURE 2-1:
Gaming on
Horizon Worlds.

As of late 2022, a collection of interesting experiences is available on Horizon Worlds:

>> **Social network:** Horizon Worlds serves as a social network where you can meet with friends, play games, work out as a group, or engage in activities such as creating a new world.

>> **Gaming:** You can play games, get into group gaming with others, and enter competitions. You can also compete, win rewards, and gain social status within the specific gaming environment by earning points.

TIP

Horizon Worlds currently features the largest number of games that can be played on a single metaverse platform. A reason for this is a thriving community of users on Meta — more than 3 billion users as of 2022, and the company's focus on making the metaverse the main area of user interaction going forward. Horizon Worlds also has first-mover advantage and has put extensive effort into attracting users to its metaverse platform. That said, you may find a more interesting game on another platform. Go explore!

>> **Fitness:** Horizon Worlds offers fitness classes, games, and other fitness apps that users can engage with, using the platform as a fitness companion.

>> **Entertainment:** Entertainment includes live concerts with celebrity performers, singers, and events worldwide. You can get access to front-row seats and watch your performers live.

Ultimately, you'll be able to use Horizon Worlds for entertainment or work. Meta is expanding the Horizon Worlds platform to offer workplace collaboration tools. This includes the ability to create virtual rooms in your workplace and meet with your colleagues and teammates in a virtual environment.

REMEMBER

Most experiences on Meta require the Meta Quest 2 headset. The headset connects to Horizon Worlds through your Meta account. For more on headsets, turn to Chapter 6.

NVIDIA Omniverse

NVIDIA is known for producing some of the best-regarded high-power graphics hardware. Furthering this work in the metaverse, NVIDIA has launched a new VR-based collaboration platform called the Omniverse (see Figure 2-2).

The Omniverse platform is best suited for designers of 3D and virtual objects, because it consists (or will consist) of a platform where activities mostly involve designing rather than entertainment. The Omniverse is an industrial metaverse, but it may host games in the future.

FIGURE 2-2:
The NVIDIA
Omniverse.

The Omniverse is a good fit for people who want to explore industrial design and other related items. NVIDIA has also announced that it's working on plans for creating the largest industrial metaverse through its industry partnerships with companies such as Siemens and Pixar.

The NVIDIA Omniverse will also help in game development to create ultra-realistic 3D models instead of becoming a gaming platform itself, at least according to announcements made thus far.

FUTURECAST

The Omniverse presents opportunities to consider how the metaverse might play a role in the future of work. With the Omniverse, NVIDIA is clearly forecasting more collaboration on 3D designs and has created a platform for creators to come together and collaborate. The Omniverse will allow designers to seamlessly collaborate in building 3D models, graphics, and real-time graphics processor unit (GPU) designs. Designers will be able to work together to design products, buildings, machine tools, and any other imaginable 3D design, such as those used in digital twins (covered in the nearby sidebar). NVIDIA is also collaborating with Pixar and using its Universal Scene Description (USD) technology, a new technology developed by Pixar that makes content creation easy.

Omniverse applications are accessible with a variety of VR headsets, although Omniverse games are only compatible with the HTC Vive HMD headset. For a full overview of the popular headsets currently available, see Chapter 6.

The technology offers an extensive level of improvement as compared to previous technologies used in graphics design. As a result, it can be used in other applications, including those used in architecture, robotics, manufacturing, and other complex design processes.

DIGITAL TWINS

In recent years, digital twins have become a popular option for manufacturers to create digital replicas of their products in VR. *Digital twins* are a digital representation of an existing industrial asset. This asset can be a turbine, a process plant, a refinery, or any other stand-alone machinery or combination of complex machinery.

Digital twins help in digitally stress-testing equipment and in simulating situations that would be too costly to conduct in real life. Digital twins are also being used to train staff in extremely difficult situations, such as training oil rig operators to operate complex machinery without flying them out to an actual oil rig.

Digital twins have become very popular in recent years and continue to grow. Manufacturers including BMW, Siemens Energy, and others have used NVIDIA technology to create digital twins of their products for applications in commercial and industrial use.

REMEMBER

The Omniverse is purely a business and development platform and is not a metaverse platform for entertainment. NVIDIA's partnerships with other companies such as Pixar and Siemens are enabling an industrial metaverse where accelerated graphics, artificial intelligence (AI), and AI-driven technologies will create a 3D virtual industrial metaverse platform.

Decentraland

Decentraland is one of the first metaverse platforms. It was launched in February 2020 and is owned by the Decentraland Foundation, a nonprofit. Most experiences on Decentraland include visiting areas within the platform, also referred to as *properties* or *lands*, owned by other users and experiencing what they've built.

Decentraland's Genesis Plaza is the first place where users land when they log in (see Figure 2-3).

Buying land parcels on Decentraland

As of this writing, Decentraland has 90,601 parcels of land that are privately owned by users. Each land parcel is also essentially an NFT. This means that each land parcel has a unique address, can't be forged, can't be duplicated on the platform, and has permanent rights allocated on a blockchain database.

FIGURE 2-3:
Decentraland's
Genesis Plaza.

To be able to buy and sell land on Decentraland, you need to have a MetaMask wallet account and have MANA to spend. MANA is Decentraland's proprietary cryptocurrency. MetaMask is something known as a cryptocurrency wallet that offers the ability to convert real-world money into a metaverse proprietary money, also known as cryptocurrency. You can find out all about different types of meta-verse money in Chapter 4. Decentraland users must first purchase the MANA token to buy digital assets, which may include virtual land in Decentraland and NFTs (such as apparel, collectibles, and digital art).

Here are the categories of land parcels found on Decentraland:

» **LAND (dark gray):** Privately owned parcels. These can be bought and sold through a crypto wallet on various marketplaces including Decentraland's own and the OpenSea platform.

» **Districts (purple):** These are themed communities and not for sale.

» **Plazas (large green squares):** These are not for sale and are community areas.

» **Roads (light gray and straight lines):** These are community pathways and not for sale.

Recognizing the types of Decentraland users

When you engage on Decentraland, you do so as one of two types of users: a cre-ator or a visitor.

Creators

Creators are users who buy a piece of virtual land (or LAND) and create experiences for other users, called *visitors*. At present, this includes a wide range of LAND owners, all of whom have various sizes of digital lands they've purchased on Decentraland and created experiences. Some of these include Chase Bank, Fidelity Investments, many fashion brands, and celebrities. So, what do these brands use the LAND for?

JP Morgan plans to use the land to build its own bank in the metaverse and use it primarily as a marketing driver.

Chase Bank is one of the first banks to open a presence in the metaverse. Its "lounge" in Decentraland features a digital portrait of the CEO, Jamie Dimon, greeting visitors, as well as a digital tiger that roams the branch. This is a great example of using the metaverse as a channel for creating public relations, marketing, and social media conversations. Although visitors in the Chase lounge can't do any real banking, they can feel the excitement and experience.

Visitors

Visitors visit the worlds created on the platform and engage in various activities and experiences. These could be entertainment, information, or games.

Finding entertainment on Decentraland

Decentraland has created a number of avenues for entertainment on its platform. As one of the largest metaverse platforms available today, Decentraland has managed to create several unique experiences. These include some of the following categories:

- >> **Arts and culture:** Art exhibitions, body paint parties, design contests, and more.
- >> **Competitions:** The ability to play games in the metaverse with friends and win prizes.
- >> **Education:** The ability to learn through courses provided by independent experts.
- >> **Gaming:** Group play and individual games.
- >> **Live performances:** The ability to attend live concerts and win NFT prizes.
- >> **TV and movies:** Providers such as Netflix are now working with Decentraland to have specific experiences for their upcoming films available on the platform.

Creating a Decentraland account

To participate in the Decentraland metaverse, you need to create an account with a crypto wallet. Chapter 4 covers crypto wallets in detail, but you really need them for just two purposes in Decentraland:

>> To create a way to securely authenticate your login credentials

>> To enable secure payments for any digital asset you may buy on the platform

As of this writing, Decentraland supports the following crypto wallets:

>> **Coinbase Wallet:** www.coinbase.com/wallet

>> **Fortmatic:** https://fortmatic.com

>> **MetaMask:** https://metamask.io

>> **WalletConnect:** https://walletconnect.com

The Sandbox

The Sandbox is a popular metaverse platform where users can play different types of games and buy land as an NFT (see Chapter 4). Sandbox is an Ethereum-based metaverse platform. This means that the proprietary token of Sandbox, MANA, is based on Ethereum protocols for authentication and exchange. It follows certain rules, and any data regarding its purchase or sale is stored on the Ethereum blockchain.

Users who own the land can develop it by creating games within their lands. Similar to Decentraland, The Sandbox provides options for gamification. It has more of a video game feel to it than Decentraland does.

Figure 2-4 shows a high-level map of the Sandbox platform, including virtual properties currently purchased and land available for sale. Zooming in will give you more details on what the pixels have on them, and further zooming in will take you to the virtual land itself.

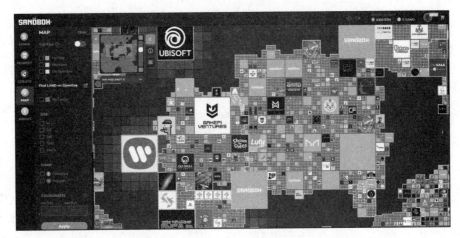

FIGURE 2-4:
A map of all properties currently created on the Sandbox platform.

Finding entertainment on the Sandbox

The Sandbox gained popularity as many celebrities and brands (including Snoop Dogg, Adidas, and others) purchased land parcels and started developing gamed experiences for visitors on them.

The Sandbox has teamed up with the Warner Music Group to bring entertainment experience to its metaverse. This includes having some popular artists such as Bruno Mars, The Black Keys, Cardi B, Ed Sheeran and Michael Bublé perform live on the Sandbox.

Sandbox plans to create live music experiences and entertainment and bring together artists and their fans on the platform. The Sandbox's partnership with Warner Music opens its doors to hundreds of different artists who are part of the Warner Music Group.

Catching a live experience at SandboxVR

Sandbox has created live experiences it calls SandboxVR at physical locations across select cities in North America. At SandboxVR, you can visit the facility and experience a gaming environment through VR glasses and accessories. This means you could play a character in a game and get your friends to join in the fun!

Creating a Sandbox account

You can create an account on the Sandbox in multiple ways, some of which require you to create a cryptocurrency wallet account and others of which use your Gmail or Facebook account. When creating an account through a crypto wallet, you aren't buying or selling anything in the metaverse or even purchasing any cryptocurrency — you're just creating an authenticated user account. The process is set up so that after you create your wallet account, you can use those credentials to create a Sandbox account.

Here are the steps to follow:

1. **Visit** www.thesandbox.game.

2. **Click the Create Account button.**

3. **Choose one of the following account opening options and follow the steps to create an account.**

   - **Coinbase Wallet:** You will need a Coinbase Wallet account, which you can create for free at www.coinbase.com/wallet. After the account is created, you can use your Coinbase account to log in to the Sandbox.

   - **WalletConnect:** Create your account at https://walletconnect.com. After you've created the account, you can use the WalletConnect login option to connect to the Sandbox.

   - **Single Sign On:** Log in through your Facebook, Twitter, or Google account. Click one of the options to log in to the Sandbox metaverse.

Voxels

Voxels is a Ethereum-based metaverse platform. Voxels consists of virtual land, roads, architecture, and other elements from the real world. Figure 2-5 shows a view of what this virtual world looks like.

Experiences on Voxels are primarily based around buying a piece of virtual land on the platform and developing it — creating games, organizing a concert, or even embedding audio or video on your land to make it into an entertainment venue.

Voxels is focusing more on the NFT side of the metaverse. (For more on NFTs, check out Chapter 4.) This means users are able to buy and sell NFTs. The platform has the look and feel of a gaming environment that looks like a city with roads and buildings organized into various districts.

FIGURE 2-5:
A view of
Voxels.

Somnium Space

Somnium Space, shown in Figure 2-6, promises a game world where the company itself has no ownership of any asset within the game. Somnium Space is based on Ethereum and Solana blockchain tokens and is focusing on player-led land parcels and in-game items.

FIGURE 2-6:
The Somnium
Space opening
page.

Experiences in Somnium Space

On Somnium Space, users will have the security of ownership of all assets and the ability to trade assets through decentralized marketplaces. Users will also have access to tools such as a software development kit (SDK) and a Somnium Space builder app that can help create your own virtual world within. With an authenticity of origin, the experiences are focused on creating a world with its own economy and currency. Users can build, trade, and play on a PC or through a dedicated VR device. Somnium Space promises a cross-browser game available on all major headsets. This means the platform will be available on all web browsers and will work with all VR headsets.

Here are some other aspects of the platform:

>> **Customizable PC client:** You can install the platform on your computer and customize some aspects of it.

>> **A forever Live mode:** User avatars can have perpetual lives.

>> **Based on blockchain technology:** Somnium Space offers strong encryption and data management capabilities.

>> **Virtual land ownership:** Users can own land on the platform.

>> **Scriptable world:** Scripting languages can be used to modify behaviors of avatars.

>> **Monetizable world:** You'll be able to monetize your land or sell goods and services.

Buying land in Somnium Space

Somnium Space held an initial land offering (ILO) in February 2019 in which parcels of land were made available for the public to buy. All parcels are connected to each other by roads within Somnium Space.

Land on Somnium Space is sold similar to the way it's sold in the real world. Land within the platform is available in square meters. You can buy parcels of land in the Somnium Space world in three parcel sizes:

>> **Small parcel:** 10 x 10 meters (approximately 33 x 33 feet)

>> **Medium parcel:** 25 x 25 meters (approximately 82 x 82 feet)

>> **Large parcel:** 50 x 50 meters (approximately 164 x 164 feet)

TIP

If you plan to buy land on any platform, a good strategy is to align your needs with a return on investment (ROI). You can find more on marketing in the metaverse in Chapter 11.

Doing business at the Somnium Store

The Somnium Store features more than 500+ custom-designed assets that include building parts and sounds that can be used by users. Users can also import 3D models from a 3D modeling software. The Somnium Store also features the ability for users to be able to sell their models and designs.

Somnium Cubes is the currency that works within Somnium Space. Somnium Cubes is a decentralized cryptocurrency that is interchangeable with other VR worlds. Find out more about money in the metaverse in Chapter 4.

Roblox

Roblox is one of the first metaverse games. It features a world where game players can create their own buildings, roads, and structures. Figure 2-7 shows a view from inside the platform.

Roblox allows users to create avatars with a variety of physical features and accessories. Users, particularly younger people, enjoy customizing their avatars. Fashion brands are also showing high interest in Roblox, because they can sell their digital avatar clothes and accessories.

Co-play and co-creation are two key parts of the overall Roblox design. Users are encouraged to play with other users. For this reason, the game has come under criticism for not being suitable for players under 12.

TIP

More than 40 million people play Roblox every day. This metaverse game has quickly scaled and is one of the most popular games available. As a popular platform, Roblox is one of the more heavily advertised spaces in the metaverse. It could be a good place for you to think about advertising your goods or services if the demographic matches your buyers. Check out Chapter 10 for more on business in the metaverse.

Creating an account on Roblox

Creating a new user account on Roblox is fast and simple. Visit `www.roblox.com` and sign up using the form on the home page. No credit card is required. Then download the Roblox game to your computer, tablet, or phone. Finally, use your credentials to log in and start customizing your avatar.

Experiences on Roblox

The Roblox experience is a very gamelike. As a participant, you can

>> Build your own world inside Roblox.

>> Gamify experiences in your world.

>> Attend concerts.

>> Visit specially curated theme worlds in Roblox.

>> Attend awards shows.

>> Throw a private virtual party and invite friends.

Roblox offers the ability to build any game you like. You can also go from one Roblox world to another without any friction — it's very easy to move around in Roblox.

Roblox is investing heavily in bringing performers to the platform and organizing more concerts. The platform has also signed deals with Sony and BMG to expand its focus on music.

Game experiences on Roblox have a very different feel from high-quality graphics games. In fact, Roblox can be considered a part of a front end or app store for users to jump into other games. Role play and participating as a character within a game along with your friends is typically the sort of experience that the platform has been created for.

Bloktopia

Bloktopia features a 21-story building with various levels that form the entire Bloktopia metaverse. The Bloktopia platform is also a decentralized open-source virtual world which means. It offers a platform based on blockchain technology. The 21 levels of the skyscraper were specifically created to pay homage to the 21 million Bitcoins that can ever be generated.

Experiences on Bloktopia

Bloktopia token holders are called *Bloktopians*. Here are some of the things Bloktopians can do on Bloktopia:

>> Buy Bloktopia land parcels.

>> Offer advertising space to generate revenue.

>> Play games.

>> Build personal networks.

>> Meet people.

Bloktopia wants to position itself as a central hub to learn everything about crypto and eliminate the confusion and deep learning curve associated with cryptocurrencies. As such, it features an open and friendly environment where people can meet and learn.

Creating an account on Bloktopia

You must purchase the Bloktopia token $BLOK in order to create an account and participate on the platform. $BLOK can be purchased from various online crypto exchanges.

Making money on Bloktopia

Bloktopians can purchase land parcels in the 21-story building. Users will also be able to monetize these experiences in different ways, such as through advertising.

Bloktopia also has an SDK available, which can be used by developers, artists, and game developers to build different scenes, artworks, and game challenges and offer them as part of the overall Bloktopia experience.

Here are three very commonly used terms on Bloktopia:

>> **Blok:** Blok is the native token of Bloktopia.

>> **Reblok:** Real estate in Bloktopia that can be bought and sold.

>> **Adblok:** Advertising revenue on Bloktopia is called Adblok. Users can build experiences and advertising space on their land parcels and even drive sponsored advertisement revenue, which they receive by selling rights to advertise on their land.

Epic Games

Epic Games is one of the largest gaming industry technology infrastructure providers in the world today, and it's considering developing its own platform for the metaverse. In 2022, Epic Games signed a deal with WPP (the world's largest advertising agency) and formed a partnership with LEGO to construct a kid-friendly metaverse.

The Epic Unreal 3D virtual scene generating technology, also known as the EPIC Unreal Engine, is a highly popular gaming industry graphics engine that allows game designers, creators, and developers to develop highly realistic 3D objects, people, surfaces, textures, lighting, and audio within a virtual environment. Epic technology has gained recognition when it comes to the quality of the Unreal Engine output. The Epic Unreal Engine is also used in filmmaking to create ultra-realistic artificial film scenes. Epic's goal is to be able to create experiences that are indistinguishable from real life and the results so far are stunning. Check out some of the virtual 3D samples at www.unrealengine.com.

Technologies such as Epic Unreal Engine will have a significant impact on the metaverse in general. As gaming companies look at developing highly experiential games (those that can provide the user the perception of being in an ultra-realistic 3D world, with real-world looking graphics, such as buildings, roads, cars, and people), the push will be to utilize technologies such as Unreal Engine to create these new metaverse platforms.

The combination of computer-generated imagery (CGI) and compute power are two important considerations in the overall development of metaverse worlds. As software and hardware technologies dramatically improve both of these aspects, seeing ultra-realistic metaverse worlds in the next few years is not unrealistic.

Epic plans to build its own open version of the metaverse in the next decade or so and collaborate with other industry leaders to build specific experiences. This goal will require improvements in both computer microprocessor technology, graphics hardware technology, inbuilt memory processing, and software for rendering crystal-clear graphics.

With technology such as the Unreal Engine, a big revolution in high-quality graphics in the metaverse could be around the corner.

Sony

Sony has emerged as a very successful gaming industry conglomerate. Sony owns the PlayStation line of products, which has sold more than 100 million units worldwide since its release in 1994. Sony PlayStation features hundreds of popular games and best sellers, including God of War: Ragnarok, Grand Theft Auto, and others. The Sony PlayStation Network (PSN) has more than 100 million active users today, making it one of the top gaming hardware consoles ever produced.

In various announcements over the years, Sony has mentioned that it would like to focus on live concerts, as well as live games. Sony has an extremely broad online network that it uses to deliver gaming experiences already, so this is a natural fit.

Sony is also believed to be working on a metaverse platform for live sports broadcasts, where users can view athletes competing or playing various sports in a metaverse space.

Sony doesn't have a platform entirely focused on the metaverse, but the company is expected to become part of various metaverse platforms through PlayStation Network and potentially look at the metaverse as a long-term strategy, according to announcements made by its leadership.

The metaverse is brand new. It's just in the very early stage of evolution,. Today the metaverse is mainly confined to a VR headset or a computer screen. But future focus and iterations can and are likely to develop as a result of the convergence of hardware and graphics technologies.

Elevating the Metaverse Experience

With all the experiences and senses engaged, the future of the metaverse is likely to be a combination of hardware, software, and sensory devices. It's very likely the metaverse participant of ten years from now is utilizing new technologies that incorporate a sense of smell, taste, and sensation, in addition to VR glasses or headsets.

Imagine being able to join a metaverse space or a virtual game and being able to visualize almost perfect visual graphics thanks to some future version of technologies such as the Unreal Engine, described in the earlier section on Epic Games. Imagine being able to taste, smell, and feel elements from your environment that take you right to that specific place you're viewing.

You could be visiting the heart of Tokyo or San Francisco. The smells, sights, tastes, and physical sensations will all make you feel like you're actually there. Experiences such as these are going to have a profound impact on the success of the metaverse, how it's used, where it's used, and why it's used. The metaverse of the future, activated through sensory devices, is going to be incredibly different from what we're seeing right now.

The following sections describe scenarios that can elevate the metaverse experience in the future.

Haptic feedback

Haptic feedback is the vibration you feel in a game controller when an event occurs within the game. Haptic feedback is extensively used in high-intensity games to provide user feedback. In fact, your mobile phone vibration is also a type of haptic feedback. Haptic feedback is something you perceive through your sense of touch.

Companies are already working on technologies that can provide haptic feedback. This feedback can come from events that happen within games and could be customized based on the type of game being played. For example, in a car chase game, your feedback device may vibrate if your car goes off the road, while in a shooter-type game, the same vibrations may happen when you throw a grenade. This feedback can also be customized to come from events within the metaverse, such as within metaverse gaming or other events. This means that within the gaming environment, special hardware (such as haptic gloves or outfits) and variables can provide feedback to the user. Imagine engaging in an activity and being able to *feel* the activity physically.

In addition to haptic feedback, advanced gaming rigs that provide highlight experiential movement are also becoming popular. In these special gaming rigs, you're strapped to a chair, which then moves depending on your gameplay. If you're playing a Formula 1–style racing game, expect your chair to move according to the turns you take; if you're playing an airplane simulator game, expect your chair to make moves just like your airplane. This hardware is currently available in the market today.

Improved auditory experiences

Current gaming experiences are either visual or auditory. On the auditory level, much more crystal-clear audio is constantly being developed with different technologies. Surround sound, Dolby, and other technologies evolved over the years to provide great auditory experiences in movie theaters. Perhaps the future of the metaverse will be about developing new ways of experiencing real-time audio and visual aids that feel and sound more like human than computer-generated sounds. This may mean a focus on clarity, timber, pitch, and other aspects of audio rather than just on volume.

Physical sensations and touch

In the future, games will also develop in complexity and the nature of being more experiential, as sensory technologies get better and more precise. Imagine wearing a gaming suit, fitted with millions of micro-sensors that are able to create a sense of touch. When you're wearing that suit, any activity happening within gameplay can be translated into a feeling of touch in your suit. Although the price point of such future technologies could be high in the beginning, it's very likely that such hardware devices will come into the market as technology costs are lowered.

Olfactory experiences

Imagine being able to smell what you're seeing within your gaming environment. Whether it's a meadow of flowers or an industrial environment, you may be able to smell it in the future. Our noses can provide a very specific experience when it comes to being able to feel ourselves in a specific environment. Close your eyes and think about a specific odor — your mind can take you to a completely different place.

Within gaming, some element of smell will emerge over the next few years. Imagine a metaverse platform able to generate a smell that all its participants are able to experience during participation. This means the development of hardware and potentially appliances, installed just like a computer and that users purchase from an electronic store, could become popular.

Taste-based experiences

Who doesn't love a good-tasting meal? The metaverse can't ignore the sense of taste, and as we progress into the future and the platforms stabilize, the sense of taste is likely to be drawn upon to improve the user experience. Metaverse platforms, technology providers, gaming companies, and anyone trying to create a highly experiential metaverse platform will likely experiment with the sense of taste. During gameplay in the metaverse, you may hold a straw-like device, or a sensor, that generates different tastes and activates your taste buds while you play.

Anticipating a Metaverse Future

The future of the metaverse is wide open, and it's impossible to predict or forecast where it will go. Just as the Internet was unpredictable in the year 2000 dot-com boom days, and little did we know all the ways it would evolve, we haven't seen all the possibilities of the metaverse.

With some certainty, we can think about the applications of the metaverse and how it could impact an industry or a sector. There are many cross-connections between a particular sector and experiences in the metaverse, so creativity will determine where innovative ideas will further take the core idea of the metaverse.

The health-care industry can utilize the metaverse to incorporate a gaming environment and help participants live an active life rather than a sedentary one. Will fitness industry companies such as Peloton and others use the metaverse as an additional channel to engage their customers and perhaps design the next exercise equipment of the future to be compatible with games in the metaverse?

New companies and start-ups such as VirZOOM are experimenting with using VR with hardware devices such as a Peloton bike to provide users with new and enhanced experiences. You can find more on VR and the fitness industry in Chapter 15.

The future of the Metaverse is highly dependent on three factors:

>> Development of the metaverse and the availability of new experiences

>> Development of hardware and software technologies

>> User adoption through lower price of entry and simplification

Chapter **3**

Staying Safe in the Metaverse

t's still very early days in the development of the metaverse. As a result, people can actively come together and work on making the metaverse a great place to hang out.

The metaverse has the potential for high growth, large investments, and fast adoption. The opportunity exists to develop security measures that keep pace with this high-growth technology. New hardware must be secured to avoid creating "doors" to your information that hackers, scammers, and others can exploit.

Imagine building a stronger foundation for your new home and taking precautions right from the beginning — having options and the right conduits for your security system, air conditioning, water pipes, and every other system needed, right from the design stage. This is exactly where we are with designing a secure metaverse: laying down the basic and yet essential rules.

This chapter describes actions you can take to stay safe in the metaverse and help make the metaverse an environment that all participants can enjoy.

Setting Up for Metaverse Safety

The following sections give an overview of some important steps you can take to secure your computer and other devices from hackers, thieves, and other ne'er-do-wells in the metaverse.

TIP

To read more in depth about keeping yourself, your family, or your business safe online, check out *Cybersecurity For Dummies*, 2nd Edition, by Joseph Steinberg (Wiley).

Creating a secure Internet connection

Whether you access the metaverse from home or from your workplace, you'll do so via an Internet connection. Incorporating the following items will help secure your connection:

>> **Firewall protection:** Make sure that the computer you use to access the metaverse has either a built-in or external firewall to secure it from cyberthreats.

TIP

I recommend getting a hardware-based external firewall even if your router comes with a built-in one to create a double layer of security. External hardware firewalls are available from computer stores, as well as from websites such as Amazon, BestBuy, NewEgg, and any large volume IT seller.

When installing a hardware firewall, you plug it between the router and the modem and follow manufacturer guidelines for configuration.

>> **Router security:** If you access the metaverse from home, you probably use your own Wi-Fi connection to access the Internet. If you access the metaverse from your workplace, you probably use the network connection provided at your workplace. Either way, it is essential to secure any router vulnerabilities such as open ports and unauthorized access possibilities that may grant access to cybercriminals, hackers, and bots to your computer, devices, and local network such as Wi-Fi.

>> **Password security:** Change the default administrator passwords for all your network devices such as routers, firewalls, and computers and follow a good routine to keep your passwords complex and securely stored (such as changing passwords every week or two). Do not share passwords or other sensitive data with anyone who should not have them, and if possible, avoid sending login credentials by email.

If you must send login credentials by email, consider sending two emails — one with the username and one with the password. You can also use different channels (such as emailing the username and texting the password). Splitting the channel of communication to send the username and password is a simple and effective technique.

>> **Guest Wi-Fi access:** Allocate guest Wi-Fi access to outsiders. To prevent any compromised devices from accessing your personal or business Wi-Fi network, don't share your internal network passwords. All it takes is a few minutes for rogue viruses to infiltrate your network. You can generate a guest password for most good-quality home routers, which gives you the option to change the guest password as you like. These days good routers come with handy phone apps that help you do whatever you need to on your fingertips.

Securing your computer and other metaverse devices

When you access the metaverse, you must ensure that your personal computer, laptop, gaming hardware, or any other device you use to interact within a metaverse world or on a metaverse platform is secure.

Best practices to secure the hardware you use in the metaverse include

>> Ensuring computers and other devices are up to date with manufacturer patches and updates.

>> Disconnecting all devices and switching them off when not in use.

>> Avoiding connecting to unsecured networks and devices unless you're familiar with them.

>> Running regular antivirus and malware scans to ensure your computer is not infected.

Hackers use unsecured Wi-Fi networks to lure in unsuspecting users and try to exploit any vulnerabilities in their devices, once connected, to get hold of private data. Unknown Wi-Fi networks may also ask you to click a link or download a small app, both of which are opportunities for the bad guys to get into your computer. Use caution and only connect to an open network if you trust it.

Look for manufacturers of metaverse hardware that provide support in case devices and equipment gets hacked or broken into. Reputable device manufacturers warn users of potential threats and vulnerabilities.

ANTICIPATING FUTURE VULNERABILITIES

FUTURECAST

Device manufacturers consider security when designing the circuit boards, open ports, and other levels of access; however, vulnerabilities can still exist, because cybercriminals constantly try to expose flaws within technology design and exploit them.

Researchers at Rutgers University recently published new research on virtual reality (VR) headsets, highlighting the possibilities of major privacy leakage known as eavesdropping attacks. Researchers compared various VR headsets and found out that headsets with built-in motion sensors could record subtle speech-associated facial dynamics to steal sensitive information communicated via voice command, including credit card data and passwords.

As the metaverse emerges beyond its initial days, application-specific hardware such as haptic gloves that can provide haptic feedback to virtually feel textures and other types of hardware that can be used along with VR glasses will become widely used. Hardware security of these components and devices will be vital in protecting users from physical or social damage.

Expect proprietary hardware for the metaverse to slowly find its way into industries such as online gaming, professional sports, health care, military applications, and more. These devices and other hardware will need to be secured as well.

Keeping your financial data safe

Most metaverse platforms offer the ability to purchase something. These platforms typically require that you have a specific digital currency that works exclusively in that particular metaverse platform. (I cover the money aspect of the metaverse in great depth in Chapter 4.)

To secure your money in the metaverse, follow these essential digital security practices (many of which also help secure your computer and other metaverse hardware):

>> Keep your computer and other devices updated.

>> Frequently schedule virus scans.

>> Install malware detector software.

>> Install a hardware firewall (refer to the section, "Creating a secure Internet connection").

>> Use a reputable wallet for transacting in the metaverse.

>> Store your cryptocurrency in a cold wallet if you're not using it frequently. A *cold wallet* is a specialized hardware wallet that plugs into your computer through a USB port and is used only when a wallet connection is needed.

TIP

To avoid anyone online stealing your credit card credentials in the metaverse, I suggest getting a credit card with a low spending limit to use exclusively in the metaverse. This separates your main banking and credit card accounts from those used for crypto transactions, mitigates risk in case your card gets compromised as a result of some crypto vulnerability, and makes it easy to track transactions.

Protecting your cryptocurrency wallets

Some of the challenges with financial security in the metaverse are not in your control (for example, the actual security of the cryptocurrency wallets).

Wallet hacks have occurred many times recently, and this responsibility falls on the wallet provider. Don't rely on third parties as much as you depend on yourself to do the due diligence needed, however.

Here are some measures you can take to protect your wallets:

>> Change your wallet password every week.

>> Use additional security features such as two-factor authentication. In two-factor authentication, double verification of a user account is typically done. After entering your password, you may receive a text message or an email with a verification code that you have to enter as a second step in order to log in.

>> Use a secure token generator, if available. Token generators are software- or hardware-based random number sequence generators typically used to generate an access code. These have become very common in the last decade to provide additional security to access systems such as banking.

>> Keep a handwritten record of your passwords in a secure location at your home, even in a safe.

>> Never share your financial or personal details with anyone in the metaverse.

>> Use both a cold wallet as well as a hot wallet to store your cryptocurrency. Crypto wallets function as a gateway to the Internet. You need a wallet to buy and sell any cryptocurrency or digital asset. You also need a wallet if you want to play a game in the metaverse or buy an NFT. Hot wallets store your cryptocurrency on the servers of the company that provides the wallet; cold wallets store the cryptocurrency on a USB hardware device that you can insert into your computer and disconnected after you're done using your crypto.

Avoiding scammers and fake NFTs

Non-fungible tokens (NFTs) are frequently called the gateway to the metaverse. This means NFTs may gain more popularity with time as the metaverse matures, and in fact, they may serve as interchangeable tokens of exchange that can work seamlessly across various metaverse platforms.

WARNING

If you own an NFT, beware of scammers who sell fake NFTs, a practice that is already quite rampant. According to OpenSea, the largest NFT marketplace on the Internet, more than 80 percent of NFTs created using its free tools are fake, plagiarized, or spam.

Staying Safe in the Metaverse

Staying safe while being part of the fast-growing metaverse should be everyone's priority. Physical safety is at risk when using VR headsets because your vision is restricted so you need to ensure that your physical environment is safe and others around you are safe, too.

Safety goes beyond the physical, though. In the metaverse, you'll likely interact with other people, so you need to be aware of the risks and take precautions to protect yourself and your personal information.

Avoiding physical injury

Pay special attention to your physical safety when you venture into the metaverse. When you use metaverse devices, you see the metaverse, not the physical world around you.

The hazard with VR headsets in particular is that you can't see where you're stepping, punching, or kicking during gameplay. People have reportedly injured shoulders, broken necks, and even developed something called *gorilla arm syndrome*, which is a fancy term for that feeling of pain or fatigue you get in your arms when using devices that require vertical motion, such as a touchscreen or handheld controller commonly used for gaming.

TIP

Here are some best practices for physical safety:

» Remove all sharp objects from your vicinity.

» Avoid using VR headsets in congested areas.

» Make sure others around you know you're unable to see them.

» Avoid areas with delicate objects around you. Don't enter the metaverse in a room full of priceless heirlooms.

» Make sure no pets or toddlers are around. You could easily step on them with your headset on.

As the popularity of VR grows and the adoption of entertainment, fitness, and other activities in the metaverse rises, incidents of physical injury and personal safety are likely to rise as well.

Interacting with others

Tracking users in the metaverse is at an early stage of development; there are limitations on what can be tracked. For example, purchases and transactions are tracked through blockchain, but individual behavior is not tracked (sort of like how you can track when a Zoom call was held but not what was said on the call if it wasn't recorded). Because legal frameworks are also absent, protecting yourself is mostly your responsibility. Avoid places in the metaverse that are R-rated places for adult-rated content, and exercise caution when meeting other participants for the first time.

Most metaverse users are not bad actors, but it only takes a few bad apples to ruin things. Serious and dangerous misconduct does occur. Misconduct by users has led to some metaverse platforms enabling safety measures that put a shield of protection around participants' avatars. Unfortunately, major legal and jurisdictional challenges exist to dealing with such incidents. For now, the metaverse community must evaluate and incorporate ideas that help create a metaverse that is safe for all.

WARNING

A huge segment of metaverse participants are potentially younger kids who are more vulnerable and susceptible to fraudsters. Take care to supervise your underage children when they're in the metaverse and also talk to them about some of the dangers they should watch out for, such as other participants asking them for their personal details such as passwords, home address, the school they go to, and other private details.

Protecting personal information

The metaverse is an open ended, regulation-free haven for scammers and con artists, and you should take every precaution when in the metaverse.

To protect yourself from scams and con artists in the metaverse, never divulge personal information or take actions that you think probably shouldn't be taken. Avoid every financial exchange of information, exchange of funds, or divulgence of any personal information in the metaverse. If you're meeting people who you know and they want you to do something, get a verification over the phone or through other trusted means.

Always be aware and don't disclose personal information that would compromise your personal safety. You wouldn't walk up to a stranger and give them your Social Security number, home address, passwords, and bank account numbers. Exercise similar caution in the metaverse. Don't disclose any information that compromises your or your family and friends.

REMEMBER

Enjoying the metaverse for what it is, a meeting place and experiential world, is a great idea. But you have to stay safe by taking preventive measures and being cautious.

Deep fakes and beyond

Deep fakes are digital personas created to appear lifelike, identical in resemblance, and impossible to tell apart from the actual digital persona of a real person. Impostors can use deep-fake technology to mimic the voice and appearance of a person. Imagine meeting somebody on a video call online, and later learning that the person was a deep fake. You may be fooled — deepfakes are as real as you and I.

In the metaverse, you're working with the complexity of meeting with and speaking with avatars of people. This means that you're assuming the person you're speaking to is the person you think they are. When you apply this rule to scam artists and impostors who are purely trying to con people and scam them, the possibilities are quite intimidating.

A master impostor needs time to study their victim. They also generally plan how they're going to scam someone. For this, they would have to know some specific information about people, their habits, or a personal piece of information. Imagine you're meeting your boss for a meeting in the metaverse, and during the meeting, your boss asks you to do something that you weren't really expecting to do. Maybe they ask you to fire someone or transfer funds to a bank account that they provide you during your meeting. Not knowing that this could be a master impostor utilizing deep-fake technology, you would do what your boss is asking you to do. The consequences of this could be devastating.

Deep-fake technology is highly specialized now, and it's not widely available. However, you still should assume that cybercriminals, scam artists, and master imposters have a way of doing things the way you least expect it, and as a result, they end up getting away with it.

FUTURECAST

ESTABLISHING REGULATORY STANDARDS

The metaverse is not evolving in a linear way, but in different pockets of innovation. There isn't one single body that regulates the metaverse or provides guidelines for operations to metaverse providers.

There are different conditions on the end-user license agreements (EULAs) for all providers, all of whom have some unique aspect to their platform connected to their intellectual property. As a user, when you sign up to the metaverse, you are in fact agreeing to your data being used as per the EULAs of individual providers.

A lot of work is currently being done by industry groups, regulators, and other stakeholders in creating a metaverse framework to establish basic ground rules and protect underage participants, privacy, and personal data. The evolution of a new Internet infrastructure also known as Web 3.0 could be a very interesting point when it comes to the metaverse, because it completely changes the foundations of how information is created and shared on the Internet.

The next few years are going to be critical for technologies and platforms that power the metaverse. As new technologies develop, it will be interesting to see how regulations and legal frameworks will help make the metaverse a safer place for all.

Chapter **4**

Mastering Money in the Metaverse

The metaverse is filled with different activities and things to do. You can visit the works created within various metaverse platforms or make your own. One thing common across all metaverse platforms is the ability to buy things such as digital assets (which include virtual branded clothes and accessories for your metaverse avatar, virtual superpowers, points, and even virtual real estate). This chapter is all about understanding how money works on the metaverse.

Understanding How Money Works on the Metaverse

From games to learning to entertainment and beyond, the metaverse is fast changing how we interact and engage with others. With hundreds of different options for engagement, the metaverse is also open and built to facilitate the exchange of money. To buy anything on the metaverse, you use digital money, called *cryptocurrency*, as described in the following sections. To understand how money works on the metaverse, though, you first need to understand the nature of digital assets.

Understanding digital assets

Chances are, if you want to buy a latte or a plane ticket, you're using your credit card or debit card to buy it. Today we use more noncash payments than ever before, and most of our money is just numbers on a computer rather than hard cash in our pockets. On the back end, banks work with money as a set of checks and balances connected to our bank accounts and credit cards. In fact, banks now carry very little cash on premises and sometimes you need to order cash a day or two before you need it (at least if you need a large sum). Money is digital more than ever before.

Digital assets are products that don't have a physical form but can be bought and sold. Examples of digital assets include software, access to membership sites that are online (such as Amazon Prime membership or a Spotify account), cryptocurrency, and nonfungible tokens (NFTs).

Grasping cryptocurrency

Cryptocurrencies are decentralized digital currencies that offer a convenient way of paying for a product or service. You can buy goods and services with cryptocurrency, invest with cryptocurrency, and do almost everything today with cryptocurrency.

TECHNICAL STUFF

Cryptocurrencies are not issued by a bank or a monetary agency. They're managed by a decentralized network of *nodes* (specialized computer servers) that enable the management of the currency. To read more about cryptocurrencies, check out *Cryptocurrency All-in-One For Dummies*, by Kiana Kanial et al. (Wiley).

The upcoming section, "Cryptocurrencies on the metaverse," covers some popular metaverse cryptocurrencies.

Knowing how tokens work

A *token* is the value of an exchange that can be used to buy or trade digital assets. A token can get you access to specific areas in an access-based platform. This access can only be available to token holders as an incentive or an assumed right. For example, a performing artist or musician may invite all token holders to a party after a concert, or an author may hold a special book signing with token holders.

Tokens are classified into two types:

>> **Fungible tokens:** A good example of a fungible token is something that is identical to another and can be used in lieu of the other in terms of an

exchange value. For example, two $100 bills are identical, and either of them can be used to buy something because they're *fungible* (interchangeable and with the same value). Two fungible tokens are identical to each other and can be swapped or used in place of the other.

» **Nonfungible tokens:** NFTs are blockchain-based tokens. Each NFT has a unique blockchain address (essentially, a string of numbers that differs from the blockchain address of every other token on the chain). You may come across different NFTs that represent similar digital assets, but because each NFT has its own blockchain address, each NFT is a singular token. The sidebar "Understanding blockchain" gives more detail on how blockchain works.

FUTURECAST

On the metaverse, NFTs are used more frequently than fungible tokens. In fact, NFTs are frequently called the "gateway to the metaverse." NFTs may gain more popularity with time as the metaverse matures. They may even someday serve as interchangeable tokens of exchange that work seamlessly across various metaverse platforms.

Within the blockchain and cryptocurrency environment, a user can acquire and own the intellectual property (IP) rights to a token. When a user buys anything that is denoted by an NFT, they're acquiring the IP rights to that NFT.

Have you heard about the Bored Ape Yacht Club (BAYC) NFT collection that features 10,000 unique pieces of art, all of which feature a bored ape? These are currently sold as NFTs in the metaverse. Every BAYC artwork has an ape on it, but every artwork is slightly different from the others.

WARNING

If you own an NFT, beware of scammers and also of fake NFTs being sold online, a practice that is already quite rampant. The largest NFT marketplace on the Internet, OpenSea (`https://opensea.io`), reveals that more than 80 percent of NFTs created using its free tools are fake, plagiarized, or spam.

TECHNICAL STUFF

UNDERSTANDING BLOCKCHAIN

In 1998, a new technology was released by an unknown person by the name of Satoshi Nakamoto. This new technology, called Bitcoin, was proposed as a replacement for traditional money. Bitcoin was based on a concept called blockchain. The blockchain database fundamentally changed how we create, store, and manage information of various types. The fundamentals of blockchain can be applied to many different aspects of information, such as video content, written content, financial data, and even money (like Bitcoin).

(continued)

(continued)

Blockchain has three core aspects to it that make it very attractive:

- Data can only be appended, never deleted.

- A blockchain can't be hacked or broken into due to its usage of complex cryptography.

- Blockchain data is decentralized, stored across a network of nodes, and hard to hack into.

In the context of the metaverse, NFTs and cryptocurrencies all use blockchain technology, although not exactly in the same way as Bitcoin does.

This sidebar is just a quick introduction to blockchain. Entire books have been written explaining the concept, so if you'd like to understand how it works (which is especially important if you're buying and selling on the metaverse), check out *Blockchain For Dummies,* 3rd Edition, by Tiana Laurence (Wiley).

Finding NFT marketplaces

An *NFT marketplace* is a website where you can buy and sell NFTs. Sellers list their NFTs and pay a small fee, also known as *gas fees,* to the platform on which they're selling. The gas fees are essentially the cost of using an Ethereum-based blockchain in order to create a NFT.

When someone buys a digital item, the back end (the Ethereum blockchain on which the marketplace is based) starts working away and "mints" the item, after which the ownership of the item is forever encoded into the marketplace blockchain. The buyer's name is now forever associated with that item.

REMEMBER

Mining is the process of creating a new block on a blockchain, which also creates a new Bitcoin (in the case of the Bitcoin blockchain). Minting is the process of using an Ethereum-based blockchain to create a new NFT. An NFT is basically a new address generated on a blockchain.

TIP

OpenSea is the world's largest NFT marketplace today, where thousands of NFT items are available to be purchased. Some other NFT marketplaces are now focused on specific arts such as film, audio, and other media.

POPULAR NFT MARKETPLACES

You can find out more about some of the popular NFT marketplaces by visiting their websites:

- **Binance NFT:** www.binance.com/en/nft/home
- **Bored Ape Yacht Club:** https://boredapeyachtclub.com
- **Enjin Marketplace:** https://enjin.io/products/marketplace
- **Magic Eden:** https://magiceden.io
- **Mintable:** https://mintable.app
- **Nifty Gateway:** www.niftygateway.com
- **OpenSea:** https://opensea.io
- **Rarible:** https://rarible.com
- **SuperRare:** https://superrare.com
- **Theta Drop:** www.thetadrop.com

New NFT marketplaces are emerging on a daily basis.

Validating NFT-based transactions

When the process that ultimately results in the creation of an NFT is completed, the NFT is said to be *minted.* In technical terms, the process of allocating a blockchain address to a digital asset is the process of minting an NFT.

Here's how NFT minting works:

1. A digital asset is uploaded to an NFT marketplace.

2. The NFT marketplace uses technology to connect to the Ethereum blockchain and request a blockchain address that can be allocated to the specified digital asset.

3. The Ethereum blockchain charges a gas fee to use the Ethereum blockchain and allocates an address that is permanently reserved for the digital asset in question.

4. The NFT marketplace adds fees on top of the Ethereum gas fees and provides the address to the digital asset.

TECHNICAL STUFF

TRACKING ETHEREUM GAS PRICES

When an application or token uses the Ethereum blockchain to validate transactions and create new blocks, the process time and compute power of different nodes within the Ethereum blockchain is calculated and referred to as *gas*. Gas fees are charged to the NFT creator.

Ethereum gas, often called *ETH gas* or just *gas,* is a fee that the Ethereum platform charges anyone who conducts a transaction on the Ethereum blockchain. In other words, *gas* is the fee you pay the Ethereum blockchain or Ethereum network in order to use it for your transactions.

Ethereum gas prices rise and fall with demand. ETH gas fees are measured in *gwei*. One gwei is equal to 0.000000001 ETH.

When NFTs are minted, the platform being used to do so will provide a breakdown of all costs, including gas and any additional fees the platform is charging for the minting process.

5. The NFT marketplace also lists the NFT in its marketplace at a sale price specified by the seller.

6. Upon purchase, the new buyer's details are appended to the blockchain address for the NFT, marketing them as the new owner.

As a process of allocation or transfer of ownership, the IP rights of the digital asset are allocated to the buyer. For this reason, it does not matter how many other copies of the digital asset are created online or distributed to others, the original ownership remains encased in a blockchain-based database that keeps it as a permanent record.

REMEMBER

Cryptocurrency is *mined,* and NFTs are *minted.*

Cryptocurrencies on the metaverse

You need cryptocurrency to buy anything on the metaverse. Say you're on the metaverse, and you visit Sotheby's auction house. If you like a piece, you bid for it and may even win the auction. For the actual transaction, you'll most likely be paying in crypto, and it may vary.

Every metaverse platform has created its own cryptocurrency that's preferred on that platform. Some may accept multiple types of crypto for transactions.

Here are some of the most popular currencies used on the metaverse:

>> **Ethereum (ETH):** Ethereum, represented by the symbol ETH, is one of the most widely used cryptocurrencies today. The Ethereum developer ecosystem is well developed, so Ethereum may gain more traction in the metaverse in the future, despite the fact that all metaverse platforms have created their own cryptocurrency tokens that are needed to transact on those platforms. This is one way for metaverse platforms to create their own mini-economies. As metaverse platforms gain users and as these users use the cryptocurrency to buy and sell, it creates a platform economy that grows with the growth of the platform.

>> **MANA:** MANA is the native token and cryptocurrency used on the Decentraland platform. MANA is used both for voting within the Decentraland platform, as well as for cryptocurrency. This means when you own MANA tokens, you get voting rights to future proposals for any changes to Decentraland and you can buy digital items on the platform.

>> **SAND:** SAND is the native utility token used in the Sandbox platform. When you own the SAND token, you can build, own, and monetize experiences on the Sandbox. You can also create NFT-based digital assets and integrate them into the Sandbox platform through the Sandbox Game Maker, a special app provided by the Sandbox platform for this purpose.

>> **ATLAS:** ATLAS is the proprietary token for the Solana-based metaverse platform, Star Atlas. With ATLAS, you can buy any in-game digital asset in the Star Atlas metaverse platform, a metaverse platform built on the Solana blockchain. This means all digital assets purchased and sold will be recorded in perpetuity on the Solana blockchain, a private game-specific blockchain designed for Star Atlas. The Star Atlas metaverse also features an in-game currency, POLIS, that can be purchased by trading ATLAS. So, you have to buy ATLAS first and then convert it to POLIS. Both tokens can work hand-in-hand, but the major differentiator is that ATLAS can help you buy and sell assets, while POLIS is used as a governance token to vote for changes in the game.

>> **APECOIN:** APECOIN is the token used on the BAYC NFT collection. It was specifically create for art, entertainment, events, and gaming on the metaverse. The APECOIN is based on a decentralized autonomous organization (DAO) architecture, where token holders have voting rights on how the token platform evolves and develops in the future.

REMEMBER

This is just a quick overview of the cryptocurrencies tied to today's metaverse platforms. For much more information on cryptocurrencies, including how to buy and sell them, be sure to check out *Cryptocurrency All-in-One For Dummies*, by Kiana Kanial et al. (Wiley).

Creating a Crypto Wallet Account

In order to buy or sell anything on the metaverse, you need to create a wallet account and fund it through your real-world financial institution. NFTs and other digital asset marketplaces typically accept Ethereum tokens or platform-specific cryptocurrencies, which you can pay using one of the wallets mentioned in this section.

Many crypto wallets are available, and while some have gotten a bad rap due to vulnerabilities and hacks, most of them promise security of your funds. Crypto wallets work because they connect with your financial institution and convert your currency (such as dollars, pounds, or other major global currencies) into a metaverse-specific currency.

Some wallets only offer a few metaverse currencies; other wallets may provide the conversion for multiple metaverse currencies.

The following sections offer a glimpse into the crypto wallets available and describe the basics of working with crypto wallets. Just keep in mind that like the metaverse, crypto is an area of growth and fluctuation.

Choosing a crypto wallet

Crypto wallets can be grouped into two main categories:

>> **Custodial:** In a custodial cryptocurrency wallet, a third party controls your private key. This means you're trusting third parties to become a transaction intermediary whenever you want to send or receive crypto funds. As a general guideline, most wallets that are based online are custodial wallets and are operated by crypto exchanges. In a custodial wallet, securing the wallet falls on the wallet operator and not the user.

Custodial wallets can be hardware-based or software-based. Typical hardware-based custodial wallets are inactive when not connected to the computer. They're similar to USB storage devices that can be plugged into the computer when needed. This also acts as a security feature because it physically keeps your wallet away from hackers.

Custodial wallets are operated and provided by a corporation and there have been many cases of custodial wallets being hacked and cryptocurrency stolen. You may choose a custodial wallet but make sure you store your long-term cryptocurrency in cold storage rather than in the wallet. *Cold storage* is offline storage of cryptocurrencies and can refer to a few different ways of storing crypto. Hardware-based cold wallets are a USB chip with special software that manages all your cryptocurrencies on the USB chip. Lose the chip, lose all the crypto. Other cold storage methods include writing down your crypto addresses on a piece of paper and putting it into a vault. Sounds very rudimentary, but it's probably the best way to store crypto as there is no way to hack it. (See "Protecting Your Money on the Metaverse," later in this chapter, for tips on staying safe.)

REMEMBER

Some Cryptocurrency wallets charge a small percentage for usage. Check with your specific crypto wallet about their policies and what they charge. This information is usually provided up front before a transaction.

Here are some popular custodial crypto wallets:

- **Freewallet** (`https://freewallet.org`): A popular wallet that manages more than 100 currencies. You can purchase crypto using a credit card, and the wallet provides a host of features to keep your crypto safe.

- **Ledger** (`www.ledger.com`): Ledger is a cold-storage wallet, also known as a hardware wallet. You have to buy a hardware device that has an upfront cost of approximately $80. This device needs to be connected to a computer in order to send or receive any crypto funds. The device features multiple levels of security.

 Noncustodial: In a noncustodial wallet, your private key is controlled by you, the user. You control who can see the information within your wallet, and information is stored locally on your wallet and not online.

A noncustodial wallet provides full control to the user, but a big disadvantage is that if the password is lost, there may be no way to recover it.

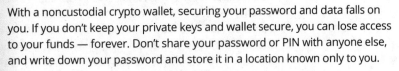

WARNING

With a noncustodial crypto wallet, securing your password and data falls on you. If you don't keep your private keys and wallet secure, you can lose access to your funds — forever. Don't share your password or PIN with anyone else, and write down your password and store it in a location known only to you.

Here are some popular noncustodial wallets available today:

- **AlphaWallet** (`https://alphawallet.com`): AlphaWallet is the first Ethereum-based wallet. It has an extremely high level of security. The wallet offers the ability to tokenize assets, which means if you're looking at tokenizing some aspects of your business model and converting it into assets that can be traded, AlphaWallet can help.

  Due to its open-source nature, the wallet code is completely accessible online, which means developers worldwide can come together and work on improving the code. This could be an advantage because developers are constantly looking at improving the code base, leading to a more stable and updated product overall.

- **Coinbase Wallet** (`www.coinbase.com/wallet`): Coinbase Wallet is a leading cryptocurrency wallet. Coinbase Wallet currently supports credit and debit cards in more than 90 countries worldwide. This means you can fund your Coinbase Wallet directly from your bank and be on the metaverse in minutes. Typically, new accounts go through a verification process that may take a few hours to a few days.

**TECHNICAL
STUFF**

The Coinbase Wallet complements the Coinbase Crypto Exchange. The wallet is not to be confused with the exchange. The exchange is one of the largest crypto exchanges available in multiple countries worldwide.

- **Coinomi** (www.coinomi.com/en): Coinomi is a multi-platform cryptocurrency wallet that includes desktop and mobile options. It supports more than 1,500 cryptocurrencies, meaning you can buy and sell these currencies in the wallet. The wallet also supports more than 125 blockchains, which means assets based on these blockchains are accessible to users. The wallet is available in more than 25 languages and is anonymous. Users don't have to undergo a lengthy verification process to add funds — the wallet is one of the easiest ones to set up.

  The initial code base for Coinomi was open source, but this was discontinued due to the appearance of malicious clones of the wallet that were created by hackers and cybercriminals.

- **Enjin Wallet** (https://enjin.io/products/wallet): The Enjin Wallet is a popular crypto wallet commonly used for storing Ethereum, Bitcoin, Litecoin, and a variety of other tokens. Users are able to trade more than 100 different cryptocurrencies with the Enjin Wallet.

- **Math Wallet** (https://mathwallet.org): Math Wallet is a new cryptocurrency wallet that offers multi-platform functionality and supports tokens across more than 100 blockchains. Math Wallet is available as an iOS, Android, or Windows app. It also has Web 3.0 support, enabling it to purchase cryptocurrencies directly in the wallet rather than going to a crypto exchange. Users are able to see the transaction cost before every transaction is conducted.

- **MetaMask** (https://metamask.io): MetaMask is a way to access Blockchain applications such as dApps. MetaMask enables you to buy crypto tokens or even exchange them with other blockchain apps across decentralized platforms on the metaverse. The wallet offers a high level of data ownership because users manage who they share information with.

Funding your wallet

A cryptocurrency wallet can be funded in multiple ways. Common methods include

>> Transferring funds from a bank account

>> Using a credit card to add funds

>> Sending existing crypto from another wallet

>> Receiving crypto funds from another person or third party

Here are the general steps you follow to buy a cryptocurrency:

1. **Open an account on a crypto exchange.**

   This involves connecting your crypto exchange account with your bank account. Typically, banks in the United States may allow transferring funds to your crypto account through ACH, direct transfer, or wire transfer.

2. **Get a crypto wallet.**

   Here, you choose a custodial or noncustodial wallet (see the preceding section), depending on whether you want to secure your account yourself or trust a third party to do so.

3. **Buy the cryptocurrency.**

   After loading your account with funds (through your regular bank account), you can place an order to buy a cryptocurrency of your choice. Depending on the crypto exchange you're using, you could have access to a few cryptocurrencies or thousands of cryptocurrencies.

4. **Exercise extreme caution.**

WARNING

   When buying any cryptocurrency, remember that crypto is unregulated with a huge daily fluctuation in value. Consult with a financial advisor before investing in any crypto. I'm not recommending that you do (or don't) buy cryptocurrency — I'm just telling you how to do it if you decide it's the right path for you.

5. **Choose your hot or cold storage option (see the preceding section for more on hot and cold storage).**

Moving metaverse money back to the real world

All crypto holdings are stored in your wallet. Converting cryptocurrency into real-world dollars (or pounds or whatever currency you prefer) works much like withdrawing money from a bank. Here are the basic steps:

1. **On your crypto exchange website, choose the option for payout or withdraw funds.**

   The wording varies from one exchange to the next.

2. **Choose the amount of cryptocurrency you want to convert to your designated currency.**

3. **Click the Confirm or Next button to start the transfer process.**

Your account will be credited with your preferred currency, which can then be transferred to your bank or connected account. This usually takes up to a few days, depending on which wallet and exchange you're using.

Protecting Your Money on the Metaverse

Securing your money on the metaverse starts by following essential digital security practices:

>> **Keep your computer and other devices updated.** Computer vulnerabilities are one of the main reasons for mass hacking incidents.

>> **Frequently schedule virus and malware scans.** Viruses and malicious programs can hide in your computer and steal information and private data.

>> **Install a hardware firewall.** Specialty hardware devices that connect between your computer and the Internet can provide added security.

>> **Consider getting an entirely new and different credit card with a low spending limit for usage exclusively on the metaverse.** This can separate your main accounts and banking from the account you use on the metaverse.

>> **Use added security features such as two-factor authentication (2FA) when they're available.** 2FA is when you have to provide some additional information to log in (for example, a six-digit code sent to your email address or texted to your phone).

>> **Use a secure software token generator, if applicable.** Banks and financial institutions are now providing an added layer of protection through secure password authentication with security token generators. Use one if you can. Token generators are either app based or a hardware device similar in size to USB storage. Software-based token generators work as an app on your smartphone; upon trying to log in, you generate a code in your token generator and use it as part of your login process. Banks provide you with instructions on how to generate a token for your login every time you log in.

>> **Keep a hand-written record of your passwords in a secure location at your home, even in a safe.**

For more safety tips on how to stay safe on the metaverse, turn to Chapter 3.

Buying and Selling on the Metaverse

On the metaverse, buying is primarily about exchanging tokens or cryptocurrency and acquiring a digital asset. Digital assets you might buy on the metaverse include virtual real estate, digital art, NFTs, fashion accessories, music, designs, and more.

Understanding what you're buying

REMEMBER

When you buy anything, even if it's an accessory for your avatar, say a new Gucci handbag, you're buying the intellectual property (IP) rights to it in a NFT format. All digital assets have an entry on a blockchain within the metaverse where the item was purchased, and each entry is unique. Even for two similar-looking Gucci bags, their blockchain addresses are unique.

A new digital economy is currently under creation through blockchain technology and its related digital assets. This includes a new creator economy where many people are participating in an extremely new industry of designing NFTs. In this book, I cover fashion, sports, healthcare, and other cool aspects of the metaverse with coverage of how these industries are leveraging NFTs and digital IP.

Buying a digital asset

The currency you use to buy digital assets on the metaverse are specific to the requirements of the platform where you're purchasing the digital asset. Most platforms accept Ethereum and provide instructions on how to buy and sell on their platforms.

Other than that, buying something on the metaverse is very simple. Just visit the marketplace on the metaverse platform, and follow the steps provided within the platform to purchase your item. Figure 4-1 shows the marketplace on the Decentraland platform.

FIGURE 4-1:
The Decentraland
marketplace.

Figure 4-2 shows an individual item for sale in the Decentraland platform marketplace. The avatar is a generic avatar being displayed with the hatchets in its hand. In order to purchase the hatchets, I would have to take the following steps:

1. Sign in to my account on Decentraland.

2. Browse to the item on the marketplace.

3. Click the Buy button beside the item.

4. Sign in to my wallet, which will be used to transfer the crypto funds to the seller.

   Upon sending funds, the item will be sent to me and my account on Decentraland will show that I own the item under my profile section.

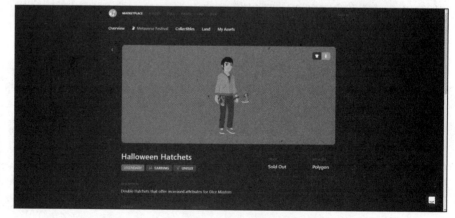

FIGURE 4-2:
Sold! Halloween
hatchet in the
Decentraland
platform
marketplace.

Receiving payments on the metaverse

When you sign up for a wallet you receive a public key and a private key. A *public key* is something you can share with others so they can send you funds; think of it as a special address, unique to you. A *private key* is for you to log in to your account and withdraw your funds; you should *never* share your private key with anyone.

In order to receive payments on the metaverse, you need to share your crypto wallet public key with the other party. Here's how that works.

1. **The sender copies and pastes your public key into their To field.**

   This is sort of like copying and pasting an email address.

2. **After selecting the amount of cryptocurrency, the sender clicks Send.**

   The cryptocurrency is credited to your account and you can see the credit in your account.

   Because cryptocurrency transactions are mostly anonymous, you won't be able to see the name and personal details of the sender, just their public key.

2
Engaging in Hobbies and Personal Interests

See how the metaverse expands the gaming experience.

Find a virtual reality (VR) headset and other hardware that works for you.

Get what you need to game in the metaverse.

Enjoy movies, TV shows, and other aspects of the gaming industry.

Find metaverse users who share your hobbies and interests.

Chapter **5**

Getting into Experiential Gaming

The metaverse helps users have a wide range of experiences they wouldn't have been able to have before. After all, this new technological concept has not become fully commercial yet.

Experiences in the metaverse are at an early stage of development. Developments and improvements in hardware and software technologies will significantly ramp up the quality and overall visual appeal of metaverse environments. Experiences will become more vivid, and activities such as skiing, hiking, and surfing can all seem very real with hardware that's custom-built for these activities.

This chapter shows how the gaming industry helped birth the metaverse. I discuss popular gaming platforms and detail how they differ from one another. I also explain how gaming is shaping the growth of the metaverse by helping creators create, as well as participate in, new gaming experiences in the metaverse.

Envisioning a Metaverse for Gamers

Gaming is how a growing number of people interact with more niche worlds within the broader metaverse for the first time. Of course, not all games are suited to a metaverse — no one is clamoring for a Pong metaverse, for example — but some games have done a remarkable job of creating what are essentially parallel worlds in the digital realm.

The "tools" of gaming — whether it's a controller, a keyboard, or a virtual reality (VR) setup — help people to navigate these worlds in a manner that's relatively easy to understand. As time passes, more and more of the world's population will have experience with different types of games. Interacting with a collection of metaverses, or the *multiverse*, will probably feel natural to people in the coming years.

Connecting games to the Internet allows people to interact with one another online *within* the digital world. Participants can talk with one another through the game or other services like Discord (`https://discord.com`), a communication tool that allows sharing of text, voice, and video seamlessly and has found profound popularity with gamers.

Many of the things you can do in the outside world have now also been translated into the game world. Within metaverse games, you can now find in-game marketplaces and/or economies where items can be bought, sold, or traded. The medium of exchange currently being used in most cases is a proprietary game cryptocurrency or digital money.

BORROWING CONCEPTS FROM POP CULTURE

The gaming industry took early concepts of the metaverse already familiar in pop culture and rapidly expanded them to create the metaverse as it exists today. In fact, the term *metaverse* first appeared in a 1992 sci-fi novel called *Snow Crash* by Neal Stephenson. Stephenson coined the term, which, in the book, refers to a digital world that exists parallel to the real world — essentially the same concept we have today.

In his novel *Ready Player One,* Ernest Cline expanded the concept of the metaverse. He made the metaverse bigger and more tangible. In the book, the metaverse is called the Oasis. People escape their troubles in the real world by retreating to the Oasis. To navigate and interact during their Oasis game experience, players use tools familiar to today's actual metaverse gamers, such as VR visors and haptic feedback gloves. In the movie *Ready Player One,* you can see what the book talks about and some of the concepts mentioned in the book are much clearer. I highly recommend you watch *Ready Player One.*

Free Guy, starring Ryan Reynolds, is a sci-fi metaverse-related film that focuses on virtual avatars developing a mind of their own or sentience. The movie is essentially based on the idea of an avatar-based world, or metaverse, operating parallel to our own world.

Both films portray a highly futuristic take on the metaverse and advancement of the gaming industry to the extent that, in the future, gaming worlds and our world exist in parallel and there is free movement between the two — so much so, in fact, that sometimes it isn't clear whether we should continue to live in our current physical world or in an artificial game world.

Developing the metaverse gaming experience

In the beginning of metaverse games, people focused mostly on experiences provided through the PC, keyboard, and screen, just like other games. Over the years, though, technology has changed and grown to allow for deeper experiences.

In the early days of the metaverse, with Second Life, for example, things played out as they would with many other types of games — you moved around with the keyboard and mouse, clicked away, and interacted with the world. The game itself had more options and possibilities in terms of what you could do, but the concept of how things worked was similar. And Second Life has grown in the decades since its release.

The persistence, connectivity, and use of an in-game economy helped to "sell the idea" of Second Life being a real world where things exist now *and* will continue to exist well into the future. (The next section covers Second Life in more detail.)

From a visual standpoint, the gaming industry greatly enhanced immersive gaming experiences such as that offered by Second Life by largely replacing simulated graphics, which are not interactive, with the following interactive technologies:

>> **Virtual reality (VR)** is the ability to create artificial and virtual worlds using computer simulation. The main difference between simulated and virtual reality is that VR is interactive. VR helps view a fully simulated or artificial world, such as in Roblox.

>> **Augmented reality (AR)** layers virtual objects on top of the physical world. Instead of replacing your field of vision with a VR visor, AR adds to the real world around you, making certain digital elements "visible" through your phone's screen or special glasses. What you see is a simulated or virtual world layered on top of the real world. Pokémon Go is a well-known game that uses AR technology.

One of the biggest changes over time in metaverse game development was making virtual reality a, well, reality. In the early days of VR, the results were less than stellar. However, over the past decade, great strides have been made in this field. VR headsets are better, clearer, easier to wear, and lighter. They can provide amazing experiences for a host of different types of games. And games with metaverses are starting to take advantage of this.

Imagine someday soon being able to have a sense of smell within your metaverse game or being able to feel cold or heat within a gaming environment. All these things are made possible by very specific Internet of Things (IoT) devices, such as wearables and special hardware devices, that can emit different odors based on the input they receive, or heat or cool your body based on the game input they receive.

Gaming hardware is already rapidly developing in the realm of specialized *haptic feedback* (the ability of computer-based systems, such as games, personal computers, and tablets, to send back physical feedback to its user). Perhaps the most familiar example of haptic feedback is the vibration you feel on your cellphone when it rings.

Examples of haptic feedback in the metaverse can potentially be felt with a surfing simulator that works with VR headsets to simulate a surfing experience or a skydiving simulator that works in conjunction with a specific metaverse skydiving app. This evolution will also spread to engage other human senses. Imagine being able to smell the pine trees or freshly baked cookies when visiting a forest or a bakery in the metaverse. Specialized hardware devices that engage our five senses will slowly enter the mainstream.

TECHNICAL
STUFF

The future of gaming is about to get more complicated and experiential. It's not a far-fetched idea to imagine that, in the future, we'll have contact lenses and similar devices that can overlay our real world with digital, augmented elements that we can interact with and manipulate. In the long term, the metaverse will likely involve brain–computer interfaces, which could include brain implants that fully integrate technology into the human experience, merging worlds.

Discovering games that use the metaverse

When people talk about the metaverse, the online game Second Life (https://secondlife.com) inevitably comes up, and with good reason. Second Life is the first real metaverse-style game. Participants in Second Life create avatars to represent themselves in the game and essentially live an alternate, "second" life where they have friends, responsibilities, a home, and a virtual social life. It's a persistent world that changes in real time.

The elements and features of Second Life are what many games today model themselves after. Of course, since Second Life debuted in 2003, the technology in today's games has advanced significantly.

Second Life is still around and going strong, thanks to improved features and graphics, ease of use, and the fact that it's free. Even though the game is free, there are plenty of things you can buy with real money in Second Life, including virtual land, clothing, and more. Second Life features a marketplace with millions of items — from fashion to a café for your virtual home and more. There are thousands of virtual experiences and communities to interact with, making it the longest-running example of an immersive metaverse experience.

Some other online games that are using the concept of the metaverse include the following:

>> **Fortnite** (www.epicgames.com/fortnite): Very popular, and one of the first interactive games that used the idea of the metaverse. Users can join Fortnite and engage in various play scenarios.

>> **Horizon Worlds** (www.oculus.com/horizon-worlds): Created by Meta (previously known as Facebook), Horizon Worlds offers users the ability to make friends in the metaverse. Users can play games, join fun activities, attend group classes, and enjoy other social aspects.

>> **Roblox** (www.roblox.com): Users on Roblox can create different worlds within the Roblox environment, make friends, and interact with others in many different ways.

>> **The Sandbox** (www.sandbox.game): As a participant you can join the Sandbox world and interact with various places that have been built by others. This could be virtual offices, play areas, art galleries, museums, and others. As a land owner, you can create a facility and create a place for others to visit.

>> **Star Atlas** (https://staratlas.com): A space exploration-based world in which users can visit various places in a hypothetical metaverse-based galaxy and interact with others through many experiences.

These are some of the larger and more impressive options that have metaverse worlds up and running right now. Some of these platforms, including The Sandbox and Star Atlas, utilize the blockchain and cryptocurrency. Non-fungible tokens (NFTs) are becoming popular in metaverse games as well.

Getting the tools you need to play metaverse games

To truly experience a metaverse world, you need the right tools. Most of the time, this includes some kind of VR hardware or headset. Here's a general list of items you should have:

» A gaming PC, console, or mobile device

» A high-bandwidth Internet connection (10 Mbps and above; in my opinion, 100 Mbps is ideal)

» A VR headset (see Chapter 6)

» Cryptocurrency or game-specific currency if you plan to buy or trade within a game

» A comfortable seat

» A safe space without any objects that may be delicate, easy to damage, or dangerous (Gameplay can sometimes get highly interactive and injury is common.)

TECHNICAL STUFF

This list may change as new hardware devices bring added functionality to the metaverse. New gaming hardware may include haptic feedback gloves, for example, that shake and vibrate during gameplay, or odor-generating accessories that may emit the smell of a forest, café, or wherever you are in the metaverse.

Upcoming technologies for metaverse gaming

Here are some other technologies that are likely to play a part within the metaverse gaming area:

» **Blockchain:** Blockchain establishes a new way of building databases and creating decentralized communities. Over the last decade, blockchain technology has grown in popularity; today, it's seen as a foundational technology that can help different industries create products, solutions, and other technologies. Within the gaming industry, blockchain can help create secure transactional mechanisms to exchange data, store information, buy and sell items, and fundamentally alter the way security works online. With the expansion of blockchain technology, its impact may also permeate online banking and asset creation. This is already seeing an uptake with the creation of NFTs.

>> **Cryptocurrency:** The exchangeable digital assets that also function as proprietary currency within gaming worlds in the metaverse are primarily cryptocurrencies. Today, many gamers use proprietary gaming currencies to transact; these include MANA for Decentral and ROBUX for Roblox. With the evolution of the metaverse, it's highly likely that gaming providers will begin creating their own cryptocurrencies to create value for gamers to stay within a platform. Other currencies in use include Ethereum.

>> **IoT:** As game controllers become more connected and functional, their usage within the metaverse is up to the creativity of creators. Game controllers typically have more functionality in one direction. This means that users are able to control many interactions in a typical game with their controller, but controllers are unable to respond back in a similar number of ways. For example controllers may only be able to vibrate through haptic feedback when an event occurs in a game environment. Future added functionality of controllers can expand in many directions. This means the addition of more sensors that can record different types of data, such as eye movement, hand humidity, breathing rate, or other factors as needed. The IoT is currently being used in smart homes and smart industries and has a number of uses that go beyond the metaverse.

>> **NFTs:** NFTs are a subcategory of digital assets created through blockchain technology. The application of NFTs is primarily in being able to provide access to a unique blockchain-generated digital asset category. As an example, an NFT created by a gaming provider could provide gamers access to specific sections of a game or unlock hidden aspects within a game period. NFTs can be purchased and sold in the metaverse and can be of value for a short term or for perpetuity. The application of NFTs also expands to digital avatar assets — for example, fashion brands now offer digital clothing for avatars, primarily sold as an NFT. These can be purchased in the metaverse or through an NFT trading platform (such as OpenSea [https://opensea.io]) or be traded within the gaming platform.

Identifying the Frontrunners in Metaverse Development

Many large companies are starting to get deeper into the idea of building metaverses of their own. Most have visions of becoming the "one true metaverse" to which everyone is going to flock. Of course, only time will tell what happens with each of their endeavors.

Some of the companies that are at the forefront of metaverse development include the following:

- » **Epic Games:** Epic Games is the founder of the Unreal Engine technology, which has been making waves due to its ability to create 3D graphics with highly impressive resolution and accuracy. The Unreal Engine is used in movie production and other applications, and as a result, it has been very well received over the metaverse.

- » **Meta:** Meta's metaverse games are primarily driven by its hardware technology. The Quest series of VR headsets provides access to Meta's Horizon Worlds metaverse. Horizon Worlds is probably one of the most popular metaverses due to the extremely large user base on Facebook that can easily join the metaverse game with a pair of VR glasses or headset.

  There is also a natural integration between Facebook (the social media platform) and Horizon Worlds (the metaverse gaming platform). Both can be accessed with a single login, which is your Facebook credential, and following the next steps is easy.

  Meta is expanding its Horizon Worlds metaverse to include live gaming, group fitness classes, and other activities that suit individuals interested in interactive group activities.

- » **Microsoft:** Microsoft has been extremely successful with its existing gaming platforms, but they're more 2D driven. (Games such as Minecraft are purely 2D.) In early 2022, Microsoft bought Activision Blizzard for $75 billion, one of the highest-priced gaming acquisitions up to that point. Activision Blizzard is a leading online gaming company, and this acquisition is likely to pave the way for Microsoft to rival Meta and its metaverse offerings.

- » **Niantic:** Gaming company Niantic has been behind games like Pokémon Go, which was probably one of the first AR games available that was accessible over a cell phone or smartphone. Niantic is believed to be building a platform for AR-based games that will also utilize a 3D map of the world.

- » **NVIDIA:** Although not a primary gaming provider, NVIDIA is building and expanding the metaverse into an industrial category. By equipping different industries to use the metaverse, NVIDIA plans to make the metaverse accessible and help designers use the 3D workspace to build better products in the metaverse. NVIDIA is creating its own version of the metaverse, called the *omniverse,* and its approach is based on building the metaverse from the ground up.

- » **Roblox Corporation:** Roblox Corporation owns Roblox, a popular metaverse game that offers users the ability to create worlds and customize game environments. Roblox is one of the newer entrants into the online and VR gaming category. Roblox also has its own currency, ROBUX, that can be used to purchase items within the game.

The types of metaverse games that are being played can vary greatly. However, with some of these companies, you should expect to see a change in the way the metaverse and games are presented. It will likely be more akin to how Second Life works, but it'll likely use VR or AR, at least, instead of requiring you to interact with a keyboard and screen. Of course, time will tell what works and what people want from these types of experiences.

Creating Your Own Metaverse Games

Depending on the platform you use, you may be able to build your own games and create the ability to engage with others through interactivity and gameplay. Different platforms offer various types of resources to do this.

In order to create your own games on a specific metaverse, you'll need to get organized and think strategically. Different metaverse platforms offer varied features for you to build your own game within that metaverse. You'll need to follow the guidelines and design limitations to best reach your game outcomes. Gamification experiences on different metaverses can be different and you shouldn't necessarily expect identical-looking games, although outcomes can be similar.

On some metaverses, you may need to work with a third-party agency to develop your parcel of land and create a game. On some others, such as Horizon Worlds, there are options to customize already built games and play with your friends.

Understanding the game development process

Metaverse game development can get complicated, so you need to strategize before you begin. If you're building a game or a gamified environment on any metaverse platform, I suggest going through the process of identifying a clear persona for your participants, establishing what success means, and creating a testing and deployment plan.

Here are some steps to get you started in game building in the metaverse:

1. **Choose the right platform to build your game.**

    Users on different metaverses may have different needs and motivations. Do your research on which platform hosts your ideal target audience.

2. **Plan the game strategy.**

    Think about how to engage with your target audience.

3. **Design the key characters.**

How will your audience members interact within the game? Will they be part of a character's journey or will they be an observer? Such considerations play an important role in overall experience design.

4. **Create the gamification steps.**

Which part of the experience will be gamified and how? Will there be rewards, and if so, how will your players win the rewards?

5. **Design the game layout.**

Designing the game layout will track the journey of your characters. This could be a simple 2D or a 3D layout. Within metaverse gaming, however, you should expect to design more 3D layouts as most game design and design tools favor 3D layouts.

6. **Build the virtual world using metaverse-specific tools.**

Depending on which metaverse world you're building your game in, you'll be working with those metaverse-specific building tools. The next section covers the tools used by the most common platforms.

7. **Start building your game.**

Finally, you'll get into building your game, experience, or world within the specific metaverse.

Depending on your skill level and expertise, you may very well be able to build a game by yourself, or may need the help of other collaborators. Most metaverse platforms work with game developers and specialized agencies that offer game design as a service.

TIP

Platform specialization is a factor you have to consider when choosing a game-building partner. Check the respective partner recommendations by each metaverse provider. Metaverse agencies and game developers may not be experts at every metaverse, but they likely possess skills in developing for a specific metaverse.

Knowing which game-building tools you need

Metaverse gaming is still evolving and while it is early days, most major metaverse providers have created tools that make game development relatively easy. Here is a selection of major metaverse providers and their game creation options:

>> **Decentraland Builder for Decentraland:** In order to create a game on Decentraland, you need to use Decentraland Builder. This tool offers a simple drag-and-drop interface with no coding experience required. You can create beautiful scenes and simple games through this interface.

>> **Horizon Worlds for Meta Horizon Worlds:** You have access to a variety of tools in Horizon Worlds. Creating a world in Horizon Worlds and gamifying it is extremely simple. An intuitive interface offers numerous templates to get started, and you can build your own specific VR world in a matter of minutes. You can use templates to create a world from scratch.

>> **Roblox Studio for Roblox:** In order to create a game in Roblox, you need to use Roblox Studio. Creating a game starts with creating an experience first. Roblox Studio offers a no-coding way to create a world and place objects in it that can be gamified. You can also use built-in templates that can be used within the gaming environment.

>> **The Sandbox Game Maker for The Sandbox:** To create a game on the Sandbox metaverse, you need to use the Sandbox Game Maker. This tool helps create games through visual scripting with no coding required.

TIP

THE FUTURE OF METAVERSE GAMING

Traditional storytelling is about following characters that have journeys designed by their creators. Superman, Wonder Woman, Winnie the Pooh, or any other comic character for that matter does what the writer of the particular comic book or episode of their show targets them to do. In a new technology-powered and metaverse-based twist on storytelling, you can now have your superhero designed in the way you perceive them to look and behave. Your character can have their own world, which you can design on metaverse platforms, and visitors on your metaverse world can interact with your superhero character the way you design their journeys. Creators of superheroes, the gaming industry, comic books, and the metaverse are all coming together and opening up a vast area of new technology-based narratives. Technology entrepreneur and founder of ACE Comic Con, Gareb Shamus, is now an artist–turned–metaverse creator. His new company, Hero Maker Studio, creates superhero characters that you can buy as an NFT and then gamify to your liking.

Chapter **6**

All About Headsets

Experiences in the metaverse are best lived through a set of virtual reality (VR) headsets. VR headsets enable you to fully experience the metaverse because they put your right in the middle of the 3D world, which the metaverse is supposed to be in the first place. This chapter introduces you to VR headsets and explains more about why you need them. It also tells you what some of the most popular models on the market are, as of this writing.

REMEMBER

One thing to keep in perspective is the compatibility of a VR headset with the metaverse platform of your choice. Every platform may not support every VR headsets available. The Meta Quest 2 headset, for example, has been designed to work best with the Horizon Worlds metaverse platform, while the Microsoft Halo Lens works best for professional use and high-complexity graphics and industrial metaverse use rather than for Roblox. Be sure to check compatibility requirements before investing in a VR headset.

Experiencing Virtual Reality in the Metaverse

The metaverse is a 3D virtual world. In order to experience the three dimensions, you need the help of VR headsets or glasses that helps render the virtual world into three dimensions. In some cases, you can participate on a metaverse platform *without* a VR headset, but the experience won't be 3D — you'll essentially be staring at a flat screen.

VR can be highly experiential because the whole visual and auditory experience can lead to actually *being* in a 3D world. It's hard to describe the experience — but when you put on a VR headset and experience it for yourself, you'll know exactly how cool it is!

TIP

To get started, visit your nearest tech store and try out some VR headsets.

In Figure 6-1, I'm modeling a VR headset.

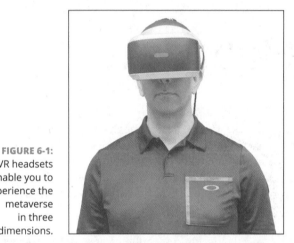 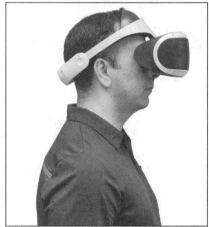

FIGURE 6-1: VR headsets enable you to experience the metaverse in three dimensions.

Photographs courtesy of Ian Khan

Understanding what VR hardware can do

Every VR headset has two components:

>> **Hardware:** The hardware component is the physical device itself — the glasses or headset you put on. The hardware should offer comfort and be light and easy to handle.

>> **Software:** The software is like an operating system that manages the headset's inner workings.

REMEMBER

Similar to how your computer had hardware and software, VR headsets have their own hardware and software. If it seems like you're wearing a computer on your eyes, that's because you are — in fact, VR headsets are much more powerful than the early computers.

Here are the ways that using a VR headset creates a VR experience:

» **Interaction:** VR hardware enables effective, time-responsive, and human-participatory interaction. VR experiences are different from typical computer experiences because using a computer generally involves using a mouse, keyboard, or touchscreen. With a computer, everything is two-dimensional. In contrast, VR uses three-dimensional data — such as physical movement in a 3D space and controller movement — which are recorded by a VR headset and used to provide feedback to the visual sensors.

» **Imagination:** VR hardware helps create the feeling that you're present, or even part of, a computer-generated world. It creates this experience by stimulating your senses (visual, aural, haptic, smell, and so on), which happens as a combination of users' eye movements, feedback on game controllers, and even voice commands.

» **Immersion:** The rich sensory experiences provided by VR hardware are completely immersive. Current research in the area of immersive virtual reality (IVR) suggests that it may allow a way for users to solve complex problems in a high-definition 3D visual environment.

Acknowledging the limitations of VR hardware

A well-known limitation of VR headsets currently available is that the hardware isn't advanced enough. Even though manufacturers have made significant progress in creating an experience that mimics the real world, people expect much more.

Headsets, for example, are currently too big and too heavy. These issues make it so that headsets really *can't* deliver fully immersive experiences. The units also have limited display capabilities and lack high-fidelity audio.

Most VR headsets also have a high upfront cost. Prices for VR technology haven't been standardized in the mass market, and although a few low-cost headsets are available today (in the range of several hundred dollars), the immersive experience users have with those headsets won't be the same as what they may experience with more sophisticated models (which can cost more than $3,000).

Looking to the future of VR headsets

Despite the inherent issues with form factor (see the preceding section), VR headsets have a promising future based on slow but eventual mainstream adoption. Although there are legitimate concerns about the short-term viability of these technologies, they're expected to find their way into mainstream adoption in the long run.

In the future, all headsets, including the most powerful ones, will be free of the shackles of wires and won't need to be connected to a computer via a cable. VR headset technologies are already progressing to the point where corded or cabled headsets will no longer be used.

True next-generation headset products will feature super-bright displays, high-resolution optics, slimline headsets, and so on, which when combined produce visuals that are so realistic that no one can tell if they're real or virtual. A future of total immersion in VR!

Buying Your First VR Headset

Although not entirely ubiquitous, VR has slowly crept into the mainstream. This evolution has been a delight for those who wanted a more immersive way to have fun and play some of their favorite games.

Still, it's a bit tricky to know where to start when it comes to buying into the prospect of VR. As a beginner starting out with VR headsets, you probably want a good balance of quality and price — or maybe you're willing to pay big bucks for the best possible performance. In the following sections, I help you consider what you're looking for from a VR headset so you can find the one that's right for you.

Why buy a headset

Headsets are becoming more popular as more people recognize how owning one can enhance the quality of their metaverse experience. Here are some reasons to consider buying a VR headset:

>> **VR headsets provide a great experience when consuming visual content.** Everyone loves watching movies on big screens. A VR headset can provide you with an even more enhanced experience because there is no limit on virtual screen size. Need a 50-foot screen? You can build your own inside your VR display. In a virtual world, you can adjust your screen size and surroundings.

>> **Specific provider add-ons further enhance viewing experiences that you may miss otherwise.** One example of this is the Netflix app in the Meta Quest 2 headset, which provides a cozy setting that allows distraction-free viewing of your favorite content. Many other apps provide cinema-like settings to watch movies and have options to customize the screen size and theme. These are certainly better than consuming content on a phone or laptop.

TIP

DECIDING TO BUY A VR HEADSET

Here are some questions to consider as you decide whether to invest in a VR headset (or which one!):

- **What are your needs?** Why do you need a headset? Is it for gaming or design? The way you plan to use your headset may impact which one you buy.

- **How much am I willing to spend?** You can spend anywhere from several hundred to several thousand dollars for a VR headset. Budget is a great way to narrow the search.

- **How often do I play to upgrade my headset?** The answer to that question could have a bearing on how much you're willing to invest.

These general guidelines are true for both consumers and businesses. However, for applications within business that work with augmented reality and other complex graphics forms, your power user may need the Microsoft Halo Lens rather than the Meta Quest 2, which a typical office worker may use for general metaverse applications.

>> **You can use your VR headset as a tool for collaboration at work.** Your VR headset can provide a distraction-free atmosphere for working. Some apps can be used to create a workplace that beats working alone in a room.

On most metaverse apps, there is an option to connect to a physical computer to share the screen, which also provides a virtual keyboard and mouse to operate it. This allows for a much better-focused experience which boosts productivity.

>> **You can use your VR headset to join a virtual workout.** Work out with a virtual avatar or other participants, track your progress, and more.

Choosing between stand-alone and tethered headsets

When you're looking into buying your first VR headset, the first thing you'll notice is two types of headsets on the market: stand-alone and tethered. Both types of headsets come in varying resolutions, which impact the overall experience you have in the metaverse:

>> **Stand-alone headsets:** You don't need to be connect to another device, such as a computer or a console, to use a stand-alone headset. Stand-alone

headsets provide a wire-free VR experience. They're portable and can be used anywhere without having to be connected to a computer.

>> **Tethered headsets:** Tethered headsets have to be connected to a game controller or a computer in order to work. Tethered VR is more graphical because it's used on a PC. It's the perfect option for gamers who want to have the best graphics.

WARNING

If you use a computer that has a lot of unconcealed cables, you may find using a tethered headset uncomfortable. It may be a hindrance during activities where you need to move around. Plus, it makes the headset movement a bit heavy on the neck and may cause neck pain after prolonged usage.

Considering VR headset features

The VR headset market is currently segmented in relation to price, so choosing between headsets depends mainly on your budget. However, in addition to a budget, there are general technical features to look out for when choosing the right headset:

>> **Screen resolution:** A VR headset with the highest resolution will have the best visual quality. A high-quality VR experience demands a high-resolution headset. If you decide to spend a decent amount on your headset, you'll want to make sure it has a high resolution.

When buying a headset, follow the iPhone analogy, which essentially is that the laest and greatest model will always have the best technology but will also be more expensive than previous models. Bottom line: Choose a model that suits your budget and application.

My personal preference is to have a headset with resolution of at least 1440 x 1600 pixels. Anything less than that would be a big compromise in terms of the quality of graphics you can see through the headset. High-end headsets, such as the PlayStation VR2, have a resolution of at least 2000 x 2040.

>> **Field of view:** The *field of view* is the width of the image in degrees. The higher the field of view, the more immersive your experience. The best VR headsets have an average field of view of around 100 to 110 degrees, which means the field of vision after you wear the headset has that width range.

>> **Panel type:** Currently, many of the best VR headsets have liquid-crystal display (LCD) panels, but in the near future, most headsets are likely to adopt organic light-emitting diode (OLED) displays due to the increased color contrast and vividness. OLED displays promise better graphics and more immersive gameplay for most gamers.

TIP

GETTING THE MOST FROM YOUR VR HEADSET

To help you get the most mileage from your VR headsets and other equipment:

- Buy a headset from a big-box retailer that provides a long warranty.

- Keep your headset in good shape and avoid damage by handling and storing it carefully.

- Keep your VR headset updated through the latest patches by the manufacturer.

TIP

>> **Tracking system:** This system tracks your movement for precision to get a better immersion. Outside-in tracking uses external sensors to track the headset's position in a room, while inside-out tracking has cameras built directly into the headphones to detect the headset's position.

Most expensive VR headsets employ the use of an outside-in tracking system, which is generally more effective than inside-out tracking.

>> **Controllers:** Using a VR headset with great controllers goes a long way toward determining the experience you get in the virtual world. The better the controller, the more immersive the experience, particularly for those seeking to use their headsets mostly for gaming.

>> **Audio:** Headsets come with very decent audio quality and in most cases support standards such as surround sound. Some new headsets are even offering 3D sound, which makes the metaverse experience more lively. You can connect any third-party or secondary audio amplification setup to your metaverse hardware to provide you with extremely good sound. Thinking about connecting it with your home theater system? Go for it!

Popular Headset Models

The following sections describe the current lineup of popular VR headsets and offer information to help you make a wise pick. This list doesn't tell you want to buy — but it does give you information to help make an informed decision.

In the following sections, I include links to each manufacturer's website as well as current prices. To see the most recent models and pricing, your best bet is to check the websites.

Meta Quest 2

The Meta Quest 2 (formerly known as Oculus Quest 2) is lightweight and provides an excellent resolution. It's wire-free, easy to set up and use, and has ease of movement.

It's also an affordable headset given that you don't need a computer or gaming console to use it. However, it can still be connected to a computer wirelessly or with a single USB-C cable.

The Meta Quest 2 also has a base model with 128GB of storage, which can store plenty of apps. As of this writing, Meta is planning to release a pro headset for more advanced users.

Visit the Meta website for more details at www.meta.com/quest/products/quest-2.

Price: $399 to $498

$$

Vive Cosmos Elite

The Cosmos Elite has almost the same features as the Cosmos has, with the first controllers and first-generation base stations. The notable difference is the faceplate attached to the headset. The faceplate allows users to benefit from extra-accurate tracking through a built-in six-camera setup.

TIP

If you already have the Cosmos, you can upgrade to the Cosmos Elite by getting a new faceplate for $200 and buying a separate base station to be able to use it.

The modularity allows for adding a wireless adapter for a price that makes it altogether expensive.

Visit the Vive website for more details at www.vive.com.

Price: $749

Vive Pro Focus Plus

The Vive Pro Focus Plus is a stand-alone VR headset made as a follow-up to the HTC Vive Focus.

It comes with more refined features than the original, such as six degrees of freedom (6DoF), a new model of controllers, which allows for more immersion and enable developers to make their computer-based VR apps compatible with the hardware.

Also, it features a new design that makes it comfortable to wear and a new Kiosk Mode that allows the headset to restrict some users with access to apps that may not be suitable (for example, in the case of an age-appropriate setup for kids).

Visit the Vive website for more details at www.vive.com.

Price: $899

Valve Index VR HMD

The Valve Index has been around for a long time, and the headset is among the best in the market.

Unfortunately, its resolution isn't great — its image clarity is a dual 1,440 x 1,600 LCD panel. But to make up for this, its variable refresh settings enable a dial-in display in correspondence to your computer's performance, which is okay for a headset with a not-so-great resolution.

The headset comes with a complete kit, two controllers, wall-mounting hardware, and two 2.0 base stations, which come at the best value for VR first-timers.

Visit the Valve Index website for more details at https://store.steampowered.com/valveindex.

Price: $1,189

HP Reverb G2

HP's Rever G2 headset offers excellent image quality. For most gamers, this is a great deal. It's lightweight and comfortable, and it has a 2,160 x 2,160 per eye resolution and a 114-degree field of view. It's basically a reality headset that launches into Microsoft's native Windows 10 VR ecosystem, links with the Steam VR platform, and works with games and apps.

The G2 features a built-in camera, which allows for easy tracking and over-the-ears speakers designed by Valve.

Visit the HP website for more details at www.hp.com.

Price: $599

HoloLens 2

The HoloLens 2 is an improved successor to Microsoft's powerful HoloLens headset. Its new carbon-fiber build makes it comfortable, lightweight, and easier to adjust.

The field of view is also a great improvement from the original, and there have been some improvements when it comes to its functionality, including a smart new interface that makes the HoloLens 2 very easy to operate.

Its price puts the HoloLens 2 a bit on the high side, but it's worth it for people who understand the benefits. This headset is geared more toward the professional user.

Visit the Microsoft website for more details at www.microsoft.com/en-us/hololens.

The Holo Lens is available in three configurations:

» **Holo Lens 2:** $3,500

» **Holo Lens 2 Industrial Edition:** $4,950

» **Trimble XR10 with HoloLens 2:** $5,199

Lenovo ThinkReality A3

The Lenovo ThinkReality A3 Smart Glasses are an augmented reality (AR) headset connected to a computer, which makes them an extension of your screen. The Lenovo ThinkReality A3 Smart Glasses use a wired connection and can make use of Android smartphone apps, in addition to being lightweight, affordable, and comfortable to wear.

This headset is more geared towards the professional user.

Visit the Lenovo website for more details at `www.lenovo.com/us/en/think realitya3`.

Price: $1,499

Magic Leap 1

The Magic Leap 1 is stand-alone VR headset that doesn't need to be connected to a computer before use. Its refresh rate is 122 Hz with a 40-degree horizontal field of view.

The Magic Leap 1 shares an identical look with products similar to it and has a transparent front that enables the user to see the environment around them.

Visit the MagicLeap website for more details at `www.magicleap.com`.

Magic Leap headsets are available in three models:

>> **Magic Leap 2 Base:** $3,299

>> **Magic Leap 2 Developer Pro:** $4,099

>> **Magic Leap 2 Enterprise:** $4,999

Vive Flow

The Vive Flow looks more like a pair of huge, very thick VR goggles than than a VR headset. It's great for a brief venture into VR, though. It requires a USB-C cable and a 10,000-mAh battery pack to power it. But it doesn't require external sensors because it has an inside-out tracking system.

The Vive Flow is very comfortable, extremely lightweight, and easy to carry about, but it only supports Android smartphones for its control.

Visit the Vive website for more details at `www.vive.com`.

Price: $499

Google Cardboard

The Google Cardboard was made solely for gamers who prefer experiencing VR on their smartphones. To use it, you only need to set up your phone and fix it into the slot.

That said, it's more of a VR *viewer* than a headset because it doesn't have a strap. However, if you're looking to get into the world of VR for a small price, this is a perfect option because it does as great a job as any other VR out there.

Visit the Google Cardboard website for more details at `https://arvr.google.com/cardboard`.

Price: $8.95 to $39.95

Sony PlayStation VR

Almost six years old now, Sony's PlayStation VR headset remains the only head-mounted display for gaming consoles, with a surprisingly sharp immersive experience.

With the highly anticipated PlayStation VR 2, those with a PlayStation 5 would have a chance to get their hands on a more sophisticated headset with a new game library.

The PlayStation VR works great with PlayStation 5, but it needs to be connected with a breakout box full of wires. For it to work, it also requires, for some games, outdated PlayStation Move controllers and a camera, in addition to a camera adapter.

Using PlayStation VR with a PlayStation 4 is a great experience because Sony has exclusive VR games. It should also be noted that the PlayStation VR is often hard to get, which might extend to the soon-to-be-released model.

Visit the PlayStation website for more details at `www.playstation.com/en-us/ps-vr`.

Price: $299.99

Pimax 8K X

The Pimax 8K X headset provides the ultimate immersive gaming experience.

Pimax continues to improve with every piece of hardware it makes, so it's no surprise the Pimax 8K X corrects some of the software oversights its predecessor had. It has dual 4K screens per eye and a field of view of 170 degrees horizontal, which is a good 30 to 40 degrees above the competition.

The ultrawide headsets don't have much use for gamers, but if you're into other types of simulations, VR seems more realistic due to its extra peripheral vision.

Visit the Pimax website for more details at https://pimax.com.

Price: $1,009

Meta Quest Pro

In late 2022, Meta announced the launch of a new headset model, the Meta Quest Pro. Positioned as a high-end headset for the professional or the more advanced user, the Meta Quest Pro has a higher hardware specification, better graphics, vibrant colors, and a new rendering technology. The headset is also priced higher than its predecessor.

Visit the Meta website for more details at www.meta.com/quest/quest-pro.

Price: $1,499

Chapter **7**

Getting Equipped to Game in the Metaverse

The gaming industry has been around for at least the last 30 years. Today gaming technologies range from advanced virtual reality (VR) graphics and crystal-clear rendering to hardware devices that provide feedback and real-time sensations of what's happening in a game. This chapter is all about getting started with gaming hardware that you can use for your metaverse experiences.

First Things First: Preparing to Start Gaming in the Metaverse

Before you consider hardware, you need to set up your accounts in the metaverse. Other chapters cover these tasks in detail, but here's the general process:

1. **Create an account in the metaverse.**

   To get started, you need a user account on a metaverse platform. I cover major metaverse platforms in Chapter 2.

TIPS FOR METAVERSE GAMING

Here are recommendations that will get you started if you're just beginning to game in the metaverse:

- Check out as many metaverse games as you can to see what you like.

- Invest in only the essential hardware first, before going all in on different gadgets. As your expertise grows, slowly expand to things such as haptic devices and gaming Rigs. You don't need to start with extreme experiences.

- If you face any health conditions, such as light and sound sensitivity, consult with your health-care provider before jumping into metaverse gaming.

- Game responsibly. Don't abuse anyone online, and don't tolerate abuse from anyone either. For more on safety in the metaverse, turn to Chapter 3.

2. **Figure out what's required to experience the game you choose.**

    From a gaming perspective, you may need a VR headset at a minimum to experience a game in the metaverse. If you don't have one, you may be able to participate in some games on a 2D screen, but it may not give you the full experience.

3. **Set up a crypto wallet.**

    Some games may need you to pay to play or to buy access. For most metaverse platforms, this means buying the proprietary token or cryptocurrency of that specific metaverse. Read more about this in Chapter 4.

After you have a user account on a metaverse platform and you've obtained some tokens, you just need to get the hardware required to experience the games you choose.

Knowing Which Hardware Is Essential

To access metaverse-like games and, by extension, the metaverse, you need to have the right hardware. For this reason, manufacturers are putting a lot of emphasis on developing new VR headsets, gaming rigs, simulators, and other gaming-specific hardware.

In this section, I fill you in on some of the types of gaming experiences in the metaverse, from the very basic to the very advanced, and let you know what hardware you need to get started.

Smartphones

Smartphones are some of the easiest ways to access the metaverse today. With an iOS or Android device, you can explore the experiences of virtual worlds and metaverse platforms. Today, most new smartphones have strong enough graphics to precisely render virtual worlds.

REMEMBER

The metaverse exists separately from VR. VR takes the whole experience a notch higher with increased immersion and interactivity. So if you're looking to step into the metaverse, just grab your smartphone to get started!

Computers

Game developers like Roblox and Epic Games have made it so that you can access their metaverse games on a personal computer (PC). Some games are available on both Windows and Mac, while others are available on only one. To enjoy the metaverse experience as a whole, the PC must have a good graphics processing unit (GPU), sufficient random access memory (RAM), and a very good central processing unit (CPU) so there is no lag. (Joining a session in the metaverse can get heavy on the computer and make it slow.)

TIP

Here's what you should aim for if you're getting ready to buy a new PC or upgrade your existing one:

>> **GPU:** At least 16GB

>> **RAM:** At least 16GB; ideally, 32GB

>> **CPU:** At least an Intel Core i5; ideally, an Intel Core i7 or above

Any less and your computer is likely to be slow and sluggish when connected to a metaverse platform.

Gaming consoles

Sony, Microsoft, and Nintendo have taken over the gaming console market from manufacturers like Atari and Sega. Gaming consoles provide a central source from which users can access a world of games. Having been used in gaming for years, gaming consoles are also relevant when it comes to the metaverse's applications beyond gaming. Major manufacturers have made changes with interoperability and level of immersion, making it so that other accessories for enjoying virtual experiences can be mounted on the consoles.

If you already own an Xbox, you're on track to having a lot of fun in the metaverse. Most gaming platforms offer the same games on a PC and a gaming console, so there isn't much of a difference between the experiences of the two.

Some of the popular recent consoles on the market include

>> Nintendo Switch – OLED Model

>> Xbox Series S and Xbox Series X

>> PlayStation 5

VR headsets

Even though the metaverse exists in a device-agnostic form — one where it can be accessed by any device — VR devices provide more immersive experiences for gamers.

VR headsets are generating the most buzz at the moment because they provide an immersive experience in a digital world — providing visual, auditory, and touch signals. Meta and Sony have VR headset offerings from $299, and companies like Apple are said to be working on advanced VR headset offerings.

Metaverse enthusiasts are preparing for the arrival of the metaverse in all its glory by stocking up on devices like this. Augmented reality (AR) glasses and game controllers can merge virtual elements with real-life physical spaces and are an important extension for enjoying these experiences.

The upcoming section "Matching a Headset to the Gaming Experience" covers the types of headsets to consider. For more information on using headsets and detailed description of the most popular headsets as of this writing, see Chapter 6.

Game controllers

Metaverse gaming is best experienced with a game controller. You can play a game on your smartphone, tablet, or computer and use your thumbs or a keyboard and mouse, but for a truly immersive experience, game controllers and new forms of accessories are highly recommended.

Metaverse games are highly interactive. This interaction includes moving your avatar around, moving items, touching surfaces, and even receiving impact feedback. This is where game controllers come in. Game controllers work well with VR headsets and other hardware to bring more immersive virtual experiences.

In addition to gaming, these controllers can be used in other fields. For example, game controllers can be used to move your avatar around a real estate property you're considering buying or to interact with other users in a virtual meeting.

VR controllers are essentially an upgrade of traditional game controllers. They have special features that make them unique and necessary for a wholesome virtual experience. There are numerous offerings on the market, but some stand out among others because of their ergonomic and sensitivity advantages.

TIP

When considering a controller to purchase for your metaverse gaming experience, here are some features you should take into consideration:

>> **Comfortable and functional design:** The games you play could run from a few minutes to hours depending. So, the controllers you use shouldn't make playing uncomfortable. The build should be sleek and easy to handle. All elements of the controller — including the weight and the spacing of buttons, triggers, touchpads, and the thumb stick — must have been put together to provide maximum comfort for you during gaming.

>> **Accurate tracking:** Movement tracking is a fundamental technical capability of a game controller. However, different controllers have varying degrees of precision. Any latency in the tracking of your hand or body movements during a game can make you miss a shot and lead to frustration as you play. Two common tracking system options used by game controllers are the lighthouse tracking system and the inside-out tracking system. The lighthouse tracking system uses base stations and laser/infrared transmissions; the inside-out system uses headset cameras and LED lights.

>> **Quality:** Gamers tend to be carried away by the virtual experience so much that they run into walls or other surfaces repeatedly. The controllers you get should be able to withstand such repeated impacts. The battery is another factor that impacts overall quality; you want to be able to enjoy long hours of play and not need to purchase a replacement battery for a long time.

>> **Compatibility:** Your game controller must be compatible with the devices you use to access metaverse games, including VR headsets and computers. Choosing one that's compatible with a wide range of devices may seem like the best option, but such controllers may lack other features that you want to enjoy, so it can be a tradeoff. The need for wide-range compatibility may also be drastically reduced when you can access multiple game stores and platforms with the device you already have.

>> **Degree of movement:** Smashing into a wall isn't the only problem you may encounter in using game controllers. The degree of mobility these gadgets offer is also important because restricted movement affects the gaming experience. You can move your avatar around and experience the virtual world in 3D with a game controller. This may require you to move around in the physical space

where you are; a wired game controller may inhibit that movement. There are wireless options that allow you to connect to your headset, smartphone, PC, or game console so you can move around freely when playing.

The next section describes some of the more popular game controllers as of this writing.

Choosing a Game Controller

Game controllers significantly improve game play and lead to a better experience. The early days of gaming saw the evolution of joysticks that have been shaped into gaming consoles, motion detection accessories, and body suits. Everything is now leading toward a more experiential gameplay rather than just being able to *participate.*

This section looks at some of the most popular game controllers and their features. The idea behind game controllers has been the same for more than a decade, but new types of motion sensors and character control technologies are quickly paving the way for the future of gaming.

Samsung Gear VR Controller

The Samsung Gear VR Controller is great for mobile VR gamers who want a cost-effective option. It features a simple build and comes as a single unit with a touchpad, volume buttons, triggers, and two navigation buttons. It has excellent tracking, too.

The Samsung Gear VR Controller is only compatible with the Samsung Gear VR headset. But because users can connect to the Oculus store, the compatibility restriction isn't much of a bother.

Visit www.samsung.com/hk_en/mobile-accessories/gear-vr-controller-et-yo324bbegww to learn more.

PlayStation Move motion controller

The PlayStation Move is the results of PlayStation's years of experience providing top-notch products in the VR gaming space. The controllers are lightweight and comfortable to use for long hours. They have very good tracking and provide a more immersive gaming experience with haptic feedback. However, this controller is only compatible with PlayStation consoles.

Visit www.playstation.com/en-us/accessories/playstation-move-motion-controller to learn more.

Meta Quest Touch Pro Controllers

The Meta Quest Touch Pro Controllers are part of the Meta Quest Touch bundle and are also available as a stand-alone accessory. The controllers have three onboard cameras for tracking movement. They also come with a pressure sensor for pinching and a pressure-sensitive stylus tip. These offer added functionality and usability.

Learn more at www.meta.com/quest/accessories/quest-pro-touch-pro-controller.

SteelSeries Stratus Duo

The SteelSeries Stratus Duo offers up to 20 hours of play with a single charge. It's compatible with a wide range of devices, including Steam. The headset offers a seamless connection with Android, Meta Quest, and Samsung Gear headsets out of the box.

Go to https://steelseries.com/gaming-controllers/stratus-duo to learn more.

Vive Controller

The Vive Controller features more than 20 sensors in its head, making it very sensitive and responsive. It sports a simple build with a grip button and trigger. It also has a multifunctional trackpad instead of a button and stick arrangement. The haptic feedback provided makes for an immersive VR experience.

Go to www.vive.com/us/accessory/controller to learn more.

Matching a Headset to the Gaming Experience

Gaming is best experienced through high-resolution displays. VR headsets provide exactly that. Today the choice is extensive when it comes to choosing a VR headset. They're available within a wide price range. But it's not just pricing that determines the outcome of your experiences — some gaming headsets are designed to only deliver VR, while others can deliver AR and some even mixed reality (MR).

Chapter 6 covers more about headsets and provides detailed descriptions of the headsets that are most popular as of this writing.

Virtual-reality headsets

VR headsets are one of the most important elements of a VR setup — they make the experience a lot more realistic. A wide range of headsets are on the market, but a good VR headset should allow you to see and hear elements of the virtual world at a more heightened level than you would with just a smartphone or PC.

Creators of these headsets have put in work to refine their offerings and provide a more immersive experience. Today's headsets are lightweight and easy to use. If you look closely, you'll find a VR headset that works perfectly for you, whether you want to play games, see movies, or work in the virtual space.

REMEMBER

Most of the VR headsets that offer excellent quality when it comes to design and overall experience cost hundreds of dollars. But it's common for the prices of these gadgets to drop over time.

Here are some of the factors you should consider when buying a VR headset:

>> **Design:** There are different headset designs, ranging from the simple magnifying lens in a cardboard case to more high-end designs powered by game consoles or powerful gaming PCs. The latter usually provide the best VR experiences, which can't be powered by smartphones. Examples of these headsets include the PlayStation VR and Vive. The Google Cardboard is the lower-end alternative, which is essentially a phone case; it works well with Android phones and iPhones. Headsets should be able to give an immersive experience, be easy to use with functional perks, and be lightweight. High-end and midrange headsets usually have some form of motion tracking that makes VR experiences such as gaming more enjoyable. The variations in design ultimately affect user experience and, by extension, price.

>> **Price:** Low-end headsets go for $20 to $40, which is understandable because of their simple build and reduced capabilities. Midrange headsets are a step up from the low-end, cardboard types, and they typically sell for $75 to $150. The high-end versions offer the best experiences and start from about $400 and may go as high as $1,000.

These prices are for just the headsets — there may be some hidden costs. For example, the PlayStation VR doesn't work without a PlayStation 4 or PlayStation 5 console, so if you don't already have one of those, you'll have to buy one along with the VR headset. Also, for high-end VR headsets that will be powered by a PC, only powerful PCs like the ones used by film and video editors (which have a lot of processing power) provide the best experiences. You'll spend about $1,000 on one of those PCs, in addition to the cost of the headset.

>> **Controllers:** The headset setup should normally allow for a button or two for controls. These buttons can be used to swipe through options, make selections, or perform some other tasks in the game. The cardboard types usually have one button for this (connected to a lever) or a space for you to put your index finger or thumb for such navigations. The midrange options may include trackpads that allow for multiple applications in addition to a separate back button. The high-end options may have a larger trackpad and more buttons; they also include motion sensors that allow you to enjoy a more realistic experience in a lot of games.

>> **Space economy:** When you're exploring virtual worlds with a VR headset, you may need to move around. You want a VR headset that allows you to move. The headset should also provide distraction canceling so you have a more immersive experience. Low-end headsets are extremely inexpensive and are the least comfortable, while high-end models are extremely comfortable and expensive. This also includes being able to provide a better field of view and eliminating distractions. For example, in a cardboard headset, there really isn't any hardware except two lenses mounted on a cardboard frame. The midrange offerings do better than the cardboard variants in this regard; because most of them are stand-alone headsets, they allow free movement. With high-end headsets, connectivity to the console or PC may be via tethering or cables, which affects mobility. If you want more freedom to move around, you may want to consider a headset with Bluetooth or Wi-Fi connectivity options.

Although some metaverse games can be accessed and enjoyed with smartphones and PCs, using a VR headset makes the experience a lot more realistic.

Here are some games that can be enjoyed with VR headsets:

>> Altspace VR

>> The Bohemian Rhapsody Experience

>> The Brookhaven Experiment

>> EVE: Valkyrie

- InMind VR
- Jaunt VR
- Minecraft Virtual Reality
- Smash Hit
- theBlu
- Thumper

Augmented-reality headsets

AR blends the virtual world with the real world. (For a full discussion of AR, see Chapter 6.)

AR gaming headsets have a more compact build — they look like regular glasses at a glance. Because of their size, they're more popularly referred to as AR "glasses," and some of them can be worn all day, like regular glasses.

WARNING

If you wear prescription glasses, AR headsets may pose a problem because you won't be able to wear your regular glasses and your AR headset at the same time.

AR glasses project virtual elements onto real-life spaces and surfaces. Although some AR glasses can be used for gaming, most of the ones on the market are preferred for more professional settings like medicine, drug discovery, and engineering. They're used to create a more immersive working environment for remote workers in this field and to facilitate collaborative communication between team members located far away from one another.

AR glasses are usually powered by smartphones or a power bank. The simple and lightweight build that the manufacturers are going for would be compromised if large batteries were included.

The glasses include cameras for streaming and some for effecting holographic demonstrations that may be used in business presentations. There are different types of AR glasses, including handheld devices like smartphones, holographic displays, smart glasses, and head-up displays (HUDs), which imprint 3D computer-generated information onto the user's field of view.

The Nreal Air AR Glasses are an example of AR glasses that are available for use by gamers. They go for as low as $599. The more professional AR smart glasses start around $1,000.

Games for which AR glasses can be used include the following:

>> Harry Potter: Wizards Unite

>> Ingress

>> Pokémon GO

>> Run

>> Zombies

Mixed-reality headsets

MR is a combination of VR and AR — it requires that the real world and the virtual world come together to offer a unique experience for the viewer. MR headsets are expected to include numerous cameras so a live feed can be taken from the user's surroundings. This live feed will then be combined with virtual elements and virtual locations for multiple applications. Most AR smart glasses already provide MR to some degree because they have multiple cameras and sensors.

FUTURECAST

Apple is said to be working on an MR headset that will sport a compact build and a lightweight structure. With multiple sensors and cameras, it's expected to provide a new perspective on possibilities for MR headsets in the future.

Some MR games that can result in better experiences with an MR headset include the following:

>> Beat Saber

>> Crystal Rift

>> SteamVR

Adding Specialized Gaming Hardware and Accessories

Gaming as an industry has developed extensively over the past several decades. Today, specialized hardware devices that further enhance the gaming experience are frequently used by passionate gamers. In this section, I introduce you to some specialty hardware that can improve the overall gaming experience and bring a new level of engagement to your metaverse gaming activities.

Hardware devices and accessories aren't cheap. Do your research on the various options available and figure out what you need. Gaming hardware is always changing, and new models are coming to the market at a rapid pace.

Gaming computers

The metaverse gaming experience relies on the proficiency of the setup. Gaming computers are high-performance computers made specifically for gaming. They sport high-end graphics processing units (GPUs), more random access memory (RAM), and multiple disk drive components. In an ideal setup, this would be at least an Intel Core i5 microprocessor, at least 16GB of RAM (ideally, 32GB) and at least a 16GB GPU. For a high-end machine this could be an Intel Core i9 or AMD Ryzen 9 processor, 64GB of RAM, and a 32GB GPU.

These rigs eliminate lagging and substandard rendering of graphics, which would occur if you used a regular low-capacity computer to play a game. Gaming rigs have cooling systems to keep temperatures in check while the central processing units (CPUs) are being pushed beyond the limits of normal computers. A stronger gaming rig makes for a smoother experience in metaverse games. You can buy them online or build them from scratch to accommodate your specific needs.

TIP

See the latest gaming computers compared on any of these websites:

>> **PC Gamer:** www.pcgamer.com/best-gaming-pc

>> **PC Magazine:** www.pcmag.com/picks/the-best-gaming-desktops

>> **Tom's Hardware:** www.tomshardware.com/best-picks/best-gaming-pcs

WHAT IS HAPTIC FEEDBACK?

Haptic feedback is essential for a more immersive experience in metaverse games. Most high-end game controllers provide these through trackpads or thumb sticks. Haptic gloves and vests that allow a more expansive range of responses in game are not yet available commercially, but they take the haptic feedback advantage to a higher degree. It's expected that advances in gaming and metaverse tech will ultimately lead to full-body haptic suits, which will have advanced motion tracking elements and provide haptic feedback all over the body. Users will be able to feel the ambient temperature in a metaverse location — higher temperatures underground and lower temperatures in winter-themed locations.

Gaming chairs

Gaming chairs are one of the earliest forms of haptic devices. Early gaming chairs just provided comfort for users when they were sitting for a long time. Today's gaming chairs, however, offer a lot more, such as customization, may have pre-installed haptic sensors, and connectivity to Bluetooth and Wi-Fi systems.

Motion simulators

Motion simulators are a full system that can includes a gaming chair, a gaming computer, and controllers. Typically, motion simulators are available as a stand-alone device that can be fitted with any gaming computer setup. Motion simulator prices can range from a couple thousand dollars for the best entry-level system to a top range of $100,000 if you're looking for a peak experience and money is no object.

Motion simulator pricing is based on the number of axes the device uses. Typical configurations are two, four, and six axes. Axes dictate the plane of movement or how a certain object moves around its axis or axes. For example, a gyroscope has three axes, the Earth has one axis, and the latest game controllers have six axes. Often referred to as *six degrees of freedom* (or 6DOF), the six degrees movement are as follows (see Figure 7-1):

>> Surge (forward and backward)

>> Sway (left and right)

>> Heave (up and down)

>> Yaw (rotation around the normal axis)

>> Pitch (rotation around the transverse axis)

>> Roll (rotation around the longitudinal axis)

Typical motion simulators are motor based, but more advanced units can have liquid or compressed air systems powering the motion.

TIP

Check out a handy list of the latest gaming motion simulators on CNET at www. cnet.com/roadshow/news/best-sim-racing-cockpit.

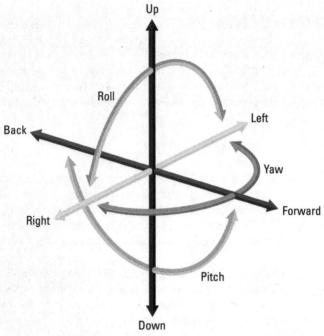

FIGURE 7-1:
The six degrees
of movement.

Haptic feedback gaming accessories

Haptic feedback is the vibrational feedback received through a device or an accessory as a response from a video game. Many controllers and devices today have haptic feedback built in, and the trend is expanding to wearables and specialty equipment.

Here is a quick primer on the types of haptic feedback:

>> **Quad haptics:** This system includes four channels, two for each hand, typically packaged into a game controller form factor. Multiple peripheral makers support this kind of device.

>> **Multi-channel haptics:** A big transition from the previous technology, Multi-channel haptics provides feedback to various devices that can include keyboards, headsets, mobile variables, and so on.

>> **Multi-modal haptics:** These go beyond vibration and force feedback. They include hot and cold actuators that provide an actual sensation of hot or cold just as it would feel by touching a surface that has those temperatures. You can also feel the texture of surfaces (for example, the smoothness of stainless steel versus the roughness of wood). And these haptic devices will be able to translate these feelings from the virtual world to the real world.

>> **Hyper-modal haptics:** With this futuristic mode of haptics, there will be no need for external peripherals. Instead, your body will be able to generate sensations directly with no stimulation. In other words, your body would have to be embedded with sensors and actuators that would make this possible. One of the products that's in an early stage of testing and development is Neuralink (www.neuralink.com), a brain implant that will help people control objects and devices with the power of our minds in the future.

The following sections cover some advanced gaming and metaverse accessories that aren't really suitable for an average user and are extremely specialized. If you really want to get into gaming, these accessories are worth a try.

Teslasuit

A full-body haptic suit developed by Tesla, the Teslasuit (https://teslasuit.io) is an interface with the gaming world. That's what defines the Teslasuit as a "human to digital interface" that monitors behavior and improves performance.

The Teslasuit is comprised of three main components:

>> **Haptic feedback:** The haptic feedback mechanism uses electro-muscle stimulation and transcutaneous electrical nerve stimulation (TENS) for simulating real-life feelings and sensations on the body. TENS technology uses a mild electric current to relieve pain. The suit provides physical feedback based on what the viewer is seeing either on flat viewing surfaces or in immersive 3D such as the metaverse.

>> **Motion capture:** The Teslasuit has 14 inertial measurement units (IMUs) that capture movement, record body positioning and monitor changes in position. The unit consists of multiple accelerometers, gyroscopes, and magnetometers.

>> **Biometric system:** The Teslasuit has a photoplethysmography (PPG) system providing information about the heart rate, oxygen saturation, and pulse rate of the user.

The suit is made from two pieces and consist of a jacket and pants. It comes in two editions:

>> **XR Edition:** The XR Edition features three integrated systems — haptic feedback, motion capture, and biometry.

>> **Medical Edition:** The Medical Edition features an added function of medical mapping, offering complete back stimulation and side zippers for anyone who can't dress independently.

Teslasuit Glove

A haptic device made to fit the hand of a user, the Teslasuit Glove (https://teslasuit.io) brings the touch and feel of virtual objects to a user's fingertips. Featuring haptic feedback, force feedback, finger tracking, and biometrics, the glove has numerous applications and is probably one of the only such advanced products on the market today.

TactSuit

The TactSuit (www.bhaptics.com) is a wireless haptic vest with up to 40 individual controllers and response transmitters, depending on the model. The embedded haptics provide feedback of more than 300 haptics patterns built across different games. Designed for gamers, the suit is packed with features such as connectivity through Bluetooth and offers a lag-free wireless connection to devices. The suit weighs 3.7 pounds and offers a play time of up to 18 hours.

TactSuit also features an additional haptics sleeve product for the arms. Imagine playing a sword fight game and receiving direct feedback on your arms. Each armband includes 12 haptic feedback points, as well as audio-based haptics, that deliver vibration feedback based on audio.

Tactosy for Hands

Tactosy for Hands (www.bhaptics.com/tactsuit/tactosy-for-hands) was specially designed as a haptic feedback device to be used for games such as boxing and other sports that need you to move your arms. These devices fit on your hands like a pair of gloves and deliver real-time haptic feedback.

KOR-FX gaming vest

The KOR-FX gaming vest (www.korfx.com/products) utilizes acousto-optic signals from games and media, translated into high-definition feedback, allowing users to feel on-screen action and environmental factors. Typical users are those playing games with vivid effects, such as military battles where you need to get an edge over your enemies.

OWO haptic vest

OWO (https://owogame.com) is another manufacturer that offers a haptic vest for "sensations technology," enabling users to feel everything that happens in the metaverse.

The OWO vest won the Innovation Award at the 2022 CES Conference in Las Vegas.

Some features of the system include

>> The ability to customize the intensity of sensations you want to feel

>> A wireless system

>> Ten sensation locations

>> Bluetooth and Wi-Fi connectivity

>> Lightweight (less than 2 pounds)

ButtKicker Gamer Plus

Immersive haptic transducers like the ButtKicker Gamer Plus (https:// thebuttkicker.com/products/buttkicker-gamer-plus) are feedback devices that can be attached to chairs, desks, beds, and other physical infrastructure. They provide live feedback through vibration, based on what the user is experiencing in a VR game.

Chapter **8**

Enjoying Entertainment in the Metaverse

Thirty-three million people watched Lil Nas perform in the metaverse for his Roblox appearance in 2020. This was roughly three times the number of viewers who watched him on traditional TV at the Grammys in 2022.

Metaverse entertainment is at an incredibly early stage of its development, but already, viewership is up for some media and broadcast events. As the infrastructure that makes the metaverse possible improves, the metaverse will improve as well. As market forces converge, we'll see a better, faster, and easier metaverse. Entertainment will likely be one of the first industries to scale.

This chapter explores how the metaverse may help shape (and be shaped by) the entertainment industry.

Choosing Your Own Experience with Metaverse Entertainment Channels

In the "Bandersnatch" episode of the TV series *Black Mirror*, Netflix experimented with a new create-your-own-ending viewing experience. Selecting a custom ending turned out to be exciting for viewers. Now consider how the metaverse can amplify this experience by allowing you to fully immerse yourself in a media experience.

Metaverse platforms seeking to stake their claim in the entertainment industry are building alliances with household names such as Pixar, Sony, and other production houses. These platforms offer the ability to integrate digital characters (controlled by the viewer, or metaverse user) into media. Imagine watching a Hollywood film or on-demand TV content in the metaverse, but instead of passively watching, you get to be a character in the film, possibly with your avatar playing the role.

Design houses such as Hero Maker Studios have already started creating individual avatar nonfungible tokens (NFTs) that can be personalized and used across metaverse platforms. This means that you can now own your own custom-designed digital avatar and participate in different narratives and metaverse-based stories in which you're the hero and you can save the world. This ability to bring the user into the story and customize their journey on a 3D platform that's visually engaging is truly a revolutionary aspect of metaverse entertainment. Visit the Hero Maker Studios website (`www.heromakerstudios.com`) for more details.

Storytelling in the metaverse may eventually include participants taking part in TV shows, blockbuster movies, and other production media in a highly personalized manner.

Streaming Content in the Metaverse

The metaverse can be used as a channel to stream content. This content or message can be in any written or audiovisual form. Thanks to the 3D environment within the metaverse, it's now possible to create virtual screens as big as the tallest skyscrapers within the metaverse world. As a creator, you can then play video content on the screen.

One reason different types of gatherings are being organized in the metaverse is because the venue size, display size, and other aspects of holding an event can be scaled. Think about it: What is a key parameter that makes an event well attended? The capacity of the location where the event is being held. In the real world, the number of people attending an event is directly proportional to how many people the venue can hold — not as many people can attend an event in a conference room as can attend an event held in a large stadium.

In the metaverse, you're operating in a world and environment with limitless capacity in terms of the number of people who can attend. You can create an outdoor metaverse venue, create a massive screen, and open up capacity for hundreds of viewers to join!

Creating a metaverse TV channel

Land acquisition is a key parameter in being able to broadcast any content on a metaverse platform. You need a landing place on the Internet, similar to a website on the regular Internet, where you can host content. In the metaverse, this may be possible by purchasing your own piece of virtual land on one of the many metaverse platforms that sell it. Check out Chapter 2 for more on purchasing land in the metaverse.

Today on the Internet, you have more than one option for broadcasting your own videos. The typical options look like this.

>> Register a domain name and create your own website where your videos are hosted. Visitors to your website can then view your video content directly on your website.

>> Create and post your videos to a website such as YouTube, which is publicly accessible to millions of other users on the platform.

>> Create the content on social media platforms such as Facebook, Snapchat, Twitter, and TikTok, where it can be viewed by users similar to you who may or may not be creating their own content.

The metaverse is slightly different from the Internet you're used to, also referred to as Web 2.0. In the metaverse, the need to register a domain name and create a website has been replaced by the option to acquire land and develop it to use it for activities such as posting content.

The metaverse is also based on a new form of the Internet called Web 3.0. (Sometimes *Web 3.0* is also used to refer to a future Internet, but that relates more to the user experience design of websites.) Web 2.0, or the Internet architecture, is heavily dependent on central players (companies that control vast expanses and services on the Internet). Companies like Google, Microsoft, Meta, and a few others control most of the Internet by providing services and infrastructure that are used by a majority of users online.

Web 3.0 is a new form of Internet built on the idea of decentralization. Users on Web 3.0 are able to create content and retain ownership of that content. Platforms are powered by multiple users who work together in the form of a decentralized autonomous organization (DAO) that provides all the legal and regulatory bells and whistles needed for a decentralized entity to operate and function.

This means you can acquire land and build it according to your needs. The building can consist of a virtual concert venue, a virtual library, or a structure of any kind that can house a virtual museum or a virtual club — the choice is yours. Subsequently creating your own content and hosting it within that environment is similar to recording video content and embedding it in the right places within this structure.

A fundamental difference between traditional websites and the metaverse is that a website is a two-dimensional asset that is available on a two-dimensional screen. Think about your computer monitor, your tablet, your cell phone, or even a billboard — these are all two-dimensional. The third dimension (depth) is missing. The metaverse, on the other hand, is a three-dimensional space where you have height, width, *and* depth for all properties that have been developed. As a result, the options to embed content and build structured content and multimedia within your developed real estate is different from building a traditional website.

TIP

Developing in the metaverse may seem complicated, but after you get into it and overcome the initial learning curve, building exciting things and structures is easy! Depending on your level of expertise (and how much time you have to spend learning), you may want to hire a domain expert or an agency that excels in metaverse construction.

This area of metaverse development — where agencies, freelancers, and individual contributors can help create assets in the metaverse — is likely going to be a big part of supporting the development of the metaverse as a whole. We're at the dawn of the metaverse creator economy.

Incorporating video and other content

A virtual world within any metaverse is an artificial, virtual reality (VR)–enabled world where you can place videos on any structure that you own or have built and retain ownership. For a metaverse TV channel, you may even connect a live-streaming software package and display it on a virtual screen in your metaverse facility. Visitors to your virtual facility can then watch this content as it broadcasts. This really changes how we look at interaction.

You can add videos, images, audio, and even videoconferencing. Here are two ways of accomplishing this (refer to your metaverse platform for any specific instructions):

>> **Embed third-party content.** Within metaverse platforms, it's relatively easy to embed content from third-party websites such as YouTube. When building your facility within the metaverse, you can create hot spots or a frame where content will be embedded.

>> **Upload native content.** *Native content* is content, such as a video, that you upload directly to your metaverse platform. If your metaverse platform uploads video content directly to it, that content is hosted on the metaverse platform's servers.

As metaverse platforms develop their ability to offer drag-and-drop interfaces and better software development kits (SDKs) to users, creating content specifically for the metaverse will become easier.

Monetizing Entertainment and Other Content

Monetizing content is a mature feature of various platforms on the Internet, and you can expect it to emerge more fully in the metaverse as well. *Monetization* means that you're able to earn and create a revenue stream by creating various types of content, such as podcasts or videos.

A very common model available today is that of influencers on YouTube — channel owners who have created compelling content that has resonated with their audiences benefit from bringing more subscribers to their channels. It's not uncommon to see subscriber counts in the millions for individual accounts on YouTube.

On YouTube and other Internet platforms, channel owners monetize their content in three ways:

» **Platforms:** Get paid by platform owners such as YouTube to drive more views and more users to the YouTube platform. YouTube has monetization policies in place that rewards content creators based on the number of views their videos receive. This may be just a fraction of a cent per view, but channels that have millions of subscribers drive a good amount of revenue through monetization.

» **Sponsors:** Influencers get sponsors to support their video content and get paid for product placement and shoutouts.

» **Affiliate marketing:** Influencers also use affiliate marketing to promote third-party products in their content, as well as in their content descriptions. Affiliate marketing rewards referrals and typically offers a percentage cut from the price of an item when a click on a link leads to a buying decision. Channel owners and content creators can do this on web content, video content, and any other content on any platform. Affiliate marketing is a big revenue generator for content creators.

FUTURECAST

Although these methods are very common on the Internet and have evolved over the last couple of decades, they haven't yet hit the metaverse, at least not as of this writing. The next step in the evolution of the metaverse is going to be the monetization of content and rewarding content creators. For platform owners, it will be important from a user acquisition perspective to push metaverse content creators on their platforms to create compelling content including video, podcast, and live content that can drive conversions.

Building a following

Before you can monetize content, you must build a following. Customers can't buy what they don't see! To grow your following, think like a content creator or an entertainer. Build a base of followers by creating compelling experiences and content that are sharable, informative, educational, and whatever your audience needs. Monetization of this content would be pivotal right from the start. (Chapter 11 provides specifics about marketing in the metaverse.)

TIP

Here are some tips that may help you succeed as a content creator in the metaverse:

>> Create a content calendar that identifies your content themes, type of content, and other key specifics. Hire a part-time or full-time content manager or a production assistant who can help build and manage a solid content plan.

>> Creating meaningful content. Ensure that your content resonates with your audiences and that you're addressing things and ideas that your viewers would be interested in.

>> Create content that's respectful and not derogatory to anyone. Quality content helps raise awareness around key issues and brings people together.

>> Post content on a regular schedule rather than haphazardly. Follow a cadence and a structured approach.

>> Measure audience reactions and responses for your content and engage with your audience by asking questions and being proactive.

>> Be authentic and original.

Offering subscription services

The subscription model is an ongoing revenue generation model on the Internet. Users or consumers pay a monthly fee to access content. In the regular world, subscription services include Hulu, Netflix, HBO Max, Disney Plus, and others.

A subscription model helps businesses have a steady source of revenue from their customers. Subscription services in the metaverse will need to follow a similar path to those on the Internet.

Here are the steps to create a subscription service in the metaverse:

1. **Create content that your followers and visitors will love.**

2. **Build a one-on-one relationship with viewers and address their problems and challenges.**

    In essence, be an incredible source of value for your target audience.

3. **Create a way for your audience to access subscriber-only content.**

    In the metaverse, this could involve giving access to a specific area within your metaverse world that only subscribers have access to.

4. **Promote your subscription-only advantages as much as you can so more of your visitors subscribe to your content.**

5. **Monetize subscription services by creating exclusivity and charging your subscribers a minimal fee for added benefits (beyond basic membership).**

Video-on-demand (VOD)

Video-on-demand (VOD) platforms include Netflix, Hulu, Disney Plus, and more. VOD platforms also support libraries of videos. You can watch a TV show, a movie, an episode of a series, and other types of content.

Netflix, one of the industry leaders in VOD, has already started experimenting with the metaverse. In 2022, Netflix built a movie experience in Decentraland to coincide with its release of the film *The Gray Man*. Users on Decentraland were able to view short clips and interact with content on the Netflix virtual property on Decentraland.

Here is how watching content in the metaverse may offer a different and in some cases more deeper experience in viewership:

>> A visually enhanced display in three dimensions rather than in two dimensions, currently available over non-metaverse channels.

>> The ability to watch content with other participants at the same virtual venue.

>> The ability to interact with video content such as through NFTs.

>> Gamification of VOD content. VOD providers can gamify video content to engage with viewers and reward their viewership habits or patterns.

>> The ability to customize the 3D environments in which VOD content is delivered. Users can design their own layouts and virtual spaces that could host more than one screen at a time, giving the users more control over their viewership experience.

USER-GENERATED VIDEO

The Unreal Engine is a state-of-the-art technology that has been critically acclaimed for breaking all previous boundaries of visual design and virtual content regeneration. The technology is being looked at by production studios such as Dark Slope, which is also the developer of the mixed-reality game, The Bogey Ogre.

Future gaming content will use visual content generation technologies such as the Unreal Engine and its future iterations, and raise the bar in experiential gaming. In addition, tracking movements of controllers and headset cameras will change the response received from the game. Future design needs to shift from a 2D to native 3D design approach, as virtual reality and Metaverse live streaming take off.

Connecting with fans through live entertainment

Live entertainment and concerts are quickly finding their place in the metaverse. In the span of the last few years, dozens of concerts have taken place on different metaverse platforms, featuring top musicians and artists across the world. Artists in particular are engaged in the metaverse because it's helping them connect with their fans. In addition to boosting album sales and helping artists gain traction and popularity, building a relationship with a fan base is an essential need of any performing artist.

One industry in particular that could thrive is the influencer industry, which would benefit from the ability of influencers to offer immersive content generated in the metaverse as a service to clients.

TIP

Decentraland, The Sandbox, and Fortnite are the three metaverse platforms actively promoting concerts.

To view a live performance, fans typically purchase a ticket for the concert and subsequently receive an access code to the performance online — similar to a real-world scenario where you would buy a ticket to a concert and go to the venue and check in.

Some popular concerts and performances in the metaverse in recent times have included the following:

>> TikTok hosted a metaverse concert featuring virtual dancers.

>> Travis Scott performed in the Fortnite metaverse. The concert featured Scott the size of a skyscraper and interacting with audience member avatars. Audience members were able to follow Scott on his journey to the concert as he headed to outer space and underwater.

>> Ariana Grande performed on Epic Games and was able to significantly elevate the bar in user engagement during her metaverse concert. Grande's avatar engaged with audience members by lifting them up into the sky as she sang.

>> Roblox has enabled individual influencers to create their own concerts.

>> Fortnite featured popular DJ Marshmello in 2019.

>> Justin Bieber hosted a virtual concert on an immersive extended reality platform called Wave.

>> DJ David Guetta had a concert on the Roblox metaverse in February 2021 featuring puzzles, dance battles, and merchandise that users could purchase for their avatars.

>> In 2021, Post Malone hosted a concert on Horizon Worlds and performed songs from his new album.

>> Popular South Asian performer Daler Mehndi delivered the first Bollywood metaverse concert on Somnium Space to 20 million viewers.

Podcasting in the metaverse

Podcasts have really grown over the past couple of decades. As of 2022, there are more than 2.4 million podcasts on the Internet and a collective of more than 66 million episodes.

Podcasts are easier to create, enable, and manage than videos are. Whether you're an individual or a business, podcasting is a great way to reach your audience.

The metaverse is a brand-new territory with numerous participants who are actively engaging in new categories of activities. As interest grows, podcasting is one of the areas that may not ride rise exponentially, but following the trend of podcasting on the Internet, you can assume that it may become a niche category of media in the metaverse. Users in the metaverse have likes, interests, and the need to engage in meaningful content, and podcasts could be a great venue for that.

Not all metaverse platforms are able to offer the ability to broadcast and embed media right now. One of the main requirements of being able to broadcast any content on a metaverse platform (such as The Sandbox, Decentraland, or others) is being a virtual landowner, where you can build a presence that can serve as a central point of engaging with your followers and audiences.

The steps to create a podcast in the metaverse are the same for individuals and businesses:

1. **Acquire a land parcel in the metaverse of your choice.**

   This could be as small or as large as you like, depending on your personal preferences.

2. **Strategically plan the layout according to the objectives that you would like to achieve from your facility.**

   This could include entertaining your visitors or engaging with them in some other way.

3. **Design your layout with the adequate amount of signage with information regarding what users can do on your land parcel or site.**

   If you're offering them a podcast to listen to, offer adequate signs that show them where they can listen to the podcast and where they should click on your land parcel or building structure.

4. **Embed a podcast media link following the guidelines of your metaverse platform.**

   Different platforms may have different ways to insert and embed media content.

5. **Get the word out and start promoting your episodes.**

   Soon users will be visiting your metaverse world and listening to what you have to say!

You can monetize your podcast in various ways, from sponsored episodes and segments to offering advertisers spots within your podcast.

INTRODUCING A NEW MTV MUSIC AWARDS CATEGORY

MTV Music Awards has created a new category for best performances in virtual spaces. The new category of Best Metaverse Performance will award performers who have delivered a concert or appeared in performances over the metaverse. In the first such award category, MTV had the following nominations:

- Ariana Grande
- BLACKPINK
- BTS
- Charli XCX
- Justin Bieber
- Twenty One Pilots

This new award category is a broader recognition by the entertainment industry, accepting the metaverse as a new channel for content dissemination and recognizing its value as a genuine and legitimate way to reach audiences and fans.

Chapter 9

Getting Involved with Your Interests in the Metaverse

People participate in literally thousands of activities that can be considered hobbies. Many people take up hobbies to learn something new, build new skills, or spend time with family or friends. Some people take up hobbies simply for the entertainment value. Others recognize that certain hobbies can provide health benefits, including boosting memory and brain health.

This chapter looks at how the metaverse can help you enhance a hobby and make it into a great *experience*.

Enhancing Hobbies with Metaverse Connectivity

Naturally, some hobbies pair with technology more seamlessly than others, but here are some ways the metaverse can enhance your hobby experience:

>> **Exposure:** Find a new hobby that you can take on and enjoy. The metaverse is a great place to find new things, ideas, and activities.

>> **Knowledge:** Learn and further enhance your hobby skills. With creative hobbies such as graphic design, 3D design, and nonfungible token (NFT) design, the metaverse can be a great place to learn what others are doing.

>> **Connection:** Meet with other like-minded people and hobbyists who have ideas to share and want to meet people like you.

>> **Community:** Build a community of hobbyists focused on the same type of activity. If you want to meet other people and create a group where one or more of you collaborate and share ideas, the metaverse can provide a place for doing exactly that.

>> **Gamification:** Be part of gamified experiences, gamify your hobby by working with others and creating more than just a hobby group.

>> **Monetization:** If you want to monetize your hobby and sell or trade with others, the metaverse can help you gain new customers for what you create or collect.

REMEMBER

Some hobbies pair better with technology than others do. For example, if you're a runner, you can just grab your running shoes and head out the door. But, you may want to go full tech with your running hobby: You may wear a smart watch to measure how far you run, how fast you run, and what your heart rate was. Using the metaverse to enhance your running could mean competing with an artificial gamified avatar so you never run alone. Such apps are already available for virtual reality (VR) systems, adding a sense of companionship and competition. Race against your own avatar? Now that's something.

The metaverse may seem like something straight out of a sci-fi film, but the reality is that as a new medium, it will have its own period of early adoption and growth. You can't expect that everyone who is exposed to the metaverse will love it and use it every day.

When it comes to interests and hobbies, the metaverse provides many new avenues of doing things. These experiences weren't available before the metaverse, and the development of virtual rendering technology, hardware technology, and Internet bandwidth is creating an exciting era where there are many new frontiers.

Here are some advantages of the metaverse when it comes to hobbies:

» You can meet anyone from anywhere in the world in a 3D environment.

» You can experience different virtual environments.

» Payments can be integrated through cryptocurrencies.

» Digital products can be sold instantly.

And here are some disadvantages:

» There is a steep learning curve, especially for the non-tech-savvy.

» It's fast emerging, so it has less credibility with some people.

» It's gotten some bad PR due to hacks and security incidents in the crypto world.

» People will need to invest in VR headsets and perhaps computer hardware to take part.

Finding hobbies in the metaverse

Finding a hobby to engage in is exciting! It enables you to be part of something that helps you grow your skills or meet new people with a single goal or interest. To find a hobby group in the metaverse, follow these steps:

1. **Sign up on a metaverse platform.**

Whether it's Decentraland, Horizon Worlds, The Sandbox, or any other, being part of a platform will open up doors and get you comfortable.

2. **Be curious and reach out to other hobbyists.**

Hobby groups probably won't come to you. Instead, you'll need to be curious and get comfortable reaching out to others and asking questions.

Get started by looking for multiplayer games and social networking apps on metaverse platforms such as Horizon Worlds and Roblox.

3. **Start your own hobby club.**

If you don't find a hobby club, build your own! Turn to "Starting a hobby club in the metaverse," later in this chapter, for more information.

TIP

The next few years of the metaverse are going to be full of exciting changes. Based on what we're seeing at the moment with big tech companies getting involved, venture capital investments, and more, you can safely assume that the metaverse may gain traction in the next two years.

FUTURECAST

This growth will open up the industry to new products and apps in the metaverse that will offer things such as the ability to create specialty groups, new networking opportunities, new job-hunting resources and even services in the metaverse. It wouldn't be surprising to find a new accountant or massage therapist in the metaverse.

As a general recommendation, be part of more than one metaverse platform to start building your communities and be part of communities that spring up across various platforms.

WHAT HOBBIES CAN YOU BUILD IN THE METAVERSE?

There is a whole world of interests and activities out there that can be categorized as hobbies. If you're looking at getting started, or even starting your own interest group in the metaverse, here are some ideas that will get you going.

To start off, most hobbies fall into one of the following categories:

- **Learning hobbies:** These are hobbies where your primary goal is to learn something new (for example, books on a particular subject that can help you gain knowledge).

- **Entertainment hobbies:** Watching movies or listening to music fall into the entertainment category. Entertainment hobbies are those where your only goal is to entertain yourself, whether on your own or with a group of people.

- **Creative hobbies:** Creative hobbies are those that help you utilize your creativity. This can include many different types of hobbies including graphic design, virtual 3D design, making beaded necklaces, painting, and many others.

- **Community-oriented hobbies:** Community-oriented hobbies are those in which your primary goal is to participate in joint activities with other members of your community to create a positive or joint change for the larger community. This could be volunteering your time to clean up the beaches and parks in your city or taking time to help newcomers in your city get oriented.

- **Games and sports:** If you like activities such as running, bodybuilding, working out, or hiking, you have a passion for sports! Many games (such as badminton, table tennis, or basketball) are hobbies, too.

- **Collecting hobbies:** Collecting coins, banknotes, stamps, seashells, and fossils are all hobbies. You could also be collecting digital NFTs or new designer outfits for your metaverse avatar.

Expanding your knowledge

Most hobbyists want to learn as much as they can about their hobby. If you're a collector, for example, you may be interested in seeing new collections that others have or viewing 3D models of your collectibles that you don't possess and would like to acquire.

You may join a class taught through the metaverse that teaches you about your area of interest. Experts from different domains have started joining the metaverse and are now teaching classes on everything from financial literacy to music production. Gym brands such as Les Mills are offering fitness classes in the metaverse with live trainers helping you with your workout in a group format.

Some hobbies demand that you stay on top of the curve and know the latest and greatest information on your topic. Combined with the sources you already use to learn about your hobby and practice your skill set, the metaverse as a media channel offering the opportunity to meet others who are interested in the same topics as you. Think about attending your favorite performer's concert in the metaverse and being able to chat with the hundreds of other people attending.

Where you take your hobbies is up to you. The ability to start a conversation, being curious and also finding different places to hang out in the metaverse are skills that need to be built. You can always start your own groups off the metaverse and use the metaverse as a channel to meet people.

The next few years are going to be very interesting as more attention towards the metaverse drives more people to do different things on this entirely new medium.

Meeting other hobbyists

Although videoconferencing and FaceTime are great ways to communicate, 3D experiences are a step ahead when it comes to delivering experiences. This is where metaverse experiences differ from video chats. It's the experience of being in a 3D space with other people and exploring together. Some hobbies require that you work in collaboration with other hobbyists to share ideas, exchange designs, build something together, or make friends. For users in the metaverse who are well acquainted with how to use a VR headset or how to join one of the many metaverses and engage in activities, meeting other hobbyists is a great way to continue building your passion for your hobby.

Unless you don't experience VR and 3D technologies, it's hard to fully comprehend the environment the metaverse offers. Viewing a metaverse platform on a computer screen is different from viewing it with a VR headset or glasses.

Visual design is an activity that is well suited for collaboration via the metaverse. As a designer, you may want to collaborate with other artists who are available in the metaverse and want to work with other hobbyists like yourself to create digital art. This could mean both of you or your friends all coming together in a metaverse platform and creating virtual 3D art or a virtual 3D building if that's what you're designing. The point being, anything can be created in 3D and many people can collaborate and be together in an immersive 3D space.

To see how you can set up meetings with other hobbyists in the metaverse, see the upcoming section, "Starting a hobby club in the metaverse."

Building a community of hobbyists

Hobbyists often meet other hobbyists in groups. I'm part of more than one group of hobbyists who get together every now and then to talk about what we've been up to and engage in the activity that joins us together.

My amateur singing club gets together every few months to sing songs and talk about the latest music releases that we find interesting. Over time, many members of our club have moved away, and some members have gone in their own direction, learning a musical instrument or coming out with an album. Members who have moved away have lost touch and some have been unable to stay in touch due to technology limitations. Collaboration and events may become a big part of social groups and membership-based organizations in the metaverse. More than that, it can be an opportunity to invite experts to talk about their expertise, musicians and singers to come together virtually to create music, and more. The possibilities are exciting!

Another group I belong to is a book club, where we jointly choose a book to read every month and then meet for lunch or dinner and talk about the book. With the metaverse, your favorite author could join you in a virtual book signing and give away NFTs of their upcoming book or access to their inner circle. The metaverse can serve as a platform for virtual book signings, book reading events, book launch events, book review opportunities, and book awards. Many of these things are yet to happen, but, based on the pace of how the metaverse has progressed so far, we aren't far from seeing many firsts happen in the metaverse in the next few years.

If you're looking at hobbyists who are in the metaverse and who share the same passions as you, creating a community group where you can all meet is extremely easy. Turn to "Starting a hobby club in the metaverse," later in this chapter, for more information.

ADDING SOCIAL CONNECTION TO SOLO HOBBIES

TIP

Here are ideas for how you might use the metaverse to make the following "solo hobbies" more socially interactive. (This list is pretty short considering the possibilities, so if you don't see your hobby listed here, be creative!)

- **Singing:** Get together with fellow members to learn songs, practice your singing skills, and enhance your voice. The metaverse can add fun to your experience by adding a chorus of virtual avatars.

- **Collecting stamps or coins:** Share videos and images of your coin collection and even display them In a virtual "museum" setting.

- **Reading books:** Share your insights and ideas in your reading club or open up a giant digital copy of your book in the metaverse for all members to read together. As a book club, invite your favorite author for a virtual book reading or invite other guests and experts to join your group in a 3D metaverse space.

- **Painting:** Use one of the digital painting apps to design 3D artwork and share it in the metaverse. Imagine being able to showcase your art on a 3D digital space to other attendees and participants in the metaverse, You can create an NFT from your artwork and put it up for sale in the metaverse if you like.

- **Baking:** Share recipes with friends and bake with others in the metaverse. With the metaverse, you can bring the party to your home in VR with your friends collaborating with you in 3D while you bake. Of course, tasting the baked goods would have its limitations because not everyone will be at the same physical location, but there's always the mail!

- **Writing poetry:** Express yourself in the metaverse by sharing your poetry in audio or video recordings or in writing. Hold a poetry workshop and bring the world's greatest poets together to teach others. Help each other improve and hold open mic nights.

- **Gardening:** Grow a virtual garden that everyone can join in. Share ideas about gardening, planting new species, or just the latest breakthroughs in horticulture. You can also take 3D pictures of plants and trees to share with your group so they can view it in 3D.

- **Pottery making:** Share strategies, techniques, and designs to create beautiful pottery. Think about using 3D models of ancient pots discovered in Egypt or Greece and replicating them with your group. You can bring collaborators from across the world and talk about intriguing pieces of pottery from time immemorial or from the Museum of Modern Art. You could hold exhibitions and even sell NFT digital twins of newly created pots.

(continued)

(continued)

- **Professional networking:** Professional groups such as LinkedIn and others are dedicated to professional discussions. The metaverse can be home to countless professional groups as remote work and work-from-home policies continue into the future. Many users have found a good level of comfort working remotely, and it would be expected that the trend would spill over to the metaverse in the future. According to Pew Research, many people are choosing to work from home because they want to. Other data suggests the remote work trend will continue.

Gamifying hobby experiences in the metaverse

The metaverse is a great venue for gamification — you can gamify any experience. Today metaverse app developers and game developers are creating hundreds of new applications that can be used to play games.

If you're a gamer, you already know the gaming industry is way farther ahead in the metaverse than any other industry is. In fact the gaming industry gave birth to the broader metaverse that we have available today. However, as a hobbyist who is looking to engage with others, you have the option of gamifying and creating game experiences on your virtual property or land.

If you build a hobby club, you can activate experiences that further engage members. Imagine for a moment that you manage a digital art hobby club with your own virtual location in the metaverse. Hobbyists from the world over can become members of your virtual club and come together every month to showcase their digital art and designs. As an ongoing engagement in your virtual venue, you can enable gamification by creating an art wall, where your group members can post their latest digital art and have other group members comment on it and rate the art on a scale of 1 to 10. As more group members post their art on the art wall, rankings rise, and the gamification encourages others to post their art on the art wall and engage with the group.

This is just one example of gamifying a hobby club in the metaverse. Depending on what you do as a hobby, your gamification could also be offline and not in the metaverse, but the metaverse can definitely provide a means and way for group members to express themselves and showcase their work if need be.

Monetizing your hobby

TIP

One way you can monetize a hobby is by creating NFTs. Digital artists are heavily involved in the metaverse and mostly generate income by selling NFT art. As a hobbyist, if you're looking to sell your creations to others, you can start building a new customer base right in the metaverse, or you can use the metaverse as a promotional channel by using some of the methods I describe in Chapter 11.

To monetize your hobby, you'll need to start by creating something of value that others would like to be part of. Then you can use the metaverse to drive visitors to your group or hobby club as members or even nonmember participants or observers. You may want to organize gatherings, exhibitions, and ticketed events for metaverse audiences.

TIP

Consider selling digital versions of your creations online and in the metaverse. Drive visitors to an actual e-commerce store with physical goods that can be shipped.

Connecting with Other Hobbyists

A metaverse platform is a meeting place and a channel of communication. It's still early days in the overall development of the metaverse, and while current VR headsets may be big and clunky, newer models are slim and sleek — and they'll get better with time. Some large corporations have already started using the metaverse as a tool for collaboration, and metaverse platform providers are working on specific collaboration tools to conduct meetings and business in general.

TIP

As of this writing, the metaverse is a place where you can meet other people, and that experience may vary depending on the metaverse platform you use. On some metaverse platforms, for example, you don't even need a VR headset.

Gathering somewhere in the metaverse

If you're looking at a metaverse-based platform or venues to meet people, one of the many metaverse platforms available today can be a good option. (For more information on the various metaverse platforms, check out Chapter 2.) Here's how to gather with people in the metaverse:

1. **Choose the metaverse platform where you want to meet your other hobbyist friends.**

   Use Google to search your hobby name with the keyword *metaverse* to find the latest search results.

Before joining a platform, be sure to find out the cost of joining, the need to buy special hardware such as a VR headset, and Internet bandwidth requirements.

2. **Establish a time and place to meet.**

   Agree on a time when you'll meet and a place on your chosen metaverse platform where you get together. This could be a public place on a metaverse or a specific location. For example, on Decentraland, you could agree to meet at the Genesis Plaza or right outside the Gucci store.

3. **Choose an activity!**

   You can choose to visit a virtual museum showcasing the latest NFT digital art, or come together for a discussion, to share skills and thoughts.

It's that simple to get started and connect.

Starting a hobby club in the metaverse

For the more serious hobbyist, an advanced option is to acquire a parcel of virtual land, and develop a virtual property on it that caters to your specific hobby. You can build a virtual venue on many metaverse platforms today and make it as a place for hobbyists in your interest lane to come together. You can create events, bring experts in to share their thoughts on the metaverse as an avatar, and collectively grow your hobby. In fact, you can do everything you would do in the real world or on the Internet, but only this time it's in a virtual 3D world with a completely different experience.

The metaverse can be a virtual home to your hobby club. To build your next hobby club "headquarters" in the metaverse, follow these steps:

1. **Evaluate some of the popular metaverse platforms available and what it would take to acquire a parcel of land.**

   Land parcels cost money and are available at various rates based on the metaverse platform. For more, check out Chapter 2.

2. **Acquire or purchase a parcel of land and develop it into a property.**

   This property can serve almost any purpose. It may be a virtual venue for concerts, for example, or a building that showcases artwork. It's up to you how you would like your hobby club's headquarters to look.

3. **Promote your new hobby club in the metaverse or off the metaverse, or both.**

4. **Use activities such as regular meetings, competitions, and expert appearances to build your hobby club's membership.**

5. **Gamify member experiences, and help members connect with each other with ease.**

   After all, a hobby club is all about giving members a great experience.

   For more about gamifying member experiences, see the preceding section, "Gamifying hobby experiences in the metaverse."

6. **Enhance memberships value adds by creating opportunities for learning.**

   Use your metaverse group not just to get together but also to hold classes, seminars, and workshops to help members learn new skills and discover new ideas.

7. **Monetize the virtual hobby club by requiring members to pay a subscription fee to be a member.**

3

Creating a Business in the Metaverse

» Recognizing that risk balances opportunity

» Selling products or even creating new ones for the metaverse

» Providing enhanced service delivery in the metaverse

» Checking out metaverse implementation guidelines for business

Chapter **10**

Getting Familiar with Business Essentials

As the metaverse gains popularity and adoption increases, businesses must make the right choices when it comes to tapping into the potential of this new technology.

This book is filled with numerous examples of how the metaverse can be used and why it should be used in the metaverse. This chapter provides a 10,000-foot overview of what the future of business may look like and what current forecasts and insights are leading us to believe. In this chapter, I look at survey results, business outlook, and other developments that tackle the metaverse when it comes to business as a whole.

Seeing How the Metaverse Can Benefit Business

In business, anything that adds value to the bottom line helps serve more customers and creates a better outcome for whatever the business does is what's most helpful.

Here are some the tangible advantages the metaverse can provide for businesses:

» A new channel of engagement to connect with younger audiences

» Speed of delivery for products and services

» E-commerce enablement for metaverse-based customers

» High-resolution digital experiences

» Ease of deployment and creation of digital engagement

» Elimination of the need for in-person availability

When assessing what the metaverse can do for business, I look at tangible benefits such as those in the preceding list and consider the steps a business needs to take to integrate the metaverse into their workings.

The following sections describe the practical challenges and advantages of integrating the metaverse into small, medium, and enterprise-level businesses.

TECHNICAL STUFF

CONSULTING INDUSTRY EXPERTS

Most industry experts agree that the metaverse has a tremendous amount of potential. A word of caution as you read through this section, though: Any indication of where the metaverse is headed is the opinion of these organizations and should not be taken at face value. As a general industry guidance, this information can help you understand where things are going, but for your own business needs, do your due diligence and consult with your advisors and investors before making any major business decisions about the metaverse.

Here are some selected insights from industry analyst firms in recent years:

- **Accenture:** Accenture onboarded 150,000 staff members in the metaverse in 2022.
- **KPMG:** In 2022, KPMG invested $30 million in creating its own metaverse collaboration hub.

- **Goldman Sachs:** In early 2022, Goldman Sachs predicted the metaverse was an $8 trillion opportunity.

- **Morgan Stanley:** In mid-2022, Morgan Stanley predicted the metaverse was a $50 billion opportunity.

- **McKinsey:** McKinsey has a very positive outlook on the metaverse and has made this very apparent with all its messaging. It has even said that the metaverse is too big for organizations to ignore.

PWC has created six steps for businesses starting to look at the metaverse. Go to `www.pwc.com/gx/en/issues/c-suite-insights/the-leadership-agenda/demystifying-the-meta-verse.html` to read more.

As more developments emerge from the metaverse ecosystem, forecasts for the opportunities arising from various metaverse platforms are very positive.

Small and medium businesses

A small business has the advantage of being able to rapidly deploy technology such as the metaverse because they have fewer stakeholders and decision-makers to deal with.

Small and medium businesses can use the metaverse to improve their brand images, facilitate hiring and training employees, and improve customer engagement. Other parts of this book describe how the metaverse can be used by specific industries, including healthcare, education, and entertainment.

WARNING

Don't make the mistake of thinking that you must use the metaverse simply because your competitors are using it. Instead, look at your overall business and ask if the metaverse can help you solve some of the problems or achieve some of the goals. The best way to do this is to hold a focused metaverse strategy session and invite the top decision makers and leaders from within the organization. Think about things a few years out, which could include sales, marketing, product launches, PR, communications, digital asset management, and other factors. You'll be risking time, money, and other previous resources of your organization if you don't take a strategic approach to implementing the metaverse.

Large businesses or enterprises

A large or enterprise-level business has hundreds of millions of dollars of revenue and may employ thousands of people. There are many opportunities for enterprise-level businesses to utilize the metaverse, including the following:

>> **As a tool for collaboration.** See Chapter 12 for more on collaboration.

>> **For design and product creation.** See Chapter 2 for more about the many ways in which creativity is emerging from the metaverse.

>> **To engage with your customer base.** A great place to start is Chapter 11, which covers customer interaction.

>> **To increase your number of customers by creating and delivering new experiences.** Part 4 covers many aspects of customers and delivering experiences.

>> **As a channel to sell products.** See Chapter 12 for more.

Most large organizations have large budgets, so implementing the metaverse from an investment perspective can be faster. Implementation within larger enterprises is always slower overall, though, because big companies have more stakeholders and complexity. Deploying such complex technological solutions is time consuming and slow.

New businesses

Entrepreneurship is possibly one of the main drivers of human progress. Most of the world's successful companies started small, and an entrepreneur somewhere laid the foundation. The metaverse is an interesting medium and can form the foundation for many future businesses. Expect "born in the metaverse" businesses to emerge soon.

The process and strategy for having a business in the metaverse should be the same as it is for non-metaverse-based businesses. Offering value, filling gaps in the market, or serving an underserved audience are great ways to approach the metaverse. The more due diligence you do on the market size and market needs, and the more you match your skills and expertise with what customers need, the better your chance of success.

TIP

THINKING LIKE A FUTURIST

Fast-forward 20 years from today. Computer graphics and imagery have reached an unprecedented level of advancement. We won't be able to tell a real person from a fake computer-generated avatar. The film industry worldwide has replaced actual actors with their digital twins. These digital twins of actors are being used by film production companies through a licensing agreement by the original actors, who are still getting paid for the work that they're doing or what their digital representation is doing.

In this incredible future, home design has radically changed, and now your home's walls are digital panels with a resolution of 50K, a big upgrade from the pasts 4K displays. These realistic-looking walls in our homes and buildings display graphics at a much better resolution than even a human eye can see. At the touch of a button, you can be transported into different scenes, places, and worlds. At extremely high Internet bandwidths, the rendering of highly detailed and crystal-clear virtual worlds is done at a rapid speed, which impacts the experience of the viewer. Perhaps your digital twin avatar is meeting a friend of yours later today or an avatar of your friend. Does that sound too futuristic?

In this futuristic world, the metaverse will no longer be a place and a space where we have to somehow take steps to enter. The metaverse will be all around us, and we'll no longer need to wear a bulky headset connected to a computer with an Internet connection to be able to use it.

Headsets will have been replaced by VR-enabled contact lenses and other technologies will be able to create a virtual 3D arena anywhere you like.

At some point in the future, the real you will have a dentist appointment. Too bad you can't send your avatar for dental treatment! The future of dentistry in the metaverse can be very experiential. Imagine your dentist being able to check your teeth in VR and crystal-clear resolution instead of bringing you in for a visual diagnosis.

Within this future environment, most tasks that we need to complete and accomplish that don't require us to be physically present will be done over virtual mediums.

It's human nature to seek better experiences and to appreciate and like those experiences. That's why we continue to use smartphones, voice messaging, and video calls and we aren't writing letters to each other the way we were decades ago. This is also the reason we love new and trendy products such as a Tesla car or a cool set of Beats by Dre headphones. People like good things, and we tend to get used to them quickly, soon forgetting what we had before. It'll be very similar with the metaverse. We'll end up using the metaverse so much that it becomes second nature, and we probably won't think about going back because of the convenience it creates.

Acknowledging the Business Risks

Especially because the technology is still emerging, the metaverse presents some potential disadvantages for businesses seeking to integrate it into their business models. Here are some immediate challenges:

>> **The metaverse is a virtual medium and lacks human interaction.** But as this new medium emerges and adoption rises, users will find way to engage with each other (for example, through e-sports, hobbies, and others areas of the metaverse where experiential opportunities arise).

>> **A widespread (and perhaps justified) lack of trust exists regarding data privacy and cybersecurity.** Securing the metaverse a fast-growing opportunity for cybersecurity professionals. As cyber laws, regulations, and new ways of metaverse security emerge, these concerns will fade away.

>> **The technology is extremely new and there is a steep adoption curve.** This steep adoption curve of the metaverse is a big challenge. It isn't just displaying high-resolution virtual graphics that's a requirement, but also enabling user privacy and safety, low-friction experiences, and a low cost of entry. With the advent of Web 3.0 technologies, customers can control data and be able to control which aspects of their data are seen by others — and that's great news, but it'll take at least a few years to a decade to become real. Building trust is key to creating communities in the metaverse and fostering digital commerce.

REMEMBER

The metaverse is not a solution for everyone and everything. It has limitations and may not be a good fit for all markets across all industries.

Selling Products in the Metaverse

Gone are the days when you could conceive of a product in a few minutes and sell it online to make millions. Buyers today are hyper-intelligent and know what they need. To be successful selling products anywhere, including in the metaverse, you need a sales strategy. (For a deeper dive on marketing and promoting your product in the metaverse, check out Chapter 11.)

Creating a metaverse sales strategy

The metaverse isn't a product but an *ecosystem* that contains multiple products, layers, and types of applications. So, to build a metaverse that is truly helpful, first consider the type of product you want to sell there:

>> **A product that solves a critical problem:** Example of products that were created to solve known problems are refrigerators, microwaves, cars, and even Microsoft Excel. All these products and solutions solve critical problems that people faced. A product being sold anywhere — whether in the physical world or in the metaverse — should be able to fill a gap in the customer's life.

>> **An innovative product:** Sometimes an innovation takes place, creating a new opportunity for a product in the marketplace. An example of this is the iPod, which was very famously created by Apple and fueled the smartphone era that we're living in today. Metaverse products can be physical, digital, financial, or virtual. Think about how your product can be unique and possibly create its own category.

>> **Scalability:** Ensure the business is scalable and can grow its customers. Having a great business idea is not the only criteria for success.

Technology products are often expected to solve all the problems around us. When we lead with a product and try to find a problem it can solve, the solution-finding problem becomes counterproductive. Finding problems and gaps and then using different approaches to solve them, with or without technology, is the better way to create value.

Selling physical products

The ability to sell something in the metaverse means that the value exchange transaction will take place in the metaverse. You may offer a product or service that your buyer may find attractive and would pay for in the metaverse but use offline.

Say, for example, you're selling toasters. Selling a physical toaster in the metaverse would mean promoting your toaster brand in the metaverse. Here are some suggestions on how you could make the availability of your toaster known to your target customers

>> Create a metaverse-based location or virtual land and build an experience on it that that utilizes VR and shows visitors the benefits or unique aspects of your toaster.

>> Bring influencers in to talk about your toaster and create a 3D experience.

>> Create a game in VR in the metaverse platform where users can engage with your toaster.

>> Create various user touchpoints where brand interactions can take place.

>> Send users to an online e-commerce page on your product website where they can buy the product.

Many brands are experimenting with such a sales model and the use cases range from tourism to coffee.

Selling digital products

Products promoted in the metaverse and consumed in the metaverse are fully digital. These products can include NFTs such as avatar accessories and skins. Some advertisers and brands in the metaverse are engaging with their audiences and offering the ability to use NFTs in a gaming environment. To create something similar for your brand, think about your brand as being an *experience* for your audience. Iconic Canadian coffee brand Tim Hortons created a brand experience for its fans on Roblox where players could receive different bonuses such as avatar skins while playing its game.

You might offer a digital product or service to your fans. This can be in the form of exclusive video content, audio content, and access to exclusive ticketed events such as concerts and celebrity meet-and-greets. NFTs can be used for various access mechanisms (see Chapter 4).

Providing Enhanced Services in the Metaverse

The global service industry includes hundreds of different categories of services, including financial services, health services, career planning, insurance, and hundreds more. The service industry is all about sharing expertise. In many cases, regulated and certified service professionals help customers achieve something. For example, real estate agents, mortgage brokers, and insurance agents are all part of the service industry.

The metaverse can open pathways for the service industry by providing customers and service providers a platform for enhanced service delivery. This section shows what this would look like.

KPMG is a global consulting company and a great example of an early adopter of the metaverse. KPMG committed $30 million to training employees to use the metaverse and to start offering services to customers focused on the metaverse. Accenture, heavily focused on the professional services business, also has made numerous efforts to create metaverse-based events and opportunities for employees to meet. Accenture also distributed more than 60,000 Oculus headsets to employees to facilitate adoption. These organizations are great examples of early movers in the professional services industries, with more to follow.

Offering enhanced government and municipal services

A big part of what governments do for their citizens is service delivery. Whether it's at a municipal, state, or federal level, governments typically offer hundreds of services to citizens. Think about it: Whether you need a driver's license or a permit to remodel your home, you need the government. The metaverse may be able to fill some of the gaps we have in this area by making service delivery easy and accessible to anyone anywhere. Imagine being able to apply for your passport in the metaverse or being able to get permits and approvals at your government office in the metaverse. This is already happening!

Here's one use case worth mentioning: The government of the United Arab Emirates (UAE) recently created a national metaverse strategy, with the goals of creating 40,000 jobs directly or indirectly related to the metaverse and driving revenues worth $4 billion by the year 2030. This is a bold and aggressive claim that utilizes the metaverse to create actual and tangible results. But it's not just on paper. The UAE government is also looking at enhancing government service delivery, which they've been working on for years.

The UAE government plans to deliver government services such as renewing of documents, passports, birth and death certificates, and more — all in the metaverse. A majority of the population in the Arab world is young, and they have experience and knowledge of computer technology. *Digital nomads* (people who work from various locations worldwide without having a permanent place of their own) are welcome in the UAE and are given a special visa status.

The government is also working on integrating many services it provides to citizens into normal channels, such as physical service delivery centers, into the metaverse. In the next few years, as a citizen or resident of the UAE, you'll be able to visit the metaverse presence or the location of the government entity you want to interact with. Let's say you want to renew your driver's license and have a new cat for whom you want to get a pet permit. You can visit the relevant government or municipal authorities in the metaverse and use either an automated bot or speak to a live person to validate your digital identity and conduct your business.

People with busy lives will probably find it convenient to visit a metaverse location instead of taking a break from their day to visit an actual physical government office.

METAVERSE FINANCIAL SERVICES

In the next few years, when the metaverse has matured, you may start your day and realize you have to speak with your financial advisor. You set up a time to meet up with them virtually in the metaverse. This could be a private meeting room within the larger metaverse or a private metaverse platform. (For more on the types of metaverse platforms, turn to Chapter 2.)

At your appointed time, you join the meeting, and you've transported virtually into a metaverse meeting room where you and your advisor's hologram (which is essentially your advisor being displayed in VR) speak to each other as if both of you were in the same room. Your financial advisor tells you they have all the information you need. They then display all the different options, growth projections, detailed statistics, and charts of possible investment options within this 3D environment. This information is displayed in a 360-degree circle around you, and you can turn around and pinpoint any specific piece of information that you need more information on and have more detailed information displayed with a virtual touch. You make your decision, and you guide your advisor on what to do next.

This is a simple overview of a very complex process that has many moving parts. This needs the integration of back-office technologies used in industries, multiple hardware technologies, and a high level of bandwidth to make everything possible. Will this be available worldwide, and would you be able to do this anywhere across the planet? That remains to be seen.

Services such as these will become very common in places where VR platforms, in general, are available.

Selling professional services

Professional services form a significant part of business today. From accounting to health care, mortgage brokers and financial undertakers, we use professional service providers daily. What could be the future of professional services, and would they be able to use the metaverse?

Image life 15 to 20 years from now. The world is entirely digital. Our homes and infrastructure are built with layers of technology. This includes ultra-high-clarity displays around our houses and businesses. This also includes holographic displays that can bring people who are remote to right in front of our eyes. There will also be no need for VR glasses. We'll possibly still need access to services and professionals who make our lives easier. Think of everyone you interact with regularly who helps you accomplish something — your banker, your lawyer, your financial planner, your mortgage broker. . . . providers within these business areas will continue to help their customers achieve their goals. How they deliver those services may just be different from the way it is today.

FUTURECAST

METAVERSE REAL ESTATE

Buying a home is one of the biggest decisions in most people's lives. The typical home-buying experience today has remained unchanged for decades, except that some aspects of technology have changed.

When buying a house, you can meet up with your real estate agent and take a virtual tour of a home that you're interested in putting an offer on. You can virtually walk to the house and view it in the most realistic display, and in some cases, even better than in real life. Perhaps you're far from the actual location, you'd like to save time, or you have other reasons for not being able to view the property in person. This would save time for both buying and selling agents and related teams such as home inspectors, vendors, and service providers. Walking through an identical twin of the property in the meta-verse would make it possible for buyers to tour the remotest properties and use a more realistic virtual tour to make this critical buying decision.

Getting Your Business onto the Metaverse

Regardless of the size of your business, here are guidelines to follow if you want to put the metaverse to work for your business.

Step 1: Conduct a market analysis

If you have a new business or product line, start by determining the demand for the product or service. Next, determine the marketing strategy that will enable you to reach your target audience, who may be new to the metaverse. Factor in their knowledge and fascination with technology, hobbies, spending power, and so on.

These essential factors will affect how you step into the metaverse to maximize engagement from your audience. There are also other factors you'll want to figure out, such as your choice of metaverse platform, your preferred digital asset or token, and the metaverse-related technologies you want to partner with. These technology providers include e-wallet and blockchain companies, VR gadget manufacturers, metaverse builders, and so on.

Step 2: Train your employees to use VR

If your team members are unfamiliar with the metaverse, you need to get them up to speed. Whether they're speaking to customers, demoing products, or booking appointments for customer service, train them specifically for the metaverse (see Chapter 12).

A number of businesses started using VR headsets for engaging employees during the pandemic.

Step 3: Embrace a metaverse-first strategy

A metaverse-first strategy may be new, but it isn't the first time a new platform had created a new strategic direction. When the cloud industry was growing, many companies create a cloud-first strategy, which meant they would focus completely on growing business in the cloud industry. Similarly, if your product is suited for the metaverse and you want to design a go-to-market strategy solely for the metaverse, there is nothing wrong with that! Your business may not need to validate itself in the brick-and-mortar or online markets before finding success in the metaverse.

Step 4: Slow down

You may worry that your business isn't fully ready, and this is usually a legitimate fear. Consider meeting with a VR consultant who will be able to guide you through the complexities of the space and point you in the right direction.

There are several ways your business can launch into the virtual space. You may list your digital asset, product, or service on popular marketplaces like the Sandbox or OpenSea. On the other hand, you may need to create a virtual space that offers your customers an immersive interaction with you in the metaverse. An example is Nike's Nikeland, where users game and can purchase Nike's products.

REMEMBER

Regardless of how you're launching, what matters most is to utilize the virtual space to create thrilling experiences that your customers won't forget. This is the basic rule of getting your audience to interact with your business in the metaverse.

As the metaverse expands and grows in adoption, millions of users worldwide will have different experiences as a result. Some will be good, and some will be bad. Regardless, metaverse platforms will continue to evolve and grow, and the best use cases and utility for this fast-growing technology will grow with it.

Chapter **11**

Getting the Word out to the Metaverse

I magine starting a brand-new business selling a physical product like high-end luxury toddler shoes sourced from Spain. Your product is handmade and is produced by a small-batch manufacturer known for quality. They also have a patented insole that has been scientifically designed and is known to be good for toddlers' feet.

You already have your finances ready and a system for order fulfillment. You have a small store on Main Street in your town. You're doing great with the local customer base, but often, trendy young parents who mostly work in the technology industry visiting from out of town say they would like to buy these trendy shoes. After speaking with them you also found out a majority of them are gamers and have been talking about the metaverse as a new thing. You want to explore the idea and figure out whether the metaverse is a good fit to be part of your business strategy.

This chapter reveals how you can market products and services in the metaverse for new and existing brands. First, I describe some of the creative ways businesses are marketing their existing brands in the metaverse. Then I show you how you can put the metaverse to work for your brand. You'll discover that a lot of similarities exist in marketing strategies between the real world and the online world, as well as some promising new opportunities in the latter through the metaverse.

Marketing Your Brand in the Metaverse

Traditional marketing is all about mastering the four Ps: product, price, place, and promotion. Of these four Ps, place and promotion benefit most directly from the advantages offered by marketing in the metaverse.

The metaverse provides a virtual 3D environment, or *place*, to promote your brand. Here are some of the benefits related to place when marketing in the metaverse:

>> It's highly customizable when it comes to look and feel.

>> You can provide customers or users the ability to engage with you in a 3D virtual environment. This includes using the platforms for communications and to conduct customer events, information webinars, and other personalized communications.

>> It's available wherever the Internet can be accessed, so it goes beyond a physical location.

When marketing in the metaverse, you can use promotion as part of the experiences your brand creates. Here are a couple of advantages that promoting your product in the metaverse can provide:

>> **Promoting a product or a service in the metaverse can be an opportunity to interact with your audiences who are already in the metaverse.** They may or may not be looking for the product you sell, but the opportunity to create a touchpoint in the metaverse may change that.

>> **Promoting products and services in the metaverse is not only being able to directly sell the product to the users you're interacting with.** If you're looking for a return on investment (ROI), this can be calculated in different ways — for example:

- Calculating the value of a direct sale
- Goodwill gained

- Brand recognition

- Continued interactions on other media such as an e-commerce website or actual store

- Press coverage gained

- The number of social media interactions created as a result

Using product placement in the metaverse

When you see a brand of soda or your favorite cereal in a movie or a TV series, this is product placement or native advertising. *Metaverse native advertising* is an option to insert your product banner or place your product within a gaming environment.

Native advertising formats with the metaverse include these forms:

>> **Virtual billboards:** Vertical displays used to showcase a product, message, or graphic within the metaverse are categorized as virtual billboards (see Figure 11-1). Different platforms have different sizes of billboard options and if you are developing your own virtual land and creating a structure, you can have any size of a billboard. Most billboards in the metaverse use static imagery and are clickable and are found in prominent places in the meta-verse. These could be a popular hangout place, a tall skyscraper, or other places of high traffic in the metaverse.

FIGURE 11-1:
A virtual billboard
behind an avatar.

>> **Audio ads:** Audio ads within the metaverse play an audio clip when clicked.

>> **In-game apps:** Within the metaverse, there are games that are built by various providers. For example, within Roblox and Horizon Worlds, hundreds of apps can be installed that will provide you access to a new game. Within these games, there are display ads and other clickable assets that can be used to advertise, market, or promote a product or a service.

>> **Virtual video ads:** Video ads are similar to banner ads, but they either are already playing a video or may play a video when interacted with. Some video ads start playing a video file when your avatar is in proximity to them, and some need to be clicked to display the video content.

>> **Virtual banners ads:** Virtual banner ads work similarly to banner ads on the web. They can either be of a standard size if offered by a metaverse platform or have a custom size if offered by a private plot developer on a metaverse property. Different metaverse platforms offer different dimension base virtual banners. Figure 11-2 shows a virtual banner ad.

FIGURE 11-2:
A virtual
banner ad.

Driving engagement with metaverse parallel ads

Your metaverse marketing efforts don't have to be completely separated from your real-life marketing campaigns. Businesses have already started using the metaverse as a new channel to run advertising campaigns and to gain traction on real-world marketing campaigns. Companies such as Deliveroo, Hellman, and others have great examples of using campaigns in the metaverse to drive real-life engagement.

For any brand, creating engagement is about connecting with its target audience and having a meaningful interaction. This can happen in many ways, some of which are highlighted earlier, where I talk about ROI.

For brands, having an omnichannel approach to marketing now consists of a new channel: the metaverse. When brands consider different channels of promotion, such as broadcast media, print media, online media, and television, the consideration for an ROI is to have a positive outcome from the advertising. Consider the opportunity at the Super Bowl every year, where brands advertise for a tiny fraction of time and yet pay millions of dollars in advertising fees. The metaverse has now opened up a new channel for advertising where the options to advertise aren't limited (the way they would be on a website, for example). In the metaverse, a brand could advertise during a metaverse sporting event, in a metaverse concert, and other places. Not only has the metaverse opened a new channel, but the options *within* the channel are not restricted.

Advertisers can benefit from data collected through ad performance, unique clicks, ad impressions, and demographic data as metaverse platforms offer deeper insights about users on their individual platforms.

Getting in on digital avatar virtual goods

Research shows that avatar customization is a top priority for metaverse participants. After all, avatars are an expression of your identity, whether you dress them in designer wear or otherwise customize them. A new direct-to-avatar (D2A) economy is also emerging in which companies make digital goods for avatars. Brands such as Balenciaga, Gucci, and Louis Vuitton have already started selling designer goods for avatars.

TIP

Brand partnerships are necessary to be part of the new D2A economy. As a business, your goal should be to connect with a metaverse provider to offer your goods and wares for digital avatars. If you're a physical goods company, think about creating digital versions of your products to sell to avatars. A bit of a mind twist, but creating, buying, and selling goods for avatars is a fast-growing segment of the metaverse.

Creating a virtual venue to attract audiences

A *virtual venue* is a place online where viewers can connect and share an experience. This experience could be a virtual conference, a virtual classroom, or a virtual entertainment venue. The metaverse is an immersive 3D virtual environment that has a significantly different experience from that of, say, a videoconference platform such as Microsoft Teams or Zoom. Virtual venues in the metaverse create a very specific engagement experience, typically enjoyed on a virtual reality (VR) headset. In some cases, it may even be preferred by users who are spending more time in the metaverse.

You could establish or create a virtual venue for your conference, meeting, or gathering in the metaverse and set your own tone, parameters, and visual elements. Perhaps you're holding a conference on climate change and you want the metaverse venue to have a green environmental look and feel, or maybe you're organizing the next conference for car collectors. You can create a 3D environment that reflects the occasion.

Creating a store

Metaverse worlds are known to have crazy virtual land–buying frenzies. Virtual land is available for purchase on the majority of metaverses and can be used to build your own virtual building, store, or even theme park within that metaverse. This store would be available for other metaverse participants to visit and possibly shop at.

Some major brands have invested in creating metaverse stores early on. Chase Bank, for example, has a tiger roaming around its metaverse branch. Other major businesses that have either created a metaverse experience or established a store in the metaverse include Alo, Disney, Gucci, Hyundai, Microsoft, Nike, Ralph Lauren, Vans, Warner Brothers, and Wendy's.

Organizing live events

Live experiences in the metaverse are very popular. In 2022, Decentraland organized the first ever metaverse fashion week. It received more attention than any other digital event before it and was the first event of its kind focused on the fashion industry.

Music concerts in the metaverse are also making headlines with major artists choosing to deliver virtual experiences for their fans by performing in the metaverse. Recent concerts have included artists such as Travis Scott and Arianna Grande, both performing virtually on the Fortnite platform.

Creating immersive experiences with advergames

In 2022, when Tourism New Zealand wanted to create a buzz around its new campaign, it chose the metaverse. It engaged with an agency to create a virtual 3D New Zealand and launched the Play NZ Campaign, in which users in the adventure game could visit sites and attractions throughout the country. This format of engagement is known as an *advergame,* which is short for *advertising in games.* If you're looking to send your customers on a journey of exploration, win prizes, and participate in an exploratory activity, then an advergame could be a good fit.

TIP

Advergames can offer opportunities to engage with your players and audience members in a highly customizable way. Perhaps you want to target adults between the ages of 25 and 40, or maybe female visitors between the ages of 15 and 19. With advergames, you can create separate elements of engagement suitable for each audience group.

Using digital collectibles and nonfungible tokens

Nonfungible tokens (NFTs) started off as digital art being sold on online NFT platforms. Artists such as Beeple gained early fame by selling NFT art worth millions in what was the early beginning of the NFT craze. Now not only is Beeple's art sold for millions of dollars, but hundreds of NFT digital artists have started creating digital art, which is giving birth to an entirely new area of the creator economy.

The metaverse offers multiple options for NFT sale. A key part of the D2A economy is converting your avatar products into NFTs and selling them. This approach can help you create a long tail of product revenue and help your buyers trace the beginning and origins of the avatar apparel they're buying.

TECHNICAL
STUFF

NFT creation could be considered a task for creative or enterprising users, but collecting NFTs is something that the average user may find interesting as a hobby.

Reaching Customers through the Metaverse

Understanding your customer base and their needs, habits, and spending patterns is extremely important when planning sales. You have to know why your customers want your product; how, when, and where they'll use it; how often they'll use it within a specific period of time; and so on. This type of information is part of the fundamental and essential market intelligence you might gather about any customer.

When you assess whether the metaverse will work as a tool to reach your target audience, you also must consider how and why (and when and where) they're likely to engage with you or your brand in the metaverse.

Think about it: When anyone visiting your store, location, or venue enters the 3D space, just like a physical space, there are many options to display messaging, showcase products, and highlight specific offers and products. Similar to an actual physical store in a local shopping mall, 3D virtual spaces can offer many opportunities to connect with visitors.

The following sections help you uncover the ways you can design your marketing strategy to cater to your metaverse visitors. I use the example from this chapter's introduction of marketing high-end toddler shoes to known users of the metaverse to show how you can apply the ideas I cover throughout these sections in real life.

Creating a customer persona

To help understand your customer base, try creating a demographic profile or customer persona. A *customer persona* is a description of your ideal customer. You might include some basics to start. For example, name, age, city, likes, dislikes, and the potential customer's buying preferences or buying patterns. You can format this description as a bulleted list with specific points, as shown in Figure 11-3.

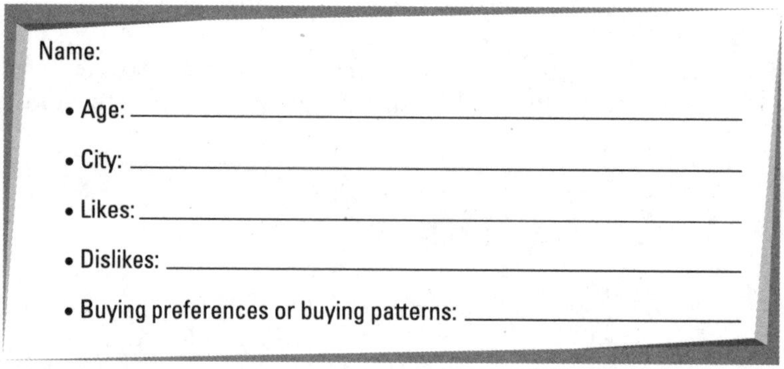

Name:

- Age: _____
- City: _____
- Likes: _____
- Dislikes: _____
- Buying preferences or buying patterns: _____

FIGURE 11-3:
A sample
customer
persona.

With this basic information, you can get started with a persona and build it out as specific as you'd like to go. The more the number of data points, or attributes, the higher the quality of your customer persona.

Refer to this description when you need to refresh your understanding of your customer base. You may update it as you gather more information about your customer base.

Depending on your products and solutions, your customer persona may have one or more profiles.

For example, if you're a retailer with clothes for ages 0 to 19, you may be better off splitting the persona into various age groups, because their buying behaviors, buyer journeys, and interactions in the metaverse will be very different.

REMEMBER

Creating a persona for a customer in the metaverse is similar to creating the persona of a customer who is buying goods in a bricks-and-mortar store, but selling in the metaverse requires that you consider an additional sales channel (or potential sales channel). Irrespective of where you promote and market your product, you should have an exceptionally well-defined customer profile.

Here is a list of basic demographics to identify when you're creating a customer profile:

>> Age

>> Gender

>> Income level (below average, average, above average)

>> Education (high school, college, graduate degree)

>> Spending habits

>> Interests

>> Computer skills

>> Online purchase habits (iffy, comfortable, master)

>> Cryptocurrency holder

>> Metaverse purchase comfort level (low, medium, high)

Consider the example from the chapter introduction of selling high-end toddler shoes. You already know that buyers are parents of toddlers and the consumers of your products are toddlers. It's up to you how deep to go into defining your audience and segmenting it; you can do it by geography, neighborhood, income level, and so on.

For example, you may further target the customer persona by noting that toddlers generally begin walking at the age of 12 months and onward. You may have also noted that the toddler stage lasts for about one to two years of the child's early life. With this information in hand, you can assume that your target user is 1 to 3 years old.

You may further choose to assume that the parents of these toddlers are at least 21 years of age and can be couples of mixed or single genders, given some generalized assumptions on when people typically have kids, although this will vary depending on geography, culture, and other criteria. You'll also assume that these parents are active in the metaverse, maybe participating in an activity in the metaverse or at least being comfortable visiting various venues, stores, and places in the metaverse. You may further refine this by assuming that most toddler buying decisions are made by parents raising their small children.

TIP

To make your sales campaign as efficient as possible, I recommend that you create a highly specific persona for your target audience. All groundwork that you put into building a solid persona will go a long way toward helping you keep your sales and marketing campaigns efficient with a better ROI. Marketing dollars quickly add up and become a big expense if not controlled.

Understanding the metaverse user base

If you already have a business, you likely know who your target customer is. But if you're thinking of establishing your business presence in the metaverse, you need to understand the *channel's* demographic and user base.

Traditional marketing today has many aspects to it. Taking the example of the toddler shoes brand, the brand can have a physical store and an online store. It can utilize traditional advertising in print media and television or use the Internet for advertising on YouTube and social media. Digital marketing can boost traditional sales, and a blend of traditional and digital marketing can create great results.

By using the metaverse to create a highly engaging experience, however, whether within a metaverse game, community event, e-sporting event, or other form of engagements, you'll end up with a more targeted, higher-quality user base that has indicated its preferences and other data points for you. As a marketer, you may appreciate the value of highly targeted data, which you can use to create a more targeted marketing strategy.

WARNING

Marketing in the metaverse is not a switch-it-on-and-forget-it activity. Because the metaverse is a brand-new medium and still evolving, you may find that marketing efforts in the metaverse are highly time-consuming and need dedicated resources. You'll need to constantly measure the efforts of your marketing campaigns by analyzing the data you receive, interactions you have with users, and how they match with your marketing goals.

Establishing whether your customer base uses the metaverse

As a business or an organization considering the metaverse as a platform for marketing, you must first ensure that it falls within your overall strategy. Here is a process that can help you determine whether the metaverse can meet your needs:

1. **Identify your customer base.**

   Ensure that your target user base, customer base, or fan base is using the metaverse. Use targeted surveys and other tools to inquire.

2. **Allocate resources.**

   Allocate a specific team, resources, and budget to be focused on the metaverse. Adding dedicated resources will help achieve the objective better.

3. **Run pilot tests.**

   Ensure you have a pilot testing stage built into your metaverse marketing to test the waters before jumping in 100 percent. Use a small sample of your target audience base, and advertise or expose them to your brand message.

4. **Measure results.**

   As with any marketing plan, allow for a great deal of testing, tweaking, and measuring results. Measure for ad impression rates, click-through rates, viewership, sales referrals, customer acquisition cost, and other metrics relevant to your business.

5. **(Optional) Engage with metaverse experts.**

   Engage with agencies, vendors, and providers who have had successful results in the metaverse. Use crowdsourcing to find broader trends and opinions.

REMEMBER

Allocate specific resources and budgets to metaverse marketing and use high standards in measuring your returns.

Building a high-quality fan following

High-engagement metaverse experiences can be used to entice new and prospective customers. Using the data you gather from respondents through these experiences, you can build a high-quality database of target and prospective customers or fans.

TIP

Here are some ideas for how you can create experiences that help build a high-quality fan following in the metaverse:

>> Create short surveys to ask your metaverse audiences about their needs.

>> Create engaging experiences and ask questions at various stages within the experience.

>> Gamify interactions to reduce abandonment.

>> Provide rewards as part of your gamified engagements.

EXAMPLE: TODDLER SHOES

Consider the example company that sells high-end toddler shoes to a customer base known to use the metaverse. Here is one-way that company could create a high-engagement metaverse experience that helps build a targeted prospect list.

Goal: To build an experience to help parents dress up a toddler virtually and win rewards for doing it in a specific amount of time.

- When the game starts, ask the parent if they have a child and how old their child is. You may also ask the gender of their child.

- Based on their answers, the game could display the avatar of a child similar to theirs.

- Next the game starts with a countdown timer and parents are provided choices of clothes and apparel.

- The game can end in a leaderboard ranking and a free coupon for shopping at the brands website or actual store.

This example shows just some of the elements of engagement that can be incorporated into an experience in the metaverse. Questions between various respondents can be taken from a larger pool and ultimately a high-quality database of target and prospective customers or fans can be built.

Creating a metaverse marketing plan

A metaverse marketing strategy has the same elements as a traditional marketing strategy; the critical difference is the channel of delivery for this marketing plan. In this case, the metaverse marketing strategy will be delivered on a single metaverse platform or on multiple metaverse platforms. For example, your plan to sell a product may be suitable for The Sandbox and Decentraland but not for Horizon Worlds because the audience demographics may not meet your specifications.

To get started, here are the critical steps to follow when creating a marketing plan.

1. **Create a fine-tuned segmentation of your target customer base.**

   Get the lowdown on knowing your customer earlier in the chapter.

2. **Position your product appropriately.**

   Decide how the product will be shown and perceived by the target customers.

3. **Decide on your marketing tactics.**

   Plan the elements that will formulate the marketing plan. These will include

   - Where the product will be advertised
   - Any unique time-related product marketing strategies to be used
   - Any partnerships that need to be built
   - Other unique aspects

4. **Create a timeline.**

   Every solid marketing plan must have a beginning and an end. Typical marketing plans start at a specific time and run for a particular duration. One of the main reasons is that marketing plans have obvious goals, and most of the time, they can be accomplished if there is great specificity. Without specificity, you might go over budget on marketing projects that balloon in scope.

5. **Develop your budget.**

   A clear budget is essential for any marketing plan. The budget should include how much you'll spend advertising your products and services to the target market within the duration of time of the marketing campaign. It isn't uncommon for budgets to start small and grow with time, and for campaigns running as tests to have small budgets. I highly recommend establishing a clear budget guideline for your project and then allocating and seeing it through.

   Two key metrics include your customer acquisition cost (CAC) and ROI.

Promoting Your Business in Metaverse Marketplaces

When you discover that you can reach your customers in the metaverse, you have to figure out which metaverse platform best meets your needs. Metaverse platforms vary in how they handle product promotion, so be sure to follow these steps when choosing one:

1. **Know your customer and who they are; learn about their habits and preferences.**

2. **Study all the metaverse platforms that are available to you and where your audiences hang out, visit, and participate.**

3. **Investigate the cost of advertising on the platforms of your choice.**

4. **Rank your preferred platforms in terms of priority.**

5. **Start with the platform and advertisement options that match your brand's needs.**

6. **Start small and expand gradually as needed.**

The following sections explore the current product promotion offerings of the top three metaverse platforms: Roblox, The Sandbox, and Decentraland.

Roblox

Roblox has created its own self-manageable advertising platform for sponsors and advertisers. As a potential advertiser, you can load your advertiser account with *ROBUX* (the native digital currency that works on Roblox) and spend it to target users, schedule ads, and set budgets per day.

The advertising platform offers detailed stats on ads currently running, funds spent, cost per click, and other useful information for advertisers.

Roblox has a younger, tech-savvy audience, so advertisers are typically companies who have products that suit this audience. Some well-known brands that have advertised on and created experiences on Roblox include the following:

» **Nike:** Nike created Nikeland as a Roblox experience. Uses can jump on trampolines, swim in Nike Lake and race with their friends in Nikeland. Nikeland also has games, competitions, and options to style your avatar with Nike apparel and gear.

» **NASCAR:** In November 2021, NASCAR created a game on Roblox called Jailbreak and held a competition for users to create new skins for cars in the game. Jailbreak became one of the fastest-growing experiences on Roblox and offered users the choice of a specific persona as part of the game.

» **Vans:** Vans created Vansworld on Roblox. Visitors to Vansworld can learn new tricks, unlock new gear, and create their own custom Vans shoes. Vansworld also offers competitions, and you can dress your avatar in Vans gear.

Here are some key advertising opportunities on Roblox:

» **Roblox-sponsored experiences:** Roblox has a native advertising platform to help advertisers connect with their audiences through paid advertisements. With this platform, advertisers can have their ads displayed in various places within the Roblox platform.

- **Products advertisements:** Advertise your product or website on Roblox. You can upload images, catalogues, or groups of items. When a user clicks your ad, they're taken to the web page you advertise.

- **Ad bidding:** The Roblox advertising system works on a bidding format as is typical with all pay-per-click advertising formats. The higher the bid, the more frequently your ad is shown. With limited ad space available, bidding can get competitive.

  Roblox offers three primary types of ad formats — banners, skyscrapers, or rectangles — which are all different types of billboards. All these ads must be bid for separately through the Roblox advertising platform.

Sandbox

$SAND is the default currency token of the Sandbox metaverse. It is also known as a *currency* or the *utility token*. To participate on the Sandbox, you must purchase $SAND tokens through the Sandbox platform.

TIP

You can convert your metaverse proprietary currency back into your real-world currency (such as the U.S. dollar) through the crypto exchange where you purchased the cryptocurrency. (For everything related to money in the metaverse, see Chapter 4.)

Here's generally how the Sandbox works:

- Users can create an account and play various games on the Sandbox.

- Brands can purchase a parcel of land and create games.

- Game designers choose which type of game to create: free to play (F2P) or not free to play.

- Games can be created by working with specific advertising agencies recommended by the Sandbox.

- Brands can monetize the land by renting it out, or selling billboard or banner ads within their games.

Advertising on the Sandbox means showing your brand on existing properties, buildings, and landmarks that have been created by others (if you don't have a property of your own on the Sandbox). The fees and options for advertising are set by landowners and game creators. You have to contact the property owners to find out about your advertising options.

Decentraland

Decentraland uses a specific utility token called MANA.

TIP

The number of tokens available for MANA can be viewed in real-time at `https://manaboard.vercel.app`.

Decentraland works on a similar premise as the Sandbox. You buy land and find ways to monetize that land. Billboard advertising on Decentraland properties could be the fastest and easiest way to get your brand noticed. Billboards are easy to create and easily noticeable on the platform. Other options to advertise on Decentraland may include

>> Interactive floors that can show information when stepped upon

>> Interactive walls that can display information when touched

>> Interactive objects that display specific information based on proximity

Billboards are generally noticed more due to their presence in high-traffic areas on Decentraland. Agency partners who own billboards in Decentraland may already have highly noticeable billboards in places such as key roads, plazas, and popular venues.

TIP

Decentraland is a third-party-led effort, so you buy billboards and other advertising assets through one of its agency partners. Typically, you would need to provide the following information to any agency that specializes in building a metaverse experience (a number of which have emerged in the past few years — you can find them by going to the partner sections of popular metaverse platforms such as The Sandbox and Decentraland):

>> A summary of what your business goals are

>> Why you'd like to use the metaverse

>> What type of experiences you think your business can deliver

>> Who your typical customer is

>> What your products and services are

With this information, connecting with agencies will give you a head start.

Here are two recommended agency partners recommended by Decentraland:

>> **Admix:** Ad management provider for multiple metaverses. Admix can help you set up advertising and ROI calculation, and plan full campaigns across

metaverses, including Decentraland. Find out more at `https://admixplay.com`.

» **Boson Protocol:** Specializes in physical product and e-commerce sales through gaming platforms, including Decentraland. Find out more at `www.bosonprotocol.io`.

Product Pricing in the Metaverse

Product pricing is key not just to the success of a marketing campaign but also to the success of a product. Many times, products are priced at levels that are not in line with what the target customer is looking to pay. On the opposite end of the spectrum, you may price your product extremely low, creating the perception of low quality, which can undermine the product's success.

To price products according to your target demographic, you must conduct market research before launching the product and continue testing it in the initial launch phases of project development.

The question now becomes: Should you price your product differently for the metaverse? As a marketing tactic, you may price your product differently and make it attractive to customers to visit your point of sale, whether it's a physical store or website where the product is sold. As a low-priced marketing tactic, you can simultaneously promote other, not as aggressively priced products. The strategy for product pricing should be carefully planned in alignment with your target revenue goals and product lineup.

REMEMBER

Take the same approach for digital products (such as nonfungible tokens) as you take for physical products. Products should be priced based on comparable brand value and what the customer is willing to pay.

Product Positioning and the Metaverse

When it comes to product positioning and promoting your goods and services to your target customers in the metaverse, creativity and innovative ideas can help. With the metaverse being a very new medium and venue for participants worldwide, and with many aspects of it still evolving, irrespective of which metaverse you use, creative targeting strategies can help. Whether you're trying to create buzz, leave a memorable impression, or sell something in the metaverse, your approach to coming up with fresh and even original ideas will be a big help.

Looking at some of the examples discussed in this chapter, some fashion brands have taken the approach of designing outfits for avatars. New Zealand Tourism created a free game in which participants could visit top attractions in New Zealand virtually. Other brands have tied a social cause to a metaverse campaign and helped raise donations.

Brands have also created unique experiences in order to engage with their fans. They're not necessarily selling at the first opportunity to engage, but building a valuable brand following, the impact of which can be measured through metrics such as public relations (PR) value gained, digital sales, NFT sales, number of interactions, social media mentions, and other ROI avenues.

These brands used a mix of creativity and innovative thinking and focused on how to create memorable experiences in their fan interactions. They also were one of the first few companies that engaged with audiences on a new medium and took a chance on exploring a new opportunity for engagement.

When you determine your product positioning, the following three elements are essential to ensure success in promoting your products or services in the metaverse:

>> **Metaverse strategy:** Create a strategy for the full marketing campaign. Include the platform and type of ads you'll run. You may also find that having an additional, separate metaverse strategy is beneficial.

>> **Design:** Design experiences that help you connect with your target audience and leave them with an experience. Make it entertaining, informative, or exclusive to bring high engagement. Create a separate metaverse design guide that helps everyone involved stay informed.

>> **ROI focused:** Create a realistic ROI goal from the campaign and evaluate results as your campaign progresses. Modify the campaign to get to your results as needed. Having a realistic ROI is necessary because new advertising platforms can sometimes be full of surprises.

REMEMBER

The metaverse is extremely new. Radical thinking and a bold vision are critical to establishing yourself and building a following.

IN THIS CHAPTER

» Improving the work experience

» Getting better results from a remote workforce

» Providing company trainings in the metaverse

» Integrating the metaverse into your workplace

» Seeing how different job roles may benefit from virtual reality

Chapter **12**

The Future of Work in the Metaverse

Amidst the buzz for more immersive games and the indifference of many people, the metaverse may be setting us up for what the future of work will be like. Although the metaverse does not yet fully replicate the ideal virtual world that is seamless and simulated to the minutest details, it does already give us an idea of what it's *capable* of doing.

Over the years, the growth of several innovations (such as smartphones and the Internet) has taught us to not underrate technology. The evolution of the metaverse is coming at a steady pace.

This chapter is all about understanding and learning about the future of work and the impact that the metaverse may have on it. I offer examples of the types of work that may be affected and opportunities within the broader industry to utilize the metaverse.

Making Work More Effective with the Metaverse

Most workers embrace new technology that improves the ease, efficiency, and effectiveness of performing their job functions. Speeding up processes, and making them more human-friendly, can be the name of the game in some industries. To be sure, work has come a long way from handwritten ledgers to spreadsheet programs to the many automation solutions growing in prevalence throughout many industries today.

FUTURECAST

Industries have long sought technology solutions to improve processes, but they're likely to embrace only those solutions that also secure their bottom-line results. The future will show whether the metaverse is up to this task in any given industry. If the metaverse is unable to improve the nature of how we work while also improving bottom-line results, then it probably won't be embraced as the best technology for the job.

Here are a few examples of how companies are already using applications in the metaverse to improve collaboration and efficiency:

>> KPMG plans to use the metaverse for collaboration across its offices worldwide.

>> Meta plans to release an enterprise version of its Horizon Worlds platform for businesses that can use as a collaboration platform.

>> Shopify, one of the world's largest e-commerce retailers, plans to use augmented reality (AR) in shopping.

>> The Microsoft HoloLens has been used in industrial applications for preventive maintenance, learning, and development.

REMEMBER

The metaverse itself is not a do-it-all solution that can help workers process information faster or automate tasks. The metaverse simply provides a 3D, virtual environment where workers can collaborate and accomplish finite goals. Workers need to access *applications* that reside in the metaverse and use those applications to perform tasks. Workers still access tools that make their jobs easier, but they do so in an environment where space is no barrier. Within the metaverse, some working environments can be customized to have a wide range of flexibility, such as having a giant screen or multiple screens. In other cases, scaling objects may be possible — something that's impossible in real life. These and other features make the metaverse an incredibly flexible and interesting medium to explore for work.

USING THE METAVERSE AS A PRODUCTIVITY TOOL

Can the metaverse be used as a tool for productivity? Here are some ideas that may work for your business.

- **Reduce workplace isolation.** You can use the metaverse to reduce workplace isolation that has been created due to remote work. Workers are complaining about being isolated from their coworkers after prolonged remote work. The metaverse can help change that by offering the ability to meet colleagues in a 3D environment.

- **Reduce Zoom fatigue.** During the COVID-19 pandemic, workers started using Zoom and other video platforms extensively, ultimately leading to a phenomenon nicknamed "Zoom fatigue," a form of exhaustion due to the excessive usage of videoconferencing platforms. The metaverse can complement videoconferencing platforms and other communications forms to offer some relief and to help workers connect with others in a different medium.

- **Enhance digital culture.** As businesses head toward digital transformation and digitization, a cultural shift is needed to adapt to new technologies. This adoption can help build better productivity models.

The metaverse may or may not be of assistance to every job role in the future, but I'm speculating about something that isn't present yet and may take years and decades to develop. We're far from an era where we can control complex factories remotely, without human intervention. Some form of maintenance, equipment change, and ensuring things are working properly needs human intervention.

Engaging Remote Workers

After learning the hard lessons from the recent pandemic, future-forward companies are putting measures in place to ensure that work processes remain uninterrupted even during moments when the world seems to slow down. Besides, the future has always been screaming "remote," and the pandemic only helped to expose that fact.

The good news is that the metaverse will possibly support remote working better than any other technological innovation so far. The metaverse can help your company migrate seamlessly into the remote work culture. Using the metaverse can help your company create a more defined and realistic virtual workspace for employees who are already working from home.

Although using the metaverse for remote work seems like a great idea, many people would rather jump on a quick phone call or into a Zoom or Microsoft Teams meeting, to talk with their colleagues. Workers will likely decide whether to use the metaverse or another mode of communications depending on their needs at that moment.

REMEMBER

When computers became mainstream, we didn't even have videoconferencing tools, and the hesitation to connect to a video call was big. It has taken more than 20 years, and the COVID-19 pandemic, to get people comfortable with other communication channels. Similarly, the metaverse has the potential to be one of the channels — not the only or main channel of communication.

The metaverse replicates real-world brainstorming sessions and allows for prompt feedback in ways that only would have been possible in a physical workspace. Adjustments on projects can, therefore, be made faster, saving a lot of time and logistic implications.

FUTURECAST

As you dive deeper into the metaverse as a tool for business, keep in mind that adoption of the technology has a cost — the actual cost of buying metaverse hardware (such as VR headsets), a learning curve (which may be steep for some people), and an overall adoption timeline (which won't be immediate). As Internet connections become faster and metaverse hardware comes down in price, more people will probably be in the metaverse. But don't assume that everyone around the world will use the metaverse. After all, not everyone has access to the Internet today, and we're decades into the Internet going mainstream.

The following sections highlight some of the benefits the metaverse promises.

Richer remote workspace interaction

The metaverse provides a more interactive and intuitive remote workspace for employees. Workers can interact with 3D models of projects they're working on, assume positions in a virtual workspace, and interact with coworkers in real-time as they would in a physical office.

In the metaverse, companies will be able to create a *digital twin* (an identical digital representation; see Chapter 2) of whatever they wanted in a physical office. There can be separate "roomlets" designated for different purposes and meant for use by different kinds of workers. You could have a corridor and a coffee room and a conference room if you want. In other words, the metaverse can even help you create an environment that is more suited for work for your employees than their home environment where they live. This will boost productivity on the part of workers, increase focus, and foster connection in the work community culture despite workers being miles away from each other.

Digital twins are a good tool for all sorts of simulations. For example, a digital twin of an aircraft engine can be visualized in VR and opened up. Then a maintenance crew can look at what's inside . . . in the digital twin. Digital twins can also serve as replicas of, say, a city or a facility or even a workplace.

Improved workplace communication

Visuals and graphics in the metaverse started with fun-looking avatars, which are now moving toward realistic, human-looking holograms — more like the actual person but in a digital format. The trend of using fun avatars may be with us for a while, but better graphics-rendering technologies will make it possible to render exact replicas of people in a digital format. Also, the development of better glasses and VR technologies will make these avatars look richer and better with time.

The metaverse creates opportunities for workers to socialize seamlessly. For example, avatars can turn to ask colleagues questions, workers can have spontaneous informal chats during breaks, and nothing extra needs to be done to achieve this. Virtual meetings may help remote employees connect, but they feature a 2D interface that isn't so immersive and often doesn't allow interaction beyond the scheduled meeting time.

Some adoption challenges to be considered are the fact that not all employees and personnel will be able to adapt to the metaverse and VR at once. There is a learning curve associated with the technology, and organizations need to plan an appropriate timeline for a specific percentage of adoption.

Lower operating costs

When running on a virtual workspace, companies are able to sideline real-world costs such as rent, transportation, electricity and other utility bills, furniture, and accommodation costs for clients.

The metaverse will require only a fraction of these costs in the long run, because the setup will be on a one-time basis and require only periodic maintenance.

Today the lowest price for a metaverse headset may be around the $300 mark, and the most expensive specialty headsets range from around $3,000 to $5,000. As headset technology gets better and adoption grows, this will lower the cost of headsets.

In the 1980s, typical personal computers came at a very high cost. In 1986, the TeleCAT-286 cost around $2,995 and came with a 20MB hard drive, 512K of RAM, and 1.2MB floppy disk storage. Today a Raspberry Pi computer of similar capacity costs about $10. On the other hand, a typical home computer today has specifications that are easily a thousand times better than its predecessors from the 1990s and would cost a few hundred dollars for an inexpensive Tier-2 brand computer.

The point: Technology costs are coming down. Headsets will eventually cost a fraction of what they cost today — and deliver a higher-quality experience.

Better work–life balance

Already, some workers prefer working remotely over working from home. The metaverse might become the most efficient innovation for getting employees to be satisfied with their work while being able to manage other aspects of their life efficiently.

Although employees are working from home, their productivity can be smoothly monitored. VR promotes the feel of a real workspace and eliminates the distraction that may crop up when working from home.

Meanwhile, workers can save money because they don't need to cover commuting costs. This goes a long way toward creating satisfaction and contentment.

A metaverse-based remote workspace has immense benefits for clients as well, depending on the nature of services rendered by an organization. The metaverse can help bridge that gap between shopping from home and the inability to determine the true integrity of goods before buying. Customers can view 3D models of what they're purchasing before deciding to buy. It gets even more interesting because customers can not only virtually view but also explore 3D projects like a building, a vehicle, or a tourist site as if they were seeing it in person.

Presenting Company Training in the Metaverse

The metaverse can do more for your company than you may have thought. The benefits that can be harnessed go beyond virtual meetings and 3D game models. You could train your employees in the metaverse, benefitting from its real-time feedback and 3D presentation features.

MGM Resorts is one company that has been quick to harness the metaverse for working with its employees. The company partnered up with Strivr, a VR-based learning platform, to give their potential employees an opportunity to try out their roles in a VR workspace before deciding to accept the offer. This isn't exactly *training* the employees in how to perform in their roles, but MGM saves time and money by ensuring that only people who have tried and maintained an interest in the job are actually recruited and then trained.

Your company could employ this model, not only to ensure the willingness of potential employees but also to train new workers in their roles. The metaverse would create the most practical training sessions ever, the kind that features just not presentations and facts and figures, but the kind that would take your workers into the heart of your organization's business model as they address real-time company projects and assume positions in a VR workspace.

REMEMBER

Employees young and old can use the metaverse if given the opportunity. Avoiding bias against any employee is a good strategy in order to give everyone a chance to learn how to operate a VR headset and how to use the metaverse to its full extent.

The metaverse is a platform that enables you to effectively leverage artificial intelligence (AI). Digital coaches can be made ready to run new workers through the working style of the company or introduce workers to a new trend. Also, training materials could be more interactive because they employ 3D displays, role-play exercises, and other VR simulations that turn learning into a fun, hands-on experience.

WHAT KINDS OF TRAINING CAN BE DELIVERED IN THE METAVERSE?

The ball is in your court to dream big and wide. However, you can draw hints from what certain companies are already doing to leverage the metaverse and VR for training exercises:

- **Bosch and the Ford Motor Company:** Bosch and the Ford Motor Company have collaborated to create a VR training tool, the first of its kind, that would utilize the Oculus Quest headset to teach vehicle maintenance to technicians. There will be no need to use real cars, but a technician can learn all about fixing a vehicle. VR provides all the practical experience needed.

- **Metaverse Learning:** Metaverse Learning, a UK-based company, has also worked with UK Skills Partnership to create training models for nurses in the UK. The training series employs 3D animation and AR to prove the skills of trainers during different VR case scenarios.

- **Medivis:** Medivis, a surgical technology company, is using the Microsoft HoloLens to train medical students using interactive 3D anatomy models.

Integrating a Metaverse Model of Work

Having explored all that can be done in the metaverse, how exactly can companies work to take that paradigm shift from currently existing models to the metaverse model?

Getting employees on board

Working remotely can be dicey. It requires lots of trust from every member of the team. Each team member must be able to trust the ability and integrity of the other to deliver quality results. Most important, communication must be clear to prevent misinformation and wasted efforts. Fortunately, the metaverse offsets these problems, because it fosters collaboration and makes communication smoother.

Perhaps the idea your employees have of the metaverse is just large headsets and cartoon animations of game characters. The only way to disprove this will be to have them try it. The metaverse may feature lots of animated characters today, but it's moving toward becoming more realistic in terms of real-world features that can be embedded in it.

Google's Starline project, for example, seems to be acing in this regard. The project aims to make communication and collaboration across a distance possible using real-time compression and a 3D display. Most interesting is that the technology uses a light field display system that provides a real-time sense of audio and visual without the need for clumsy VR glasses or headsets.

Workers may even find that the metaverse provides a source of fun. That's right, *fun!* People can better express their individuality using customized avatars and better project who they truly are to others, even though none of them have ever met before.

TIP

Some workers enjoy exploring new technologies. Younger generations, in particular, tend to be more comfortable learning new tech. Perhaps unsurprisingly, these are the users who are already flocking toward the VR platforms in the metaverse. They head to the metaverse to view concerts, meet people, and play games. One specific driver that is leading to this is the fact that younger generations get involved in gaming at an early age and as a result are exposed to gaming technologies early on. The metaverse is a platform that came from gaming, so there is much lower resistance in learning. That said, *everyone* has the ability to learn how to work a VR headset in a matter of minutes and, ultimately, a person's curiosity and approach to learning new things are what matter, not which decade they were born.

Knowing what to expect

Despite the told and untold benefits of the metaverse, the early stage of integration, as with any new thing, is usually the most difficult. You should expect work to slow down a bit as workers transform their working systems to something entirely new. Sometimes, the most effective way to plunge in is to have trial explorations. You could have your company split into different teams and work on mini projects using the metaverse.

WARNING

Company owners and stakeholders may need to understand that this change won't happen all at once. Besides the complexities involved in getting humans to change and adapt to new models, such major transitions will also come with huge costs for the company, but this will only be at the initial stage.

A good way to implement the metaverse, therefore, is to introduce it slowly and then watch it invigorate the whole work system of the company. It's a good thing that most companies are already familiar with remote models of working and many are already operating hybrid, if not fully remote, models. It could help if companies explore how working remotely could change them first, before incorporating more sophisticated technologies like 3D VR and AR.

The good thing is that work in the metaverse is yet to go mainstream, so there is absolutely no reason to rush. You have time for proper planning, perhaps some form of consulting, and very accurate budgeting to determine how the transition will affect the economy of your company.

Coming up with a rollout strategy for using the metaverse in your workplace

TIP

The following steps outline a metaverse rollout strategy that your organization can try (or modify to suit your needs):

1. **Ask yourselves why your organization would use the metaverse.**

   To answer this question, you'll need to analyze key areas of impact such as sales, customer service, or product design and how the metaverse can help. Getting your teams involved in helping create a compelling business case is essential before you commit to anything. Start by planning out a timeline by which you should have captured all the requirements; conducted a strengths, weaknesses, opportunities, and threats (SWOT) analysis; and looked at your broader strategy to see if it can benefit from the metaverse.

2. **Allocate the right resources to the implementation.**

   This could mean allocating tasks to even hire new people who would be dedicated to the metaverse implementation. The roles can vary from a pure project management role (which is nontechnical) to software architects (who may even be involved in designing a specific app for your organization to use in the metaverse).

3. **Lay down the timeline, the source of funding, and other key aspects of the project.**

4. **Identify marketing, operations, public relations, brand management, and other relevant teams that will play a role in the pre- as well as post-implementation phase.**

5. **Clearly identify the right time for the metaverse implementation.**

   Try to avoid it coinciding with other important projects or initiatives underway at your organization so you don't stretch yourself too thin.

Exploring Job Roles and the Metaverse

This section looks at some job roles to see how the metaverse may be able to augment them or complement them. In the end, the goal is to help people do a better job. Read on to see how some jobs of today may transform with the metaverse tomorrow.

HR goes VR

Human resources (HR) professionals play a critical role in managing the successful operations of an organization. From recruitment to exit interviews, HR manages it all in a typical organization.

A critical role of HR is to be able to meet new hires. Some of this is done in person through interviews and face-to-face engagements. This process has been greatly improved through technologies such as videoconferencing. In recent years, platforms such as Zoom, Google Hangouts, and Microsoft Teams, have become popular tools for the HR department.

Based on current trends, HR may be a good candidate to utilize metaverse platforms. Imagine your interviews being held in the metaverse in an immersive VR environment. You can ask candidates questions or even get a feel for their collaboration skills virtually, which is especially useful if your work environment is hybrid or fully virtual. The metaverse can provide an option for recruitment and exit interviews alike. Especially for younger candidates who are accustomed to VR, this would be a very comfortable way to interview for a job.

Operations and digital twins

Operations teams within organizations deal with managing a company on a daily basis. This can include everything from complex operations such as those in a factory to back-office operations such as in an accounting firm. Every role within operations relies on knowledge and information gained from multiple aspects of the business. This could be the number of customers acquired (such as in marketing) or the number of shipments sent (as in shipping).

Operations can easily use the metaverse for collaboration. And when you consider the advent of digital twins being used within the business context, it may give operations personnel an advantage within some industries and company sizes. Imagine operations teams being able to look at the real-time digital twin of a warehouse and do an inventory count virtually. That would be incredibly time-saving. As a warehouse operator, the metaverse would allow your avatar to fly across shelves virtually (without wings, of course) and do your job to your satisfaction.

Sales pros go virtual

Selling can be a one-on-one process, such as in consultative sales, or fully customer driven, like what you find online. In cases where sales is done on consultative basis, and products or services are discussed before the actual transaction takes place, some form of communication is likely to happen.

Sales professionals today across different industries rely on phone communication and videoconferencing. As the new creator economy emerges, we've seen the evolution of nonfungible tokens (NFTs) and digital goods that are only available online. As these economies have grown, salespeople will need to be able to talk to customers on metaverse platforms, where they're buying these digital goods.

Not only digital goods but other services will also start being sold in the metaverse. These may include products in industries such as insurance, car sales, accounting, financial products, and more.

Within the sales function of an organization, the metaverse can play an important part serving as a new channel for sales. This new channel, the metaverse, can help sales professionals qualify and nurture their sales prospects.

Future roles in sales will include positions such as a metaverse sales manager or a metaverse sales consultant.

Marketing meets metaverse

In addition to proving a fertile ground for sales, the metaverse can serve as a marketing channel. You may not be able to sell everything in the metaverse, but depending on the demographic you're targeting, using the metaverse as part of your channel strategy could prove useful.

The future of work for marketing teams in the metaverse and utilizing metaverse platforms completely depends on the products and services that you're promoting. Marketing may find the metaverse an interesting playground due to its scale, unique audience, and virtual environment. It's possible that marketing professionals will use the metaverse as a place to collaborate, share designs, and test marketing campaigns.

There will also be a time when marketing in the metaverse will become a specialization, just as Internet marketing has transformed into a multi-billion-dollar industry over the last 20 years.

Turn to Chapter 11 for more on marketing in the metaverse.

Design done virtually

Design may be a critical piece of the metaverse. Companies such as NVIDIA are already banking on a big growth within the design community. NVIDIA is creating the Omniverse, which focuses on providing designers with metaverse design tools that can be used for creating digital artifacts for industrial use, enabling collaboration between designers, and facilitating the process of digital design that will help create a better metaverse. Designers may be able to collaborate over the metaverse.

Think about fashion designers who want to incorporate designs from around the world or collaborate with others who aren't located in the same office. Imagine being able to collaborate with artists and other professionals in your profession, who are all using VR to come up with better products. The metaverse is already very design-focused — 3D buildings, museums, and NFTs are making big waves in the digital community as a whole.

Will creators find more avenues to create and sell their products in the metaverse? This has already started to happen.

The metaverse as a management tool

Leaders who manage organizations and help them scale can use the metaverse as a means of collaboration, oversight, and taking their organizations into a

VR-powered era. Companies today can easily hold all-hands meetings in the metaverse or go on leadership retreats in the metaverse.

The metaverse, as we know it today, was never imagined to be that way. It started as a means to enjoy entertainment better — a platform to satisfy the need to play video games in a more realistic and sophisticated world. But the metaverse means more than just video games and VR today. It has crept into different systems of life, from social media to cryptocurrency, to finance, and the workspace culture.

Here are three things that are making the metaverse expand beyond its early days and opening doors for organizations to undertake more complex tasks:

» **Investment:** There is a huge amount of interest by tech giants and venture capital firms. As a result, billions of dollars are being spent on developing the technology further.

» **Involvement:** Users are now signing up not only to play games in the metaverse but also to purchase virtual land, visit virtual museums, and meet other users, among other things.

» **Development:** Fast-growing technologies are changing how the metaverse works and how it delivers user experiences. New tech, such as Epic Games Unreal Engine, is making VR graphics almost lifelike.

FUTURECAST

DID SOMEONE SAY "DIGITAL HUMANS"?

We may not be able to fully grasp all that the metaverse will open up to at the moment, but we know that the metaverse has opened the world to new ways of going about our daily work activities.

Before now, the world was screaming digitization. Organizations had opened up to using different sophisticated applications and AI to get things done. Data science and analytics tools took over paper surveys and social media platforms made remote working and work integration easier.

We're in for even more interesting features with the metaverse. It shouldn't be considered a disruption to the technical flow of your organization. In fact, consider the metaverse a technological addition to complement already existing methods of solving problems like AI and virtual conferencing.

(continued)

(continued)

The metaverse and the whole idea of VR offer the opportunity to harness AI and robotics. Beyond the avatars that represent human characters, the metaverse may open us to a world of other digital beings — AI-powered robots and digital doubles who talk like humans and can sustain intelligent conversations, provide smart answers to questions, and make decisions as a human would do.

UneeQ, a platform that aims to "revolutionize customer experiences with scalable human connections" has leaped ahead of many to create several digital humans, including a digital double of Albert Einstein. Some of UneeQ's digital humans like Nola and Daniel are already working as digital workers. Nola is a digital shopping assistant, while Daniel is a digital double of UBS Chief Economist Daniel Kalt. Daniel is able to give personalized wealth management advice to clients, while the real Daniel is being productive doing something else.

Technology is using AI and autonomous animation to ensure these digital workers match up with human emotional standards. They should be able to make lifelike gestures and recognize humor. More fascinating is that humans may have their digital doubles who would converse and work just like they would. Learn more at `https://digitalhumans.com`.

Chapter **13**

Hiring, Training, and Connecting Employees

I f you have employees, you need human resources (HR). HR is responsible for hiring, training, and supporting employees. This chapter looks at ways the metaverse is changing the workplace, creating new ways to manage people, and creating new processes and initiatives for hiring people and keeping them engaged with organizations.

Extending Employee Training to the Metaverse

Employee training sessions are usually provided in either self-learning or facilitated modes. The metaverse can assist in both modes of training — even if your business isn't based in the metaverse. You can also extend training in the metaverse from soft skills training to technical training.

REMEMBER

Of course, not all training is best delivered in the metaverse. You can use the information in this book to identify the possibilities, and then match your training needs to what the metaverse offers.

The following sections show what the metaverse brings to existing training formats you may be considering. I also provide a framework for considering the cost, time, and other logistics of delivering training in the metaverse.

Engaging with interactive training

Here are some ways you might use the metaverse for training:

>> Have two-way interactions with your instructor.

>> Engage in group learning in a live classroom.

>> Meet with third parties and go on virtual tours as part of the training.

>> Engage in project work and deliver the deliverables over the metaverse.

>> Execute on a specific training and learning goal, such as receiving a credential.

WARNING

Don't overcomplicate your employee experiences by compelling them to be part of metaverse trainings unless doing so adds value and significantly enhances results. Excessive and unnecessary complications in experience delivery can lead to technology overload and mental fatigue, ultimately leading to job dissatisfaction and burnout.

Interactive training over the metaverse should be designed to suit your business needs. Some industries, such as industrial design or preventive maintenance training, are more likely to use the metaverse. Even these organizations, however, should exercise caution and not cause organizational anxiety and employee stress.

Choosing a training format

Organizations determine the best format for employee training sessions based on job role, upcoming project needs, individual career paths, and other determining factors. Training formats naturally vary by industry. In some cases, organizations may benefit from holding employee training in the metaverse.

Here are some common formats organizations use for employee training:

>> **Self-learning:** Self-learning video content, self-study without any instructor input are both types of one-way delivery. A metaverse-based option would help learners learn in a 3D environment that can offer interactivity.

- >> **Workshops:** This is where more than one person works together over a stipulated duration of course work and acquire skills. Imagine meeting other participants and collaborating with them through 3D models of equipment, art, or even music, all in the metaverse.

- >> **Breakout sessions:** Typically held at conferences and larger gatherings, breakouts are shorter-duration sessions that focused on a niche area. A smaller set of participants can get an intimate learning experience and even collaborate with remote metaverse participants of the conference.

- >> **Lunch and learn:** This is very common where employees learn during lunch hours in a nonformal format. Many companies moved to virtual-reality-based meetings and learning during the COVID-19 pandemic and continue to use it for team building.

- >> **Instructor led:** These can be in person or virtual, but in either case they're facilitated by an instructor. With a metaverse option, adding to the immersive nature, working with instructors who wouldn't be able to make it in person, or designing trainings with expert instructors from all over the world would be invaluable.

- >> **Interactive workshops:** Workshops can be entirely digital, where software tools are used, or a blend between the virtual and real worlds. Examples of this can include workshops on specific aspects of work where students are given an assignment to complete after the workshop is over. Findings can then be shared back in the metaverse platform. A key aspect of a workshop is the ability to work with others in a classroom format where teamwork would facilitate the learning process.

- >> **Technical training:** Conducting technical training in the metaverse requires that you build technical resources within the metaverse platform. For example, the aerospace industry and others use Microsoft HoloLens to visualize digital-twin models of turbines and jet engines. This way, technicians can work on virtual equipment to learn the usage of complex machinery that they typically don't have access to. Metaverse-based training could save a lot of time and money for organizations with continued trainings for personnel, especially with a complex work environment.

Performing a cost and time analysis

Every business or organization is different. Just because other organizations are using the metaverse as a strategic tool, that doesn't necessarily mean that it will suit your needs. You need to analyze the cost and time impact involved in training in the metaverse.

Cost

Take time to understand if your employees are able to learn better through the metaverse. Does it add an advantage to the process of acquiring a skill? As an example, when we look at digital twins and the cost of training in real working environments, it is sometimes not possible at all to train employees and workers on a hot, or constantly operating, equipment. Equipment shutdown are expensive and industries need solutions to train workers on parallel systems. The metaverse can definitely help. Some other cost-related aspects could include cost of hardware equipment (VR headsets are expensive), and the need to own digital land and develop it.

Time

A metaverse-based system may outweigh training situations where time is of the essence.

After investing in things like a training environment, an instructor, VR headsets, and other expenses, consider what benefits you'll gain that couldn't be find in training outside the metaverse. For example, maybe you have a large number of employees to train and they're located all over the world; maybe training them in the metaverse can save you a ton of time and effort. Moreover, time away from desks can balloon out of control for large gatherings.

When building a case for metaverse based training ensure that you calculate the impact over short and long-term durations. Sometimes it is hard to recoup costs over a short time and much easier to extract value on the long run. Some additional time-related factors could include the time required to create metaverse awareness for employees and keeping up with a fast-changing industry with rapid developments.

Delivering training in the metaverse

Not all learning and training will be able to be delivered in the metaverse. As an organization, you have to evaluate which parts of your training can be delivered in the metaverse and what benefits it brings.

After you've analyzed the cost and time involved in training in the metaverse, if you've decided it makes sense to proceed with metaverse-based training, follow these steps:

1. **Create a metaverse learning and development policy.**

   Organizations typically have learning and development departments that manage all aspects of delivering training to employees. The metaverse is a radically new medium, so learning and development managers must create metaverse usage and impact specific organizational policies to protect employees, the organization, and third parties in order to create an effective training environment. For example, forcing employees to use the metaverse excessively may impact their health, or some departments may not use the metaverse at all, which could possibly hamper their overall technology adoption, in turn impacting the organization as a whole.

2. **Invest in metaverse hardware such as VR headsets.**

   Turn to Chapter 6 to learn more about headset types and find the ones that are suitable for your business needs.

3. **Train instructors and students on the usage of the metaverse hardware and in-platform applications.**

   Creating a solid foundation for employee training means getting them acquainted with the tools they'll be using. Start by making sure they're comfortable using VR headsets and any other software tools needed. This may mean conducting trainings prior to the actual program starts.

4. **Launch a small group initially to iron out any delivery issues.**

   Before you launch a company-wide learning and development program, work with a small batch of students and trainers to perfect the process of training delivery. This will give you a good opportunity to iron out any hiccups.

5. **Create specific programs with learning outcomes that employees can use in their jobs.**

   Being goal-oriented in creating a training program is essential for any learning and development program. Make sure that your employees receive tangible skills and benefits.

6. **Make learning enjoyable through the usage of different tools within the metaverse.**

   The metaverse can be fun if designed properly. Make your training program fun and gamify any aspects of it that you can. Fun makes learning stick!

7. **Keep in mind inclusivity while promoting metaverse training within the organization.**

   Be sure to balance the needs of the organization with inclusion and cultural appropriation in mind. Some learners may not be comfortable wearing headsets due to cultural or faith-based garments, for example. Learning and development teams must create alternatives for people facing such challenges, if any.

8. **Offer resources for the learners to be able to learn about the metaverse and overcome any initial fears they may have.**

   Help employees and trainees continue the learning journey beyond the metaverse. Provide adequate resources such as books, reference manuals, and any training needs freely. Build a metaverse-focused digital library where employees can borrow and read books and magazines and watch informational videos.

Early adopters who have embraced metaverse–based employee training include the Hyundai Motor Group, which has created its own metaverse experience. Hyundai Mobis has started carrying out new employee trainings and summer training camps in the metaverse.

Hiring and Onboarding Employees in the Metaverse

Adding new people to an organization is an ongoing task for HR. This section shows you how you can use the metaverse as a tool for employee onboarding.

Recruiting talent in the metaverse

Today many organizations are struggling to attract talent. Reasons for this are varied but include attrition, more career choices, unfavorable social and economic factors, and a demand for workplaces to work harder to attract and retain talent. Competition in some industries, such as tech, is fierce.

Here are some circumstances in which conducting hiring processes through the metaverse makes the most sense:

» The business is focused on the metaverse.

» The organization would like to showcase its metaverse-based business environment to candidates.

» Connecting over the metaverse is a standard operating procedure for the organization.

If your organization plans to leverage the metaverse, or it has standardized on the metaverse as a channel for communication, HR can easily use the platform to hold job interviews in VR. Holding job interviews in the metaverse has some advantages. You can

>> Provide candidates with a 3D experience rather than a face-to-face conversation over videoconferencing.

>> Provide candidates an opportunity to engage with the organization in a new medium.

>> Offer candidates the ability to peek into the culture of your organization.

>> Enable better collaboration for interviews with teams that are spread out and need to interview the candidate simultaneously.

>> Hold interviews with senior leadership and decision-makers in two virtual rooms within private metaverse platforms.

REMEMBER

Whether you're conducting interviews in a common meeting place in the metaverse or in your organization's metaverse headquarters, digital inclusivity is crucial. Candidates who don't have access to VR headsets may not be able to attend interviews or meet you in the metaverse, which would exclude them from the opportunity. Arrange for a VR headset to be sent out to candidates for the interview process so you don't miss out on a great candidate!

FUTURECAST

The push of HR into hiring through the metaverse or creating these initial interactions in the metaverse also opens up the opportunity to develop custom infrastructure in the metaverse. This push to the metaverse adoption can take the form of creating a virtual office in the metaverse that replicates or is a digital twin of your actual headquarters. You can design the experiences that candidates have when they interact with spaces and staff within the facility.

Organizing virtual hiring events

The next frontier in creating the first touchpoint with prospective employees is to connect with them through a metaverse job fair or hiring event. Here are steps for organizations to hold their own hiring events in the metaverse:

1. **Start small for your first event.**

2. **Create a brand presence in the metaverse.**

3. **Launch the event at a specific time and date.**

4. **Meet and greet visitors to your virtual booth.**

5. **Provide information on jobs and culture, and answer any questions attendees have.**

Holding a virtual hiring is similar to how you would hold an in-person event, except with a metaverse-based option you can reach candidates in faraway locations. If your organization is spread out geographically or trying to tap into the metaverse for suitable candidates, a virtual hiring event could be a good option.

In an online poll conducted by ExpressVPN, 46 percent of Gen Z respondents said they foresee working in the metaverse within two years. This means a huge segment of the younger generation is likely to be a big part of metaverse employees.

Organizations that have held metaverse recruiting events include AIS and Accenture Malaysia, which have used different metaverse platforms to speak to prospective candidates for new job opportunities at their organizations.

Creating a virtual job fair

At job fairs, employers and employees get a chance to learn more about each other and break the ice. The metaverse can help tap into a segment of job hunters who are extremely comfortable on such a platform. Think of it as another channel to meet and greet potential candidates who could be part of your organization and vice versa.

Here are some steps you can take to organize a virtual job fair:

1. **Create your organization's virtual space on a metaverse platform.**

   Make sure you have relevant digital assets in place. This could include virtual brochures, video content, and a place for visitors to meet your staff and ask any questions. Check out Chapter 2 to learn more about which metaverse platform could be the most suitable for you.

2. **Organize your virtual fair as you would in the real world.**

   Announce the job fair through corporate communication channels and any other media relevant to your organization. Spread the word and let it be known that your business is tapping into the metaverse. Chapter 11 provides ideas on how to promote your business in the metaverse.

3. **Make sure you have enough staff members attending the virtual fair and provide them with the adequate training.**

4. **On the day and time of the event, connect with visitors and engage in conversation.**

5. **Create a plan to follow up with prospects who attended the virtual fair.**

   Make sure to create a lead capture process either in the metaverse or off the metaverse.

TIP

A number of Metaverse job fairs are coming up everywhere. Check out `https://web3jobfair.hy.pe` to get an idea of what's happening.

TIP

If your organization is conducting outreach to recent graduates, holding metaverse-focused events at university graduate fairs might help differentiate your organization from the competition.

Increasing Team Engagement

Today many organizations find that remote work has created challenges with employee engagement. Working remotely puts strain on employees to build bonds with colleagues and have a sense of teamwork. It also can create a sense of loneliness and detachment from the organization and coworkers. No water cooler conversations or going out for casual lunch with colleagues — it all adds up.

VR-based platforms can help foster a sense of camaraderie within the virtual workspace. Many organization are experimenting with VR and the metaverse as a mode of engagement.

For example, KPMG recently announced its investment of $30 million to create metaverse-focused learning and collaboration opportunities for its employees. KPMG plans to use the metaverse as a tool for collaboration between teams located in different places and geographically separated.

TIP

Here are some tips to help you use the metaverse to increase employee engagement:

>> **Complement your overall engagement strategy with different channels of engagement, including the metaverse.** Don't use a spray-and-pray type of campaign.

>> **Be very specific with your goals and targets for teams to have an engaging experience in the metaverse.** No two teams are alike, and their job responsibilities can be highly varied.

>> **Launch pilot trials to gather feedback from participants.** Then fine-tune your engagement strategy before launching it company-wide.

>> **Offer employees the opportunity to freely access metaverse hardware and platforms.** This way, they can get acquainted with the nuances of the metaverse and be able to use it as a tool for collaboration.

>> **Support employees' needs for training to learn more about the metaverse and how to get better at it.**

4

The Future of Industry in the Metaverse

Chapter **14**

Teaching and Learning in the Metaverse

The metaverse offers new ways for the education and learning sectors to plan and deliver structured learning programs. The application of virtual reality (VR) elements in classrooms can already be seen across the learning spectrum with the use of head-mounted devices and certain applications that even use artificial intelligence (AI). This chapter looks at some key aspects of metaverse-based learning and how to get started.

Teaching in the Metaverse

The metaverse offers an opportunity to enhance modern learning models by introducing immersive and interactive learning experiences.

With metaverse technology, processes that are invisible to the human eye, such as chemical or biological processes, can be brought to life in 3D VR. Imagine being able to zoom into the actual protein structures of cells, seeing the crystalline structures of metals in immersive 3D, or taking a 3D walking tour of the human circulatory system.

Here are some ideas for how teachers and other instructors might use the metaverse to enhance the learning experience:

>> **Games:** Using games to engage learners and allow them to put the knowledge they've acquired to test can prove helpful in helping students retain what they've learned. Games can be particularly beneficial for children and teenagers.

>> **Immersive storytelling and role-playing:** Immersive storytelling and role-playing help participants relate to the concepts being taught at a deeper cognitive and emotional level. With a 3D environment and participation possibly with other participants, learners can immerse themselves within the story by being active participants or playing characters.

>> **Visual aids:** Humans are more likely to retain information when learning is aided with visuals rather than just text. The visual element of metaverse learning can be used to explain relatively abstract concepts.

>> **Personalization:** Experiences in the metaverse can be personalized to suit particular demographics. For example, it might make more sense to cover diseases that are more prevalent in a certain geographic area than to go deep into conditions that healthcare professionals in that area would probably never see.

>> **Immersive and collaborative field trips:** Field trips allow students to access locations in groups and make meaningful connections with people from different locations around the world. For more about using VR and augmented reality (AR) in group learning, see the sidebar "Group learning in the metaverse."

Extended exposure to VR may cause discomfort. Future education models must have strategies in place to avoid any healthcare concerns for students, at least until the relevant industries develop high-performance, more comfortable, and lower-cost hardware for accessing the metaverse.

TRAINING FUTURE FIREFIGHTERS WITH 3D SIMULATIONS

Imagine future firefighters being trained in the metaverse. Candidates would be transported to scenes showing varying danger levels and would be able to immerse themselves in real firefighting scenarios. With VR technology, the teaching models would include sensory details (heat, flames, victims, and so on) that help the students get an actual feel for the firefighting scenario, just as they would if they were there in reality.

Perhaps specialized metaverse hardware such as scenario generators that impart a feeling of hot or cold could be part of a wearable device that trainees would wear during this stage. Students could also be trained to manage crisis in different types of terrains and environmental conditions, all through VR and the metaverse.

Creating a Learning Experience in the Metaverse

In order to create good learning experiences and outcomes in the metaverse, you need to ensure that you design these experiences the right way. The metaverse is different from an actual classroom. It's also different from a video-based class that you can attend via a computer with an Internet connection. With the metaverse, virtual headsets are a default, putting the learner in a three-dimensional environment as opposed to viewing a two-dimensional computer display. When you're designing a curriculum for the metaverse, you have to take into consideration the environment itself, and how students will experience the "classroom."

Understanding the metaverse learning environment

A metaverse *learning environment* is a 3D learning space that has been created with one thing in mind: immersive learning. This learning space can be a virtual facility, a virtual room, or an open space. You're no longer bound to having the boring walls and windows of a classroom. Imagine being able to create an environment where learners feel they're in the right space. For a visual arts class, you could create the look and feel of an art gallery; for a photography class, you could use award-winning photographs as your wallpaper. Within this virtual environment, you could be sitting in a virtual swimming pool or on top of a virtual mountain, the possibilities are endless.

Masterclass (www.masterclass.com) offers courses taught by people who have reached the top of their careers. What if you could view and join one of these courses in VR in the metaverse? You'd feel as if you were sitting right in front of your teacher and be able to interact in many ways with their lifelike avatar. This realism and interactivity make metaverse learning stand out from current forms of remote and online learning.

With this level of flexibility and the ability to create different three-dimensional environments where users can immerse themselves, perhaps one of the exciting features of a metaverse learning experience is how learning providers will design these environments.

Assembling a metaverse learning design team

Designing any metaverse learning program is likely to be a multi-person task. Here are some of the team members who may be involved:

>> **Program managers:** To create the high-level objectives and own the project

>> **Instruction designers:** To design the actual steps learners will take through the learning journey

>> **Metaverse programmers:** To take the instruction design and build a virtual world around it

>> **Instructors and trainers:** To assist students and learners through their learning journeys

These roles are some of the typical ones and the nonobvious ones that could be part of metaverse learning.

Designing an effective learning environment

As experts from various faculties and areas of learning — such as human behavior, psychology, instructional design, technology, and others — come together to make metaverse learning better, better models and learning methods will arise for the metaverse.

In the meantime, here are some recommendations for designing a learning environment that ensures learners get the most from a metaverse learning experience:

>> **Consider the needs of your learners.** As you design your metaverse-based learning experience, perhaps some aspect of your program should be in the metaverse while another part can be in person. Or maybe all of it should be in the metaverse. This decision will depend on aspects such as whether your learners have all the hardware available, whether they have the necessary connectivity, and whether they're attending classes from different time zones. Such questions need to be considered at the beginning of the design process.

>> **Align the environment with the learning experience.** The virtual learning facility that students are accessing remotely through the metaverse should be aligned with the type of education students are getting. For example, if you're

teaching a class for future diving instructors, having a virtual metaverse environment that looks and appears like a bank or a restaurant may be cool but may not put the learners in a proper mindset. Instead, perhaps design an environment that looks like a beach or a pool.

>> **Create a tidy, organized digital learning space.** For example, you may be teaching a class of factory mechanics who work on very specific machinery. Within factory environments, it's common to train technicians to store tools in a very specific way. A *shadow board* may be used in a factory environment to mark the position of each tool when it's stored in a wall hanging system. A metaverse-based training system should consider such environmental needs and incorporate them where needed.

Avoid incorporating distractions and unnecessary enhancements of your learning space. Overdesigning your environment with elements that are distracting may hamper the learning environment. Imagine teaching a class of teenagers in a metaverse designed to look like a Las Vegas casino. That environment would be extremely distracting.

>> **Establish a code of conduct.** Create rules to follow within the learning space to ensure the learning space is safe and inclusive for everyone. Create a process for any complaints to be raised anonymously. Make sure there's a process in place to deal with problems when they arise.

>> **Avoid sensory overload.** VR applications for learning can employ spatial audio and stereoscopic imagery that create an illusion of depth and increase the learner's sense of agency. The learning goals must be clearly defined to prevent confusion in the face of sensory overload.

>> **Measure learning goals.** Metaverse hardware and software haven't been developed to a point where they can be used to measure how much learning has been achieved. The next few major developments to see within the metaverse learning industry would be the ability to track and measure learning outcomes. At present, trainers should find secondary systems for measurement.

>> **Practice sensitivity.** The program design team must take into account the suitability of the learning environment being developed concerning the target audience and context of use. For example, maintaining a neutral stance with cultural, religious, or social sensitivity would be a good choice.

>> **Measure learning progression.** Enabling progression and measurement of learning success in any learning environment is a necessity. This means ensuring that students are learning and that there is a clear success case instead of focusing just on the technology and not being able to actually help students learn.

GROUP LEARNING IN THE METAVERSE

When people learn together, they can share knowledge and experiences that may not be possible in solo learning. Group work helps build a collaborative work habit and creates a team spirit. Learners within groups form a bond and work toward helping each other succeed. As a group that's responsible for learning together and perhaps completing a project together, learners see the value of friendship, kinship, and reliance on team members. These qualities can come in handy later in life.

The metaverse will provide an opportunity for group interactivity and collaboration through VR. This will allow participants to put the knowledge and skills they acquire to the test. For example, you may design activities and games that help participants learn together and share ideas.

Research is currently lacking in this area, but the next few years may shed light on how useful group learning is proving to be using VR technologies.

Preparing for Class in the Metaverse

The more people can personalize their learning experiences, the more likely they are to retain the information they learn. Metaverse classes and learning experiences must allow participants to enjoy immersion, interaction, and the ability to retain information. Educators must work together with researchers and developers from the scratch towards the development of learning programs that facilitate learning. In this section, I look at the major components of a metaverse class and point out ways that they can be optimized for the best results.

A number of startups, venture funds and established tech companies are now working on the idea of a *metaversity,* a metaverse-based university. Meta has created a $150 million immersive learning project to bring ten U.S.-based universities into the metaverse. This includes the University of Maryland Global Campus that has no physical location and has more than 45,000 enrolled undergraduates. Meta has participated by donating headsets, and students will use these in biology and astronomy classes in VR. Visit `https://about.meta.com/immersive-learning` to learn more about Meta's immersive learning program.

Finding a suitable physical location

Although class participants are likely remote, connecting to the classroom from around the country or around the world, they might be in the same physical location, attending a metaverse class together. If so, you need to find a location for the class that's safe for everyone involved and conducive to learning.

The first step is ensuring you have enough space available for participants to move around. Students should be able to interact with metaverse elements, free of distraction during class hours.

Access to infrastructure such as a suitable Internet connection that can work with multiple VR headsets and has a high bandwidth would be necessary. Depending on what's being taught, you may need custom metaverse platforms.

TIP

If schools or professional settings can bring participants together in a designated classroom fitted with screens and movable chairs, it might positively impact the learning experience. Students would be able to connect both in person and in the metaverse. This may increase the collaborative element and eradicate discrepancies concerning Internet access and homogeneity of the learning material. A healthy goal would be to see how we can improve the efficacy of what we already have instead of seeking to completely replace it.

Getting the right gear

To access the metaverse, students need VR headsets, smartphones, tablets, PCs, and many other devices.

There are ongoing conversations about how to make these gadgets more afford-able and accessible for as many people as need them. Most of these gadgets are very expensive, so some learners may not be able to afford them. Schools will need to come up with new solutions that can eliminate the digital divide.

Because the metaverse and its expansion are currently in progress, there have been certain issues concerning inclusivity. For example, motion sickness experienced with VR headsets has been linked to the *interpupillary distance* (the distance between both pupils). Motion sickness is observed more in women and people with smaller head sizes. Work needs to be done to provide multiple sizes or adjust-able variants of VR headsets that everyone can use comfortably. Similarly, people living with certain disabilities may experience difficulty using the controls of VR hardware when learning.

REMEMBER

More inclusive and affordable hardware options are necessary for the progression of the metaverse's successful adoption in the universal education system.

Installing all the needed software and apps

Before starting a program, instructors should pretest any software tools or apps that learners must download onto their VR devices. Also, be sure the overall pro-gram design includes protocols for technical support in case a student or learner is unable to get their VR hardware or software not working.

APPRECIATING THE VALUE OF HUMAN INTERACTION

The importance of the educator and guide in metaverse classes can't be overemphasized. This person highlights the learning trajectory for every participant, leading them to focus on and pick out points that are instrumental for achieving the learning objectives of the class.

Attempts to replace a human instructor with AI are currently underway. Automated, chatbot-based systems are slowly being integrated into the World Wide Web. For simple tasks and instructions, bots seem to work, but for specialized learning, more complex systems are needed. We're still far away from being able to get a degree in medicine or engineering through self-study.

Education and training in the metaverse can be very interactive. Instructors can provide a tour of learning environments, types of learning outcomes, and interactions between leaders even before the actual training starts. This way, learners can get comfortable before the training begins.

Dealing with Logistics and Technical Challenges

Metaverse learning experiences can be 100 percent in the metaverse or be part of a blended approach, with some form of in-person learning, videoconferencing-based sessions, or a mix. How these learning experiences are delivered would completely fall in the hands of instructors, curriculum designers, and schools.

There are also specialized learning management systems such as Blackboard (www.blackboard.com), Moodle (https://moodle.org), Canvas (www.instructure.com/canvas), and countless others that are already being utilized within learning environments. Whether these integrate with metaverse platforms and are able to create better transition into metaverse learning will probably be apparent in the next few years as these providers step into the metaverse.

This section expands on some of the challenges and limitations of the metaverse when it comes to learning.

Ensuring access to the metaverse learning environment

Both hardware and software aspects of the metaverse continue to become better in terms of speed, resolution, delivery, and overall experience, so easy access to the metaverse as a learning tool is a must. Access to high-speed Internet isn't a problem in many places, but it may be a challenge in rural areas or underdeveloped countries. Accessing the metaverse isn't cheap — for example, VR headsets need to be procured. Hardware costs will come down over time, but headsets are still quite expensive (possibly prohibitively so).

REMEMBER

Statistics reveal that more than 35 percent of rural America does *not* have reliable high-speed Internet access. The United Nations says that nearly half of the world's population lacks Internet access of any kind. For the metaverse to be universally acceptable and adopted, the digital divide must be eliminated or lowered.

Finding programs and instructional materials

There is a scarcity of programs and instructional materials for learning in the metaverse. This is largely because its adoption in education is still in the shaping stages. There are no databases with materials that enable educators to search based on subject areas, learning goals, or age groups. Most instruction design professionals and teams have so far worked with 2D screens as a channel and have yet to fully immerse themselves into a metaverse-based design. At this stage, even designers and course creators have to undergo a learning curve to be able to design learning content that is successfully adapted.

TIP

A number of future-focused companies are breaking new ground in the metaverse learning industry. Here are some companies to check out:

>> **Hatch Kids** (https://kids.hatchxr.com): AR/VR coding for kids

>> **Edverse** (www.edverse.com): Education at various levels in the metaverse

>> **Marvrus** (www.marvrus.com/index-eg.html): Korean metaverse education startup

Also check out a chart of companies making waves in VR and metaverse according to industry analyst firm CB Insights: https://research-assets.cbinsights.com/2022/04/14140733/metaverse-market-map.png.

Creating an inclusive learning experience

The metaverse is an extremely new environment for learning, and it has a long way to go when it comes to being adopted by the majority. A challenge with the adoption of any new technology is the cultural and regional appropriation by audiences worldwide. The planet has a population of 7 billion, and it's projected to grow to 9 billion by 2030. These billions of people speak hundreds of languages, practice numerous religions, and have countless customs, belief systems, and traditions. Some of these are very conducive to technology, while others may not be, at least in the early stages.

Users with accessibility challenges face their own challenges to adoption of the technology. For example, visually impaired learners may encounter difficulty in using VR headsets and other head-mounted devices.

People who use religious hair coverings or have certain hairstyles may find the headsets especially cumbersome. This points yet again to the need for inclusivity in the design of VR tech.

Inclusivity should also be a consideration when designing classroom layouts, graphics, and imagery to ensure any form of offensive content is avoided and that educational places look and feel welcoming.

REMEMBER

VR headsets can make people uncomfortable with prolonged usage, so they're better suited for shorter periods of learning. Newer headset models look and feel more like eyeglasses. More futuristic models of headsets look slimmer, lighter, and are easier to adapt to.

Accommodating Learning Groups

From preschool kids to seniors, everyone can, and probably will, be part of a learning experience in the metaverse. The following sections describe how the metaverse can best serve various learning groups.

Preschool

Children at the preschool level (ages 3 to 4) are in the early years of cognitive and sensory development, not to mention learning how to use their hands! Children at this age are driven by sensory experiences, such as touch, sound, and sight. At this age, children shouldn't be exposed to harsh sounds and lights because it could permanently damage their vision and hearing.

Getting a preschool child to wear VR glasses or use a technology that constricts them in any way isn't recommended. In addition to the hardware inconvenience, wires can get tangled easily and create a choking hazard.

The metaverse isn't just VR, though. Non-headset VR — such as three-dimensional holographic displays — may be able to assist in the development of children's brains. Children's brains develop at an extremely fast speed from birth to age 5. Most of the neurological development is shaped by every interaction that a child has. Genes play a big part, but the environment and environmental stimuli are factors, too.

The metaverse is so new that there is no evidence available yet on the impact of VR on children. For this reason, we should tread with caution and not use VR and metaverse technologies with kids of such a young age due to the heavy size of headsets and the strain on their eyes.

Kindergarten

By the time they're in kindergarten, kids have a good vocabulary and are able to recognize objects and speak in clear sentences. At this age, exposing your kids to an online world may be conducted in a very supervised manner. Introducing VR as a tool for learning and utilizing virtual 3D spaces can assist in expanding kids' knowledge and learning ability.

Scientific evidence suggests that kids at a young age think in symbols and engage in role playing with imaginary friends. Specialty hardware such as cave automatic virtual environment (CAVE) systems can transform an entire room into a virtual environment with interactivity. These are interior project-based immersive environments that can be customized to create 3D and interactive worlds to help children learn, play games, and interact with lifelike objects.

I don't recommend using VR headsets on kids at this age, at least not for a prolonged amount of time, due to the constricted nature of the headsets and its impact on their eyes and possibly brain development. Plus, ill-fitting and large headsets could put stress on children's necks and create long-term damage.

Elementary school

Elementary-school kids today are learning about computers and robotics in their schools. Children of this age group are curious and have a good sense of understanding of both real and virtual worlds. Today gaming is very common, and kids this age often play computer games. As a learning tool, the metaverse may be able to help explain some of the aspects of their learning curriculum in a better format then others. For example, consider the metaverse showing kids actual 3D models of the Jurassic Era or immersing them into environments of Ancient Egypt — the metaverse could really help them learn about things that they're curious about! In such a scenario where VR, AR, and mixed reality are used in conjunction with the metaverse or virtual worlds, learning may improve on multiple levels.

The next few years will determine how these systems will emerge. As providers come out with new educational tools and products, it will open up a new area for the convergence of technology and learning for students and children of all ages.

Middle school and high school

Today's middle school and high school kids have already adapted well to technology, are using computers within a classroom environment, and may be very comfortable using tablets and even productivity software. Kids this age are likely well versed with general technology and may also have a social media presence. High school students especially are adept at meeting friends and staying connected with them on social media platforms such as Snapchat, TikTok, and Discord.

At this age, kids are also starting to think about college and studying to get into a specific university. They're learning subjects such as biology, which could be one of the subjects that may have an earlier rollout when it comes to the metaverse and VR. Currently a huge focus in the healthcare industry is on being able to visualize the human body in 3D format. This can expand into other areas, such as studying plants and animals.

College or university

The metaverse will make its way into some areas of study before others. Health sciences is one of the areas that it may develop first. Some other fields that may develop fast could be architecture and industrial design, facilitated by platform such as Nvidia Omniverse.

Adult education and seniors

Adult education classes are popular for people who want to continue learning throughout their lifetime. Adult education is self-motivated (unless it's mandated by a person's place of work).

The adult education and skills improvement industry can benefit from the metaverse by providing an alternative to in-person and traditional online learning. Learners can experience classes in a VR environment, build connections and a rapport with their peers and trainers, and have a positive learning experience.

Metaverse learning could be a good opportunity for seniors, enabling them to avoid long commutes or harsh weather conditions, because they can attend classes from the comfort of their homes.

Some challenges with adult education, however, could include the steep learning curve when it comes to VR headsets and related technology. More advanced designs and lighter headsets would be a step in the right direction toward higher adoption.

Ongoing Education for Professionals

The learning and development (L&D) industry is worth more than $400 billion globally. This includes not just training organizations but collectively what the global business community spends on L&D every year. Today organizations are spending time, effort, and energy to keep their teams up to par with the latest training and education needed to keep them sharp, competitive, and engaged. The metaverse can serve as a tool for upskilling and helping employees learn about job- and industry-related training. The metaverse can serve as a tool of engagement in your overall L&D strategy.

That said, the metaverse may *not* be needed for all professional learning and development needs. The cost of technology enablement is high, and user adoption for new and emerging technologies is slow at the beginning. It remains to be seen how younger generations will adopt it over the coming years.

TIP

As a professional, you may choose to use the metaverse and VR as a learning tool for ongoing education. Here are some ideas for how you can use it:

>> **Experiential:** Experiential learning in a three-dimensional metaverse environment can have many applications. Imagine learning through digital twins of machinery or building. Being able to learn in a 3D environment will be very different from traditional learning.

>> **Immersive:** Working with others, collaborating, and being part of a world where the digital and physical worlds meet is thrilling. Immersive learning will take you into virtual campuses, the world's leading institutions, libraries, and places that were previously inaccessible.

>> **Connected:** You might be part of one or multiple metaverse worlds such as those specially built for your profession. As the metaverse evolves, niche learning spaces and groups will also emerge in various metaverse spaces. You'll have the opportunity to attend conferences and other professional events from where you are, without the need to travel.

CREATING LEARNING OPPORTUNITIES FOR PROFESSIONALS

Here's a quick rundown of how different areas of learning and education may use the metaverse:

- **Engineering:** Visualize complex machinery and design new equipment. Possibly use digital twins to operate infrastructure, learn about machinery, or train technicians.

- **Medicine:** Visualize the human body, plants, and animals. Understand the building blocks of biological organisms and be able to zoom in and out of micro-structures that would need specialized equipment or a lab to see otherwise.

- **Architecture:** Design buildings in 3D, and share your designs with collaborators across the world. Make changes to designs in a matter of seconds and stress-test the designs to see how they hold up. Perhaps in the future, the final stages of projects in master's degrees will be done with VR and on a 3D platform such as the metaverse. No more writing reports on paper!

- **Arts:** 3D art is already being developed and in a good stage of adoption. Digital artists are creating 3D art figures and objects. Think about creating the next *David* in 3D. Artists such as those working within digital design, and even traditional arts such as painting, pottery, and sculpting, could do all that within three dimensions in the metaverse. Does this open up the opportunity to create new schools of learning within these subsegments? Yes, it can new streams of learning in schools and universities. With students learning metaverse art in school, that may open up a path for metaverse art as a career choice in the future.

IN THIS CHAPTER

» Using augmented reality for surgical procedures

» Discovering group and personal fitness activities in the metaverse

» Considering how metaverse technology can help pharmacies

» Seeing how metaverse technology is currently used in healthcare

» Watching out for issues affecting privacy, entry cost, and interoperability

Chapter **15**

Health Care, Fitness, and Well-Being

This chapter explores metaverse developments related to health, fitness, and other aspects of the medical field. From early adopters to advanced use cases such as surgeries, many exciting things are happening and on the horizon.

The healthcare industry is complex. In this chapter, I use the term *healthcare* to encompass several disciplines. I describe each of these areas and consider how the metaverse is growing within some of them.

The future may appear distant, but with developments that are taking place today in our world and in the industry, it's safe to assume that technology is having a tremendous impact on healthcare and medical breakthroughs. Although a lot of work needs to be done on basic healthcare reaching every individual on the planet, breakthroughs are also underway.

Metaverse in the Medical Field

Medicine is all about understanding the human body. Medical students have to work with real human bodies — whether real patients or human cadavers — to understand disease. New breakthroughs in healthcare have always occurred because doctors and scientists have developed a better understanding of the human body.

The field of medicine is probably one of the earlier ones that will transform as a result of 3D visualization and virtual reality (VR). Through VR technology, new ways of managing various stages of surgeries are being pioneered. From pre-surgery analysis to in-surgery visualizations, surgeons are looking at utilizing VR technology.

Family doctor visits

Meeting your doctor in the metaverse isn't very common today. One of the reasons for this is that metaverse experiences are mainly avatars and have a steep adoption curve. But more and more people are using metaverse-based technologies than ever before. According to industry experts, by some estimates, 25 percent of Internet users in the United States will spend more than an hour per day using some area of the metaverse by the year 2026.

So, how long will it be until we start our doctors' visits in the metaverse? Perhaps not too long. A key development that needs to take place before this happens is for hardware technology to support better graphics and 3D visualization technologies to render high-resolution graphics with ultra-realistic avatars or personas. As adoption of the metaverse rises, a majority of the users will be younger adults, a demographic at ease with technology and the metaverse. As a result, they'll be much more comfortable meeting a doctor in the metaverse.

Emergency medicine

Will it really be possible one day to visit the emergency room in the metaverse? Although many physical injuries need immediate in-person attention, connecting with emergency room doctors and nurses in the metaverse could be a great service.

Imagine being a witness to an emergency and being able to access 911 on a VR platform. What if you had VR glasses with a much better form factor, similar to today's eyeglasses? And what if you had the ability to follow the instructions of the emergency room staff to take care of an injured person until help arrived? This could mean stopping blood loss, performing CPR, removing a breathing blockage, or performing other critical and lifesaving measures. Bringing the ER to you is something the metaverse may be able to do.

As the metaverse develops, hospitals and health-care institutions may explore the option of multiple services on VR platforms, including outpatient consultations, or even offering emergency service consultations on VR platforms. The technology could save many lives because some form of lifesaving intervention could be taken until an ambulance arrives or the injured person could be taken to the emergency room.

Dentist visits

Who doesn't want healthy teeth and gums? Visits to the dentist typically fall in two categories:

>> **Preventive:** At these visits, typically every six months, your dentist checks your teeth to make sure your oral health is in good shape.

>> **Emergencies:** At these visits, your dentist treats any conditions that may require immediate attention, such as toothaches, infections, broken teeth, and other pressing issues.

With advances in VR, it may be possible for your dentist to conduct preventive visits over VR. Imagine your dentist being able to view your teeth in VR, and through the usage of ultra-high-definition cameras within devices, being able to enlarge and zoom into the video to crystal-clear quality.

FUTURECAST

Ample opportunity exists for startups in the remote health and dentistry domain to create solutions that will make this kind of care possible. Dental health professionals can also use the metaverse and are able to show patients simulations of potential dental corrections, the usage of implants, and possible outcomes even before a dental procedure or surgery has been conducted. Dental consultations will become way more technology driven. Of course, with the adoption of VR and metaverse-related technologies, the dental industry, dental health diagnostics, education, and regulatory authorities and bodies are definitely required to get involved to make an industry-wide change.

Physiotherapy, chiropractic medicine, and osteopathic therapy

Physiotherapists, chiropractors, and osteopaths rely on physically treating patients. As a result, in-person treatment is essential. Follow-up visits and consultations can be done remotely, but these health sciences remain in-person therapies with a few exclusions. When patients are given exercises to do at home, they can be supervised through VR to ensure they're following protocols.

With new developments and innovations within the health-care industry, especially in the field of physical therapy, there is an opportunity to create new equipment that connects with metaverse and VR platforms to provide feedback to patients when used. For future inspiration, imagine equipment that patients can wear and that can be operated by the patient or the remote physiotherapist. Treatment may happen over the metaverse, saving time and money and creating efficiencies in treating patients.

Mental health services

Mental health fields treat conditions such as depression and anxiety. Treating such conditions has a lot to do with understanding the challenges patients face or have faced and working with them to establish a treatment plan and approach. Mental health is a complex field of health care with many different aspects to it. The clinical use of the metaverse is subject to a big debate as we try to understand how it can help and which gaps it can fill when treating patients.

Psychiatry is a very big field and complex in its undertakings. At a surface level, psychiatrists can use VR headsets to create therapy sessions that are experiential and possibly developed and delivered on metaverse platforms. I would find it difficult to adjust to a counseling session held on Decentraland or the Sandbox, but if there are specialized metaverse platforms that serve the medical community, it may be much easier to use the metaverse or patient benefits to its full extent.

In Chapter 1, I introduce the idea of private metaverse worlds; health care can significantly benefit from such private metaverse platforms. Patient confidentiality and privacy wouldn't be a concern, and practitioners would have full control over seeing their patients virtually. Future health-care systems such as diagnostic metaverse platforms could emerge where only health-care providers could have access to seeing patients, and in turn, patients could have full control over giving access to specific practitioners and health-care providers. This subject is currently emerging as part of a Web 3.0 debate.

Acupuncture

Health-care disciplines such as acupuncture are highly unlikely to evolve as part of the metaverse. Some things will never transform into technology and never should. Disciplines such as acupuncture require precise delivery of acupuncture needles, and unless we have robots who do this with 100 percent accuracy, it won't work.

However, there is an opportunity for an extremely large patient base in Asian countries where acupuncture is very common. China itself has a population of 1.4 billion as of 2022, and Chinese traditional medicine is used predominantly as a form of health treatment in China. It is estimated that more than 33 million patient visits were recorded for acupuncture in China in the year 2018 alone.

FUTURECAST

An opportunity to develop robotic technology that could perhaps remotely deliver acupuncture to patients in remote locations could become a possibility. China is one of the fastest-growing nations in the world when it comes to technology. Perhaps the next big business idea is to bring the metaverse and traditional Chinese medicine into one place, and help patients receive health-care services when and where they need them.

Studying Human Biology and Anatomy

The study of human biology and anatomy is done in all health-care disciplines. One of the advantages of VR- and AR-based anatomical models is the ability to view the human body in three dimensions, and dive into specific body parts to observe, diagnose, and study. For this reason, VR-based systems are being well received in the study phase of medicine.

An extension of VR- and AR-based systems, when connected to the Internet or viewed in the metaverse, is the ability to share anatomical models with others. Does this mean that future surgeries can and should happen in the metaverse? In the hospitals of the future, smaller metaverse worlds and platforms may emerge and offer a virtual home for medical practitioners, surgeons, and diagnosticians to view their cases and treat their patients. Although we're far from such a time and era and a lot of work still needs to be done to develop this the right way, the possibilities of remote medicine are very exciting.

Currently, a number of hospitals and medical facilities are experimenting with VR-based medicines and surgeries. These are being used to visualize patient scans in 3D and plan surgeries, including pediatric neurosurgery being pioneered at hospitals in Europe and the United States.

Performing surgeries in the metaverse

Some initial attempts have been made at helping health-care professionals realize the potential of VR-based technologies — for example, doctors and surgeons actually using the technology in their practice. Due to the high amount of care and caution needed to treat patients within the health-care field, progress has been slow. From a teaching and learning perspective, VR has been welcomed. But actually performing a surgery through the metaverse isn't possible at the moment — it's far too complex. In the future, metaverse surgeries are unlikely to be conducted on cartoon-looking avatars and would need specialized health-care industry metaverse technologies to become a reality.

What does that mean for public and private metaverse platforms? When you consider this question from the perspective of public metaverse platforms, it seems like an obvious no. But when you look at the evolution of highly specialized metaverse platforms, such as those that can potentially be used as AR surgery rooms with specialized hardware equipment, zero-lag connectivity, and precision robotics developed specifically for surgical purposes, then things start falling into place. Metaverse-based surgery might become reality in the distant future.

TECHNICAL STUFF

Alvin Toffler, one of the pioneers of futurism and foresight, rightly said that technology feeds on itself. In other words, we have to develop technology to develop even more *complex* technology. In the evolution of further enhancing surgeries in the metaverse, we still need to work on extremely high-precision robotics in order to execute very specialized tasks and then at the next level add remote-control abilities. Surgeries are highly complex, and it's impossible to categorize all surgeries in one category, but the path would have to be created for easier surgeries to take place remotely and then more complex surgeries could be attempted once the infrastructure and skills exist. Some types of surgeries will probably never be conducted over the metaverse or on a virtual platform, while some may become common. It may seem simple in concept, but it needs the simultaneous development of technology, skills, and regulations.

Using augmented reality in surgery

The lines between AR, VR, and the metaverse are closely joined together. Surgeons of the future may use VR for surgical training and AR for actual surgeries. They may also use the metaverse for meetings, collaborations, and learning. As more health-care facilities, institutes, and faculties use these technologies, their use will also mature with adoption.

In the first surgery of its kind, Johns Hopkins Hospital performed its first AR-based surgery in June 2020. The surgery involved placing six screws in a patient's spine during spinal fusion surgery. In a second AR-based surgery, also at Johns Hopkins, surgeons performed tumor removal surgery from the spine of a patient.

Both surgeries used AR and consisted of a high-resolution headset projecting the image of bones and other tissues based on CT scans. The specialized headset manufactured by Augmedics was used in the surgeries, and these findings were published in the *Journal of Neurosurgery*.

INNOVATION IN HEALTH CARE WITH VR

London-based pediatric neurosurgeon Dr. Owase Jeelani's work involves pioneering VR-based surgical techniques to visualize what surgical outcomes can look like and provide patients a realistic 3D model of what their appearance may be post-surgery.

In May 2014, another pioneering surgeon Dr. Shafi Ahmed performed an operation that was broadcast live to 14,000 students across 132 countries and 1,100 cities. Also known as "Doctor Snapchat," in December 2016, he performed the world's first live operation using Snapchat spectacles and trained 200 medical students and surgical trainees.

Medical practitioners such as Dr. Ahmed and Dr. Jeelani are creating new frontiers in remote health and digital surgeries.

FUTURECAST

Although these surgeries were not performed in the metaverse, performing them through AR is a huge step, and it also opens the doors to metaverse surgical procedures. The evolution of the metaverse is at a very initial stage, and the next few years will dictate a clearer direction as hardware and software technologies developed to deliver more cutting-edge and crisp imagery and graphics.

Taking Fitness to the Metaverse

The fitness industry is always innovating. In the last decade, we've seen the emergence of companies such as Peloton that have created a highly experiential way to work out. Fitness is one of the biggest subcategories within the larger health-care industry, and technology has been continuously changing the way the industry works.

The metaverse is an interesting playground for the fitness industry. Within some of the popular metaverse platforms, such as Horizon Worlds, a number of gamified experiences now offer the ability to participate in games and use body movements to progress, which ultimately leads to a rigorous workout, at least in some cases. Gamification within the metaverse is helping fitness companies create new apps that facilitate fitness. The convergence of gamification, body movement, music, and high-resolution visuals is creating a new metaverse-based fitness industry.

Fitness is not just an activity; the industry is creating platforms that bring together coaches, trainers, and students in one place. If you're a fitness instructor, you can not only hold classes with students from anywhere in the world, but also partner with equipment manufacturers and monetize your skills.

With cryptocurrencies and the emergence of nonfungible tokens (NFTs), brands are exploring different avenues to engage with consumers. One possibility I envision is a fitness metaverse platform where different brands come together and offer incentives to visitors in the form of crypto and NFTs.

Brands that are looking at ultimately converting users into consumers of their products can create experiences on a platform such as Horizon Worlds, Decentraland, or the Sandbox. They can deliver a sense of excitement and competition and at the same time help users achieve their fitness goals.

Through VR and wearable technologies, recording fitness activity is easy. Brands will be able to incentivize fitness activity and offer users exclusivity, access, and discounts through NFTs. How motivated would you be to do 50 pushups and get tickets to your favorite singer's concert?

Having an active lifestyle where fitness is a part of your everyday activity is about to get a lot more exciting. If you also consider the future development of VR headsets and extremely high-resolution rendering of metaverse platforms, the ability to take the metaverse anywhere with you is an exciting possibility.

Brands such as Nike and Garmin have multiple opportunities within the metaverse ecosystem. From digital activations of the brand within a metaverse platform to designing games and offering membership-based NFTs, the possibilities are fast opening.

TIP

As if the future isn't exciting enough, you can buy a VR headset *today* and start working out on a gamified VR app within minutes. Head over to Chapter 6 to find out how to get started.

FUTURECAST

TRENDING IN "EXERTAINMENT"

The idea of *exertainment* (exercise and entertainment brought together with technology) is appealing to Gen Z and younger audiences. According to the Welltodo *2022 Consumer Wellness Trends Report* (www.welltodoglobal.com/just-launched-welltodos-2022-consumer-wellness-trends-report), key trends emerging in the future include the following:

- **"Fitutainment":** A convergence of fitness and entertainment
- **Wearables:** The rise of tracking technology and wearables, from wrist watches to smart mattresses

- **Brand reinvention:** A new direction in which consumer brands are developing products that are more suited to the temperament and liking of health-conscious and environmentally conscious consumers

- **Nutrition:** Custom-tailored nutrition solutions

- **Inclusivity:** The rise of inclusivity at every stage of the product life cycle within the fitness and health-care categories

- **Sustainability:** A focus on sustainability and caring for the planet

- **Home health care:** A rise in home-based health and wellness services

All these observations point toward key trends emerging from the health and fitness industry that can be potentially augmented through technology.

Yoga, Zumba, Pilates

Just about any group or one-on-one training activity can take place in the metaverse. In fact, a number of games and sports apps today are focused on the fitness industry. Here are some popular fitness apps in the metaverse:

- » **FitXR** (https://fitxr.com): On-demand fitness classes

- » **HOLOFIT** (www.holodia.com): VR fitness especially suited for stationary bicycle, rowing machine, and elliptical

- » **Liteboxer VR** (https://liteboxer.com): The first VR platform to have live trainers

- » **OhShape** (https://ohshapevr.com): Especially designed for the Quest series featuring unique ways of moving your body and getting fit

- » **Supernatural** (www.getsupernatural.com): Exhilarating virtual locations and music while you workout

Using the metaverse for yoga could become very fulfilling as you change your scenery to what your heart desires.

Group fitness classes, such as Zumba, might begin with specialized apps followed by live classes and training, all taking place in the metaverse.

This is fresh new ground for apps and business use cases to be realized. There may not be an app for each category of sport today, but experimentation and new launches are happening frequently.

Martial arts

VR can assist users on their journey of learning anything, including martial arts. The utility of technology in this case would be in removing the barrier to attend a class in person.

More than 18 million Americans per year practice a form of martial arts. Globally the numbers are much higher. Would VR help more people learn and acquire new skills? Would students find it beneficial to attend classes in the metaverse? Would it require specialized training centers in the metaverse? The simple answer to all these questions is yes.

Immersive VR and the metaverse at an interesting point of convergence today as different industries are creating first use cases and testing the ground in the metaverse.

TIP

Instead of thinking about whether the metaverse will *replace* in-person activities, try to think about how the metaverse can complement in-person activities.

Fitness for seniors

As fitness providers enter the metaverse, a growing opportunity is to create fitness options for seniors. These options could include apps that offer everything from physiotherapy to dance classes. The options are endless.

Research is proving that although senior care is complex, there are aspects of it that can be made enjoyable for seniors. Early pilot projects have included retirement communities using VR to help residents travel to faraway places and visit landmarks such as the Egyptian pyramids. The Engage VR app was designed for the Watermark Residential Communities in Tucson, Arizona, and has served as one of the early pilots of VR for seniors.

In other cases, and in the area of mental health, the following apps are breaking early ground:

>> **MyndVR** (www.myndvr.com): Helping improve lives of seniors in assisted living facilities, specifically in the areas of Alzheimer's and dementia to create meaningful experiences

>> **Rendever** (www.rendever.com): Working on helping seniors with social isolation

>> **Viarama** (`https://viarama.co.uk`): Helping seniors needing end-of-life care revisit the places they used to live

>> **VR Genie** (`https://eqlab.global`): Helping seniors visualize various environments, such as a new retirement community, in VR

Within the domain of senior fitness, Aalborg University Copenhagen has made initial efforts to research how senior fitness can be transformed through VR by making physical excursions enjoyable.

A lot more work is ahead for the senior health-care industry in terms of creating solutions for the world's aging population. According to Reuters, the world will have more than 1 billion seniors by the year 2040, which opens up a huge market for VR and metaverse-based care.

Personal coaching

The rise of the fitness industry has also led to a growth in the personal trainer and coaching profession. Personal coaches are now delivering services on platforms such as Zoom, Microsoft Teams, and Google Hangouts. The next natural transition of this industry is to offer personal coaching services and training using VR.

The future evolution of personal coaching in the fitness industry can lead to a few different possibilities:

>> Independent fitness companies and gyms will start offering metaverse classes.

>> Freelance fitness professionals will open their own metaverse presences.

>> Collaborations between multiple parties can create metaverse-only gyms, where every coach, trainer, and instructor will be available only in the metaverse.

Metaverse fitness hardware

A number of manufacturers within the sports and fitness industry have started developing equipment that can be used in conjunction with the metaverse. These devices include not only headsets but also equipment and machinery that can connect to metaverse worlds and provide feedback and share information with others.

Here are some examples of such devices that are making the waves:

» **KARA Smart Fitness Mirror** (https://karasmartfitness.com/products/the-mirror): Products like the KARA Smart Fitness Mirror are changing how people work out from the comfort of their own homes. The device uses artificial intelligence (AI) technology to track and analyze body movement and help optimize workouts. At the moment, the KARA Smart Fitness Mirror is a 2D mirror, but future iterations of such devices can be built into VR and connected to the metaverse.

» **Tonal** (www.tonal.com): A smart mirror with an option to use resistance training, Tonal offers a virtual display, do-it-yourself (DIY) recommendations for workouts, and a new way to get fit at home. A part of the smart fitness mirror category, Tonal was one of the first entries into the market.

» **Peloton** (www.onepeloton.com): Peloton is more than just a treadmill or a cycling apparatus. Peloton has created an engaged community of teachers and learners who all speak the language of fitness. A big reason for Peloton's success has been the large screen positioned in front of the user. Users can take virtual trips to different countries and different scenic rides while using the fitness equipment. Taking this to another level by using VR technologies and immersing the participant in a 3D environment would be incredible.

» **VirZoom** (https://virzoom.com): Companies such as VirZoom are working on creating VR experiences for fitness enthusiasts come true. With the VZFit app, users can visit snowcapped mountains or sun-kissed beaches while working out. Selecting a VR scene is easy — it uses Google Earth technology and maps to take you where you want to go. The app is additionally able to work with headsets such as Meta Quest series to enable full-body workouts and with bike manufacturers to offer a cadence sensor that can track pedaling during a workout and display the appropriate visuals.

Considering a Metaverse Pharmacy of the Future

Pharmacies can easily utilize the metaverse as an option to consult with patients, refill prescriptions, and deliver customer service. For an audience and user base that is already in the metaverse and using it for their daily activities, education, and work, being able to visit the neighborhood pharmacy in the metaverse and consult with the pharmacist would be convenient.

The initial few use cases from the pharmacy world will take innovative and pioneering efforts from the largest pharmacies. Imagine being able to speak to your neighborhood pharmacy to get a prescription refill. Pharmacies also rely heavily on retail opportunities and sell commonly used groceries and essentials. Browsing the pharmacy shelves virtually and picking up milk and bread seem like a real possibility.

In fact, in March 2020, pharmacy giant CVS revealed that it had filed a trademark with the U.S. Patent and Trademark Office to open an online metaverse store. CVS plans to offer patient advisory services, wellness programs, and counseling and nutrition services, among many in the metaverse. The global pharmacy market is worth $1 trillion and has ample opportunity for growth.

The pharmacy industry has already started using voice-activated virtual care such as that on Alexa and other voice-activated systems.

FUTURECAST

Is the future of pharmacies in the metaverse a distant dream? As a channel, the metaverse is available and ready to be used by the pharmaceutical industry. However, the rollout will take years if not decades. Regulations must be developed, privacy ensured, and most of all misuse and abuse of any drug avoided at all costs. This means possibly tighter controls on dispensing drugs will likely happen as the pharma industry moves to the metaverse.

Seeing How the Metaverse Is Already Being Used in Health Care

Some of the exciting use cases of the metaverse in hospital health care include

» **Digital twins of hospitals:** Full digital replicas of hospitals and facilities can be created in the metaverse. This, in turn, can be used to plan for capacity and manage the hospital facility.

» **Digital twins of the human body:** Digital twins of the human body can be created to precisely identify the conditions that are impacting one or more people. They can be used to create a blueprint of a human body that can be digitally viewed for diagnosis. This has already been done, in fact — scientists are using digital twins of people to predict the impact of a medication.

- >> **Space travel health care:** NASA plans to use the digital twins of astronauts before they undertake long journeys into space. Being able to create a baseline body of the astronauts and then continue measuring it to their journey in space would be useful to measure the impact of space travel on the human body.

- >> **3D training:** In an early use case, the University of Connecticut Medical Center used VR to train orthopedic surgery residents. Visualizing 3D surgeries and procedures allowed the students to make mistakes and receive feedback from the faculty.

- >> **Trauma training:** At the University of Miami Miller School of Medicine, VR and mixed reality (MR) technology was used to train first responders to better treat patients who had trauma (including strokes, gunshot wounds, and heart attacks). With VR headsets, students could see internal damage on a mannequin and come up with a treatment plan faster.

- >> **PTSD treatment for former military members:** One of the use cases in the treatment of post-traumatic stress syndrome (PTSD) and mental health is a company called Bravemind, which is developing solutions around VR and AR that can be used to treat patients with PTSD. This treatment will include therapy and other visualization and relaxation treatment plans that will be delivered with technology as a partner.

Important Considerations for Health-Care Applications

This chapter covers a number of metaverse applications for the broader health-care industry. Here are some of the pressing needs of implementing the metaverse within the health-care context.

Privacy

Predicting the information and data of participants is a major challenge across all technology industries, not just within health care. Data governance, data management, privacy, and security are more important than ever before. For the metaverse, regulatory frameworks are not fully developed, and we're still far from a time and a place where we have global standards of information exchange and data management developed for specific use in the metaverse.

Policies around the management and handling of private data and the storing and retrieval of patient information all are key when it comes to the potential of the metaverse. Local, regional, and even national regulations such as those under the *Health Insurance Portability and Accountability Act* (HIPAA) and others are a good guideline in the regular world, but when it comes to the metaverse, there's no specific jurisdiction. The question is: How will health-care practitioners and providers manage data and ensure the privacy of participants? Perhaps HIPAA and its usage will be expanded to the metaverse and related platforms in the future or a new set of regulations and standards will be created.

High entry cost

The barrier to entry includes the high costs of equipment and hardware. As hardware technologies evolve and VR headsets become more economical and less bulky, more people may be part of the metaverse. Until then, growth in some areas may be slower. The fitness industry will have an easier time moving into the metaverse than the health-care industry because there is less personal and private data exchange in the former.

Interoperability

All metaverse platforms are likely to exchange a significant amount of data with other systems. There are many different hospital management systems and technologies used daily by staff. Will the metaverse data seamlessly interoperate with hospital systems? Is there a need for developing connectivity technologies and interconnectivity sub-programs? There is a great opportunity for technology companies to build solutions that will help connect everything together.

Chapter **16**

Moving Events into the Metaverse

The global events industry is big business. Corporate events, concerts, entertainment, and all sorts of other events are held every day all over the world. The events industry already makes wide use of the Internet for virtual events. Accordingly, the events industry has been one of the first industries to experiment with the metaverse. With the metaverse, you can host events that are more accessible to more people. In this chapter, I show you what hosting events in the metaverse can look like and steps you can take to get started.

Bringing the Metaverse to Events

Events generally bring people together for a purpose. People host events to support causes or further business goals, and people attend events because they want to support the cause or have a great experience. The metaverse offers an opportunity to attend events virtually in immersive ways that may appeal especially to younger audiences seeking new ways to experience events.

Location is an important consideration when creating events and organizing them. Thanks to the Internet, events can be virtual or in person in a specific location.

The global events industry is a multi-billion-dollar industry that impacts many others, including airlines and hotels. Local economies benefit from events, as do countless others in the value chain of the events industry as a whole. The metaverse can change all that and expand some of the limitations of the global in-person events industry.

There may be an initial hesitation in embracing the metaverse — and rightfully so. Not everybody is tuned to very complex technology, but as the technology becomes easier and more accessible, more people will jump into accepting it.

Increasing attendance

There's a limit to how much you can increase attendance of in-person events. Attendees may not have the time or money to travel to your event. And you may not have a venue big enough to host everyone who wants to attend. The metaverse changes all that with virtual events, which work in tandem with in-person events. This is adding more viewers and participants to events, creating opportunities for sponsorships, and offering attendees a chance to still be part of the event, despite being remote.

Creating memorable experiences

People are generally attracted to attend events that promise a memorable experience. Smart event organizers capitalize on this fact. You've probably heard people rave about concerts they attended and how they felt in the presence of their favorite musician or rock star. It's not a coincidence that successful events leave us with experiences we can remember.

The metaverse is different from the Internet. The current web is 2D by nature, but the metaverse changes that by immersing viewers in a 3D environment. Two key aspects of this 3D environment are customization and interaction. For his metaverse concert events, Travis Scott uses both customization and interaction to create a truly memorable experience for metaverse concert attendees. Attendees of his metaverse concert were able to fly with Travis in the metaverse and enjoy a sense of being an integrated part of the whole environment.

You can watch a video of the Travis Scott concert at https://youtu.be/wYeFA1VC8qU. Of course, if you were attending his concert in the metaverse, you would have been able to view this content in 3D!

Here are other some events that really took to the metaverse for the first time:

>> **CES** (www.ces.tech): The Consumer Electronics Show, held every year in Las Vegas, held sessions in the metaverse.

- **Dubai Metaverse Assembly** (www.dubaifuture.ae/dubai-metaverse-assembly): The Dubai Future Foundation, a government entity in the United Arab Emirates, held its first metaverse event focused on growth through the metaverse economy in the region.

- **GITEX** (www.gitex.com): The largest tech event in the Middle East held a metaverse experience. Parts of the event were available to be viewed in the metaverse.

- **Metaverse Summit by The Economist** (https://events.economist.com/metaverse): The Economist group held its first metaverse conference, with the event available both in person and in the metaverse.

Building on the successes of others

One way for event managers to get started is to attend as many metaverse events as possible to fully experience the possibilities of the metaverse. Learn from other events what works and what doesn't.

Some celebrations, such as the Tomatina Festival in Spain (www.tomatofestivalspain.com), require a person's physical presence. Would anyone who is missing out on the in-person experience of the festival want to throw and crush virtual tomatoes? If the option exists, you bet they would!

Large-scale events such as the Olympics, large conferences, and social and faith-based events draw global audiences. Many of these events are simulcast on TV and online through livestreams. Event organizers are now looking at the metaverse as an option to help attendees who are unable to attend the in-person events still be part of these experiences.

FINDING FAITH-BASED METAVERSE WORLDS

Faith-based metaverse worlds are already here. These include a virtual Mecca and the Holy City experiences that allows Orthodox Christian believers to follow clerics in religious ceremonies. The Vatican is building its own metaverse presence in collaboration with metaverse company Sensorium. Muslims similarly will be able to follow the steps of worshippers during Ramadan at Al-Aqsa Mosque. Other religious experiences that have been created include a Haitian voodoo ceremony and a Hindu funeral last rite. Creators of these experiences want to attract younger generations to religious and faith-based communities despite the fact that they're glued to their phones and other tech devices.

Organizing a Metaverse Event

So, you're ready to host your first metaverse event. How do you go about it. Here are the essential steps you should take, with modifications based on your industry and specific case.

Deciding whether a metaverse event is right for you

Why should your event be in the metaverse? How would it change your event or the experiences it delivers? How much effort would be required from you, and do you have the resources available? These are some off the basic questions you should answer even before you get started.

Work with your team and circulate the business case with others who are involved in the decision-making process. Developing a business case for your metaverse event will help you get clarity on the *why* and also help answer questions you may not think about at the beginning.

REMEMBER

Here are some considerations to keep in mind when organizing metaverse events:

» The way to attend an event in the metaverse is primarily through a VR headset. This means the event organizers aren't just broadcasting an event to a virtual screen within a metaverse platform, but adding interactive and other elements of engagement.

» Think about how your metaverse event will differ from an online or in-person event. In some cases, a VR-based or metaverse-based event may have a much higher level of personalization and one-on-one interaction with individual attendees versus live in-person events.

» Consider the costs, including the cost of creating an event location on a metaverse platform, assigning staff to manage metaverse attendees, and broadcasting logistics (such as ensuring the event experience in the metaverse is smooth).

Planning your approach

Assuming you're all clear to proceed with the metaverse event, you have to plan it right. Here questions to ask:

» Where in the metaverse will the event be held?

» Do you need to procure any virtual land or can you rent it?

>> Do you need to create a virtual facility or premises?

>> What are the key goals of the sponsors or organizers?

>> What is the experience attendees will get?

>> How will attendees view and listen to the conference?

>> How can attendees engage and contact others?

>> How will you ensure the security and privacy of attendees?

Delivering on your promises

You've planned everything for your metaverse event, and the plan is in action. Here are some ways to make sure your attendees walk away satisfied with their experience:

>> **Make sure to provide adequate resources to manage engagement in the metaverse.** This could mean assigning the right number of customer service reps or creating a complaint resolution policy.

>> **Plan for unforeseen events such as loss of electricity, bad Internet connection and others such possibilities.** Always create contingency plans in case something fails.

>> **Ensure your team has all the information to do their tasks.** Ensure your team has clear instructions and that you have access to all event performance data in order to make quick decisions based on reliable data.

Monetizing Metaverse Events

As an event organizer, you face many challenges in delivering a successful event. Making money from an event is a top priority. In the following sections, I cover the main ways you can monetize your metaverse event.

Metaverse access tickets

The primary revenue for an event is through ticket sales. Whether these are free, early bird, or sold in a category such as general or VIP, segregating tickets by type of access is a common strategy. More access and better engagement usually mean a higher ticket price.

Selling tickets with a metaverse viewing option for an event is an opportunity to draw audiences who want experiential aspects of a performance to be delivered to them. This may mean an additional investment on the part of the organizer to create that experience that metaverse attendees want.

Access to events can be through traditional tickets for sale. However, access can also be provided as part of an NFT purchase where NFT buyers have access to the event. Tickets can be sold on platforms such as OpenSea or through a specific link within the metaverse where a credit card or cryptocurrency can be used as a form of payment.

TIP

Organizing events in the metaverse means more attendees attending virtually. You'll need a strategy for your event for meeting the needs of these additional viewers along with in-person and online audiences.

Swag sales in the metaverse

Event organizers also try to monetize their events through swag sales. You often see this happen in sports events where memorabilia are available for purchase — everything from T-shirts and baseball caps to mugs, towels, and more. Metaverse swag can be sold digitally and delivered physically — you can create a virtual kiosk to sell swag within the event and then ship the goods to buyers.

Buyers could also have the option of getting a free NFT of the item they just purchased. Many combinations of physical and digital goods can be created that resonate with buyers and event attendees.

Metaverse membership sales

Many events are held for members only, and a paid membership can get you a free or better price to access an event. Such events are typically organized by experts (for example, leaders and celebrities). Special access may include specific industry events and other digital products, such as access to one-on-one events, special downloads, access passes, and more.

Here's how a membership model typically works:

1. **You invite users to be part of a community or group.**

   The event or series of events are only accessible to members of the group.

UNDERSTANDING HOW EXCLUSIVITY WORKS

Exclusivity is when you offer a selected group of people the ability to be part of a unique group of members that receive added benefits and takeaways. Exclusivity can be created for various aspects of an event — for example, after parties, unique one-on-one meet-and-greets, access to book signings, and other cool things that fans, attendees, and guests enjoy.

When it comes to the metaverse, creating exclusivity can follow the same process as in online or in-person events. However, the delivery may be different. You might offer a unique takeaway for members of the group, the option to receive a free NFT, discounts, coupons, or limited edition events and goods.

2. **You charge a monthly recurring fee to be part of the group's exclusivity.**

   Exclusivity is when you offer a selected group of people the ability to be part of a unique group of members that receive added benefits and takeaways. (See the sidebar, "Understanding how exclusivity works.")

3. **You provide members with access to experts, advice, or some other unique aspect.**

NFT sales for events

NFTs are a new opportunity for innovation and creativity when it comes to access. For example, NFTs have been used in basketball and other sports as a digital collectible that featured a "Top Shot" during a game. This "Top Shot" digital collectable was a very short video clip of the best shot taken during the game and was sold as an NFT.

For event organizers, lot of possibilities exist with NFTs. Here are some ideas to consider:

>> For concerts and performances, consider creating audio or video clips and converting them into NFTs.

>> For trade shows and events, provide attendees key takeaways with a digital NFT. It might be a PowerPoint presentation or a video file that opens up when the NFT is clicked.

>> For celebrity events, think about creating personalized NFTs with a combination of audio, video, and digital art.

There are many ways of creating NFTs — it's just a matter of being creative and offering your attendees something they'll cherish.

TIP

The idea of creating exclusivity is deeply ingrained in NFTs. You can use an NFT to provide unique access. In other words, the NFTs become a gateway to exclusivity. It's up to you how you monetize and create exclusivity with NFTs. There are hundreds of different ways NFTs can help you create excitement and deliver engagement at your event.

Attending Entertainment Events in the Metaverse

When pop artist Travis Scott held his first metaverse concert, attendees saw a giant virtual avatar of Travis within the metaverse. Individually, each attendee was able to have close proximity to the show, as well as a one-on-one experience of being lifted into the sky and flying with Travis. If this event were to be held in person and had the front-row seats to the concert, you would be watching Travis perform on stage for the entirety of the concert, right from where you were standing. No other experience other than loud music and close proximity to the stage would be available. So in essence, your experience in person would be great, but in the metaverse, it can expand to have a one-on-one experience or multiple levels.

REMEMBER

When metaverse technology becomes commercialized and freely available, the more we use it, the more it will integrate into our everyday lives. In its early days, videoconferencing felt very different and many people shied away from it, but now most of us are used to it and it feels like a part of everyday life. The same will happen with the metaverse.

Concerts in the metaverse

Many high-profile performers have taken to the metaverse, including Travis Scott, Justin Bieber, Ariana Grande, and others.

The events industry is looking at more options of tapping into the youth market and bringing new fans on board. Metaverse events offer an opportunity to deliver exceptional new concertgoing and other experiences as they never have been in the past.

Whether contemporary composers such as Yanni broadcasting to the world over the metaverse or classical violin players like Yo-Yo Ma playing to audiences in the metaverse, everything is possible.

As metaverse technologies become more affordable and platforms become more high-definition and easy to use, the entertainment industry will likely increase its focus on the metaverse. In fact, this has already started happening. The metaverse offers unique programming opportunities, one-on-one engagements, and interactions with fans. It also adds a significant revenue stream to existing opportunities. Although the entertainment industry is unlikely to move completely to the metaverse, after artists such as Travis Scott took to the metaverse, others followed. South Asian singer Daler Mehndi held his first virtual concert online and drew almost 20 million viewers. Old records are being broken as new breakthroughs take shape.

The best way to get started with the metaverse is to attend some events and go from there. Check out the events directory on Decentraland, the Sandbox, or Horizon Worlds to get started.

ENTERTAINMENT OPPORTUNITIES IN THE METAVERSE

I would like to see different forms of entertainment and concerts being held in the metaverse. These can include book signings, a speaker series where someone is being interviewed on stage, or an event such as TED Talks that spreads awareness. Here are some ideas:

- **Think tank events:** Experts could come together to find solutions to real-world problems.
- **Thought-leader events:** A single thought leader could talk on stage.
- **Expert talks:** One or more expert could talk about a specific industry pain point.
- **Metaverse studio sessions:** Musicians could hold metaverse jam sessions with students.
- **Master classes:** Experts could talk about their craft and teach others.

Chapter **17**

Woo-Hoo! Going Meta in Sports and Gaming

This chapter explores what the metaverse can do for the sports and gaming industries. I also fill you in on how some professional sports are already using the metaverse and how they may use the metaverse in the future.

TECHNICAL STUFF

Before I dive in, a quick overview of some of the terminology I use in this chapter. *Sports* are activities like tennis, badminton, football, or golf — regardless of whether they're played on a team or solo. *eSports* are sports online — including online games and metaverse-based games. *Gaming* is video games, whether played by amateurs or professionals in the real world. And *eGames* are professional videogames played online or in the metaverse. I use the terms *sports* and *eSports* and *gaming* and *eGames* interchangeably.

Bringing the Metaverse to Gaming and Sports

Gaming evolved first as computer games that were played by people individually. They advanced to becoming eGames, professionally played in arcades and then played online with millions of participants involved. Sports include traditionally played professional-level sports that now have metaverse counterparts, or eSports. Both games and sports are now entering the metaverse.

The metaverse provides opportunities that are similar to those it provides for other forms of entertainment:

>> A unique fan engagement in a virtual 3D environment

>> Reaching broader audiences with the metaverse as a channel

>> Attracting a new generation of fans

>> Monetizing by selling virtual tickets and nonfungible tokens (NFTs)

>> Generating exclusivity and buzz

I cover each of these opportunities in the following sections.

Increasing engagement

As with other entertainment industries, the professional sports and eGaming industries thrive on fan engagement, whether it's about building more followers or drawing a worldwide fan base in the case of international events. Fan engagement and sponsorships are crucial aspects of the profitability for both categories.

Professional players can demand a lot of fees, which puts tremendous financial pressure on sports league and eGaming team owners. Any way to increase fan engagement and expand the fan base is crucial.

Reaching broader audiences

One way to increase the size of fan bases is to expand the overall breadth of your marketing efforts. As an entertainment company, sports organizer, eGaming organizer or team owner, getting a larger pool of attendees increases the chances of converting those audiences into newer models of revenue such as ticket sales, subscription sales, and selling merchandise. Using digital channels can help reach broader audiences, including digital natives, because they're possibly already using or have begun to use the metaverse. Selling more digital goods and collectibles such as NFTs is easier when your audience already knows how valuable they are.

Attracting younger fans

The metaverse also serves as a new channel to reach younger audiences. Many sports and entertainment categories are seeing a decline in their fan bases and there is a dire need to attract younger generation fans. Professional sports need fans and generating more fan following needs more channels of engagement. The metaverse can serve as a key channel as it grows. One differentiator with the eGaming industry is that eGaming players as well as audiences are younger in age and growing in numbers.

As the world of sporting, eGames, and the metaverse converge some of the future possibilities include

>> Events organized only for metaverse viewers

>> A hybrid approach to event broadcasts with live, pay per view, and metaverse delivery options

>> The ability for fans to purchase NFTs during metaverse events

>> Tournaments between fans or at local and regional levels

All these generate a lot of revenue, not to mention new fan acquisition opportunities for organizers. Organizations such as the World Wrestling Entertainment (WWE), Ultimate Fighting Championship (UFC), and other professional sports are likely to tap into the metaverse in the future by taking these highly popular brands into a virtual medium.

Industry analysts have predicted the metaverse sports industry could be worth $8 trillion in the next few years alone. Moreover, with a tech-savvy and young audience base, the growth of the sports industry could be heavily impacted through the metaverse. On the other hand, the eGaming industry is valued at over $180 billion and growing.

Making money

eGaming and sports organizers typically monetize their events in the following ways:

>> Live event tickets

>> Collectibles, such as limited edition collections

>> Swag, including T-shirts, decoration, and other items

>> Exclusives, such as VIP events and appearances

>> Sponsorships

>> Media rights (with specific media given the rights to broadcast)

>> Streaming (subscribers watching the event online)

On the Internet, subscription models to view exclusive sporting events is already available. Sports such as UFC have long been known to have a pay-per-view model, because it draws a vast audience. eGaming, on the other hand, has remained mostly virtual, but live in-person eGaming events are now more popular than ever.

For more information on global rankings on different eSports leagues, Players, Teams and Tournaments, check out the Electronic Sports League at `https://pro.eslgaming.com` and the Electronic Gaming Federation at `www.egf.gg`.

New additions to monetization with the metaverse potentially include

>> Pay per view in 3D using ultra-high-resolution graphics

>> Exclusive meet-and-greet events with pro athletes in the metaverse

>> Experiential delivery of events with one-on-one experiences

>> Sales of digital goods including NFTs and collectibles

>> Virtual training academies for fans

>> Live metaverse entertainment

Current use cases for professional sports monetizing the metaverse is primarily through selling NFTs. It's still early in the full development of the metaverse, and it's hard to predict the changes that will happen within professional gaming and sports in the next few years.

Based on trends today and data that is emerging from the industry, professional sports will likely continue to explore monetization by selling virtual passes, special access, exclusives, and NFTs to drive event ticket sales. Examples in this chapter include those of the Australian Open, which raised more than $800,000 in NFT sales in 2022. On the other hand, the entry of big players in eGaming, such as Epic Games, is changing the industry.

Professional players and teams are also likely dig deeper into building communities around their brands.

Creating exclusivity and buzz

Using the metaverse to create buzz for your sporting or gaming event is all about tapping into existing audiences, not only making them feel relevant but also finding ways to further enhance fan engagement. In the metaverse, this means not only being able to capture the attention of attendees, but also getting them involved on pre- and post-game activities, including the following:

>> Continued engagement throughout the year, not just during tournaments

>> Contests and fan competitions such as ranking charts

>> NFT design contents and giveaways

>> Pre- and post-game fan events and activities

>> Exclusivity

Exclusivity through the metaverse within the industry can result from any of the following:

>> Using NFTs to create exclusive content and access to sporting events that are only available to NFT holders. Even NFT holders can be given exclusivity for in-person events rather than just metaverse events.

>> The metaverse is a brand-new medium with an experiential aspect to it. Gaming events accessible through the metaverse can create new experiences for fans as they engage in a medium of connection.

Creating "buzz" is all about making your platform, product, or service known to others. Turn to Chapter 11 for the full scoop on how you can use the metaverse to market your business.

Experiencing Sports in the Metaverse

Digital viewership of sports is gathering momentum as more audiences switch to digital platforms that broadcast them. Every year, billions of people watch some kind of a sporting event. Think about viewing these events in a digital 3D format where viewers can immerse themselves in the viewing environment. The metaverse offers the ability to be part of a virtual universe that has been digitally created and delivers visually engaging experiences. Interacting with other participants worldwide and engaging with performers and fans will be exhilarating. All this from the comfort of your own home.

Using digital money

The metaverse enables you to participate in a sports event by viewing it on a VR headset within a 3D environment. Imagine being able to view a sporting event right from the front line while still being at home. Experiences delivered in the metaverse are going to be ultra high definition and will feel very real. This is partly because of rapidly developing technologies such as the Unreal Engine technology being developed by Epic Games. The metaverse will bring the viewer into the event and perhaps even more closer than they could get in person. Plus, being able to access exclusive content will forever change the way sports are experienced.

TECHNICAL
STUFF

The Unreal Engine technology created by Epic Games is a remarkable breakthrough for games and even film production. The Unreal Engine functions as a real-time 3D creation tool that generates extremely complex environments based on programmed algorithms. Unreal Engine can take a complex scene and create high-resolution, detailed imagery, including the right type of shadows, textures, and other elements that add definition to a scene. This was never possible before. Its applications are also being utilized in creating architectural drawings to high accuracy, creating cityscapes to exactly replicate the major cities of the world, generating scenes in Hollywood movies, and more. For more information, visit https://www.unrealengine.com.

Today, cryptocurrency may not be absolutely necessary to participate in a metaverse sporting event, but as sporting events get into creating and selling NFTs to fans, offering exclusive access, it's possible that you'll need to ultimately dip your toes into cryptocurrency.

Generating revenue

During the COVID-19 pandemic, live attendance at events declined, and most in-person sporting events suffered because they couldn't operate. As with the types of events covered in Chapter 16, the metaverse offers new revenue opportunities for organizers of sporting events. New forms of revenue include ticket sales for metaverse events and digital subscription models for membership-based attendance. The ability for viewers to participate remotely from any corner of the world opens new possibilities in sporting event delivery, revenue, and fan experiences.

FUTURECAST

Estimates suggest that by 2024 there will be more than 577 million viewers of eSports worldwide. Not all of these are in the metaverse right now, but this opens up the possibilities for the future of eSports, eGames, and other VR-driven competitive professional industries.

Using NFTs in sports

Major sports teams are exploring NFTs as a way to monetize their professional clubs. Professional players have started creating their NFTs to create new revenue streams. One way the NFL has started to monetize the sport is by selling fans short video clips of players making good jumps during NFL games. These short video clips are then attached to an NFT and sold to fans.

One such offer by the NFL is NFL All Day (`https://nflallday.com`), which is being created in collaboration with the Flow blockchain from Dapper Labs. According to NFL All Day, this is where fans come together to own officially licensed NFL video collections. The NFL will produce possibly millions of short video clips featuring exciting moments from future games. Fans will be able to purchase these video clips and retain the intellectual property rights to the NFTs they own. This information will be recorded in a blockchain ledger that will hold this information in perpetuity. This information is also verifiable publicly. If you decide to sell one of your prized NFT videos, the buyer will be able to verify that you're the owner within seconds. This will help the NFL generate revenue through a new channel and step into the future.

See Chapter 4 for a detailed explanation of how cryptocurrencies and NFTs are used in the metaverse.

Discovering popular sports in the metaverse

The following sections over a view of some major sports categories so you have a sense of how the sporting industry is getting into the metaverse.

Basketball

The National Basketball Association (NBA) is one of the most prestigious professional sports leagues in the world, and it has already started taking the digital world seriously. In early 2022, the NBA announced the launch of its own NFT initiative called NBAxNFT. This new initiative includes creating new NFT collections and engaging with fans in new ways, including online chats, online video, metaverse events, and others.

In 2020, the NBA released NBA Top Shot, as well as the Golden State Warriors responsive NFT collection. The new project aims to leverage new and evolving technologies, including blockchain and the metaverse, to help monetize and popularize professional basketball.

FUTURECAST

The outstanding success of the NBA's NFT launch (with more than $800 million of sales) ended with more than 16 million fans buying NFTs. The NBA also launched a Discord channel; it currently has more than 35,000 members. So, there is reason to anticipate that if the metaverse develops in the direction it's headed right now major sports leagues will continue to experiment with its usage, and future sports viewership through VR may grow fast.

Baseball

Major League Baseball (MLB) has jumped into the metaverse world by releasing an NFT collection (www.mlb.com/news/mlb-nft-partnership-with-candy-digital-to-expand-in-2022). The MLB is now collaborating with creators and a company called Raider, one of the many who helped bring the idea of baseball cards into the digital realm. Baseball cards are highly prized and traded frequently among fans. Some MLB cards are sold for millions of dollars, given their rarity and uniqueness. NFTs can be equally prized and expensive, depending on the supply and exclusivity.

TIP

Some of the popular NFT marketplaces that have hosted baseball NFTs are

>> **Candy:** www.candy.com

>> **OpenSea:** www.opensea.io

As younger viewers and baseball fans gravitate toward the metaverse as a medium for engagement, they'll likely want to view the game in VR and 3D platforms in the metaverse. Imagine viewing future baseball games in the metaverse in crystal-clear clarity and having the ability to be an active participant with other viewers. You could feel part of the experience, similar to the way metaverse concerts have made fans part of the experience. In one metaverse concert, attendees were able to fly virtually with the performer and experience something better than they would have in an actual in-person event. Something similar could happen in sports in the metaverse, too.

Hockey

The National Hockey League (NHL) has started looking into the metaverse as a possibility for the future. Matthew Tkachuk, who created and minted the first NFT in 2021, was the first professional player to do so within the hockey league. More players followed his lead, including Auston Matthews, Wayne Gretzky, and others. NFTs are definitely finding their way into the NHL. Future possibilities could include the NHL creating NFT's similar to the NBA and using it as a tool to generate more revenues. This also opens up doors for more fan engagement and bringing events to the metaverse.

In fact, in June 2022, the NHL officially stepped into the metaverse during a finals Game 6 between the Tampa Bay Lightning and the New York Rangers. The game incorporated metaverse technology from Beyond Sports, rendering players in 3D. Through existing NHL data, players were rendered as block-shaped cartoons, mirroring the activities on ice, and could be viewed on VR and regular computer screens. Imagine getting kids into the NHL by showing players as cartoon characters or watching the NHL games with your family and replacing players' faces with your own!

TIP

You can watch a video clip of what the avatar-based play looked like at https://youtu.be/9eiQLFUTqRw. Visit https://www.nhl.com/news/nhl-nhlpa-announce-nft-partnership-with-sweet/c-334699756 for more information.

NASCAR

NASCAR partnered with the technology sector to bring an NFT collection to its fans in 2022. Other collaborations within the NASCAR ecosystem include the collaboration between Candy Digital and the Race Team Alliance, which features 12 NASCAR teams. The collaboration created NASCAR NFTs that were freely available to ticket holders.

NASCAR is looking to attract younger audiences, most of whom may be kids of NASCAR fans. NASCAR's strategy in stepping into the metaverse has been to provide free NFTs to younger fans to get them into the fold.

In other collaborations, NASCAR has tested the grounds for advertising in digital media and metaverse activities. NASCAR is featured in a digital horseracing game, Zed Run, and horses within the race, are branded with NASCAR team logos. Check out the races at https://zed.run/racing/events.

Visit the NASCAR website (www.nascar.com) for more information and news releases.

MotoGP

Pro motorcyclist Valentino Rossi is one of the most popular MotoGP personalities of all time. Rossi is working with a partner to create a new metaverse presence for his team, VR46. The objective of the platform is for fans to interact with the digital avatar of the MotoGP legend. Rossi wants to take MotoGP to the younger generation by creating a global platform dedicated to learning more about the sport and creating an academy where fans can meet officials.

Technology brings access to events that audiences can't attend in person. Imagine being able to attend any concert or sports event without being there. As events struggle to drive new participants and fans, engaging with them digitally and bringing the event to them on a medium they're comfortable with seems like a great option.

Visit Valentino Rossi's metaverse at `www.vr46metaverse.com`.

The Olympics

The Olympics are one of the world's most popular sports events. The Tokyo Olympics in 2020 drew more than 3 billion worldwide viewers. More than 200 countries participate in the Olympics, on average, making it a globally viewed event. Olympic event organizers have used the metaverse to enhance audience experience for the sporting event, and the potential exists to build further on these experiences.

The 2022 Beijing Olympics Games, for example, created its own NFT game as part of the launch strategy. Released for iOS and Android devices and based on the Olympic Games, participants are rewarded with NFTs as they progress to different stages of the game.

Opportunities to create more engagement in the future can include NFT drops, providing event coverage in VR, and partnering with digital platforms to help attendees be part of the games and be immersed in the metaverse.

Imagine being able to virtually swim with Olympic athletes and win exclusive opportunities to join your favorite countries in highly personalized experiences in the metaverse.

Read more about the Olympics initiative to create NFTs for the official pins at `https://olympics.com/ioc/news/officially-licensed-olympic-nft-pins-announced`.

Golf

In 2022, the Professional Golf Association (PGA) submitted its initial applications to the U.S. Patent and Trademark Office to officially be part of the metaverse.

The PGA intends to use the metaverse to create NFTs, sell digital collectibles, and expand its reach to golf fans worldwide. The PGA is a lucrative professional sport with a healthy sponsor ecosystem and a history and reputation that spans decades. Technology is already a part of professional sports such as golf, where analytics and visualization platforms are used to track players, shots, ball movement, and end rankings. By embedding player equipment and golf courses with digital sensors, generating even more insightful data that can be used in the metaverse is easy.

Based on the developments in other professional sports, it wouldn't be surprising to see a professional golf tournament broadcast in real time in the metaverse and fan engagement taken to a new level. With specialized hardware and software suited to the metaverse, fans may even be able to engage in the act of walking with their favorite golf players between holes. One-on-one fan interactions, exclusivity, and the ability to monetize multiple aspects of the sport are some of the possibilities.

In 2022, professional golfing also saw the establishment of a new golf league, LIV, which has attracted many professional golfers to it due to its high payouts and big sponsorship deals.

The next few years will dictate which pro golfing league will leverage the metaverse to grow more extensive engagement and fans.

Tennis

In 2022, the Australian Open partnered with Decentraland to launch a series of initiatives dedicated to the tournament. Attendees could view exclusive content and get behind-the-scenes footage from 300 cameras around the venue. With more than 400 matches in the tournament, digital technology was also used to track data from each ball and use it to create match highlights. A total of 6,776 Australian Open Art Ball NFTs were created in partnership with local and international artists. Each digital ball also corresponded to a section of a virtual tennis court.

The Art Ball collection, which sold out within minutes of a public drop, was sold for around $875. Subsequent activities include resale of some of the NFTs for a charitable auction.

In this year's tournament, some new technologies that connect human senses with technology were also tested. One of these was audio technology that captured sounds from sensors placed across the venue and converted them into 3D sounds.

Visit the Australian Open website for more in-depth coverage on what the event in 2022 entailed https://ausopen.com.

Football (American)

The National Football League (NFL) kicked off NFL Tycoon, the league's metaverse experience on the Roblox platform. Within NFL Tycoon, released in February 2022, fans can now get a taste of team ownership and build custom stadiums end team rosters for two competing teams, all within the metaverse.

The objective of NFL Tycoon is to test the waters of the metaverse by educating fans on the game and provide a platform for social engagement. NFL Tycoon also gave fans the ability to purchase limited-edition NFL New Era draft virtual caps within the game. There were a total of 33 caps representing the NFL, including a complimentary league-branded cap that was unlocked within the game.

To access the NFL Tycoon app, you need to visit the Roblox platform, which means creating your account on Roblox. Head to Chapter 2 to read more about the Roblox platform.

The NFL previously collaborated with Epic Games on Fortnite in 2018, and NFL Avatar NFT skins representing 32 teams were released. In 2022, the NFL collaborated with Meta to provide Avatar T-shirts featuring Super Bowl LVI.

Soccer

Spanish Football League team La Liga teamed up with Decentraland to digitize its engagement to bring experiences to fans in the metaverse. With this, La Liga will bring fans worldwide together in a new virtual world on Decentraland. A major objective of La Liga is to bring younger audiences together with those who are already connected on digital platforms, including new fans and existing fans.

Other Spanish teams have also experimented with the metaverse, including FC Barcelona, which launched Barca Studios to develop its metaverse activities. The club has already seen significant investments in its platform. Finally, another Spanish football club, FC Real Madrid, has filed trademarks for intellectual property (IP) registration.

TIP

Visit the Decentraland platform (https://decentraland.org) to find La Laga and other cool virtual spaces that are emerging daily.

Gaming and the Metaverse

The eGaming industry, essentially professional video gaming, is projected to grow to a $470 billion industry by 2030. The industry today comprises all the video-gaming industries such as video game consoles, PC games, mobile, and online streaming games.

eSports is the professional side of the eGaming industry. Competitors from various leagues compete against each other in sold-out gaming arenas with prize money worth millions up for grabs. These competitive games include electronic games such as Fortnite, Call of Duty, NFL Madden, Counterstrike, and others that are played by millions of gamers worldwide.

Games such as Fortnite paved the way for the metaverse in a way where gaming has become a primary reason for the growth of the metaverse. Developments within the gaming industry are headed toward more immersive experiences for players who are already participating in these games online.

Fortnite's parent company, Epic Games, is now planning to release a Fortnite-specific metaverse where participants can experience a higher-resolution live gaming experience.

Enhancing the gaming experience

Here are the main benefits that the metaverse provides to eGaming players:

» Play-to-earn helps gamers win virtual gaming money that can be converted to real-world money

» You can collaborate and play with your friends in the metaverse.

» Interoperability will help gamers jump from one game to another and retain their star status, points, or virtual assets.

» You can be part of sporting leagues and compete with players worldwide.

» Use NFTs to drive fan engagement by launching your own NFT or collaborating with others.

» Drive sponsors to your brand.

Finding games in the metaverse

The best way to get started with eGaming is to check out which games are making a splash. Here are some popular eGames and where to find them in the metaverse:

>> **Counter Strike** (`https://blog.counter-strike.net`): Counter Strike Global Offensive has more than 1.3 billion players worldwide and has awarded more than $96.5 million in award money.

>> **Fortnite** (`www.epicgames.com/fortnite`): Fortnite has between 2.4 billion and 4 billion active users and has awarded more than $89 million in award money.

>> **League of Legends** (`www.leagueoflegends.com`): League of Legends has 11.5 billion active users and has awarded more than $75 million in award money.

>> **Dota 2** (`www.dota2.com`): Dota 2 has almost 8 billion active players and has awarded more than $225 million in award money.

>> **Overwatch** (`https://overwatch.blizzard.com`): Overwatch has more than 7 billion users worldwide and has awarded more than $21 million in award money.

FUTURECAST

Monopoly is the world's most widely played game. More than 1 billion people are estimated to have played the game since its inception in 1935. The digitization of games such as these is now on the horizon with technologies such as the metaverse. Imagine participating an immersive version of Monopoly while playing with your friends and family in other cities or countries.

Getting involved in metaverse gaming

If you want to get involved in metaverse eGaming, here are the pathways you can try:

>> **Players:** As a player of any major eGame, you'll find opportunities to be part of the respective metaverse as and when these gaming platforms connect to a metaverse platform or build one of their own.

>> **Provider:** As a game service provider or a company that specializes in building or enhancing gaming platforms, get in touch with gaming companies to see what their road map is. If you're a creative firm that wants to build or develop gaming assets for the metaverse, your best bet is to start speaking with game manufacturers. There is ample opportunity for services providers in various areas including

- **NFT designers:** Helping gamify content by providing the digital goods that will be exchanged or purchased, NFT-based art crosses many different realms. NFTs can be art, a skill within a game, an audio file, a video, and more.

- **Graphic artists:** As 3D and VR graphics come into play and with newer technologies such as Unreal Engine, graphics artists will need to take an active part in designing these worlds. This means learning new platforms and digital creator tools.

- **Console developers:** Hardware consoles are a key part of a gamers' interaction. Console developers will need to come up with new designs that can provide more control to players and higher dexterity within game play and beyond.

- **Specialty hardware manufacturers:** Body suits, haptic gloves, and other devices have begun appearing on the market. Other specialty hardware that needs to make a commercial debut could be anything that provides a better experience. This is a hot area for development.

Anticipating a metaverse future for gaming

As both sports and eGames move into the metaverse, multiple changes are expected ahead. From fast-growing technologies such as Fortnite's Unreal Engine technology to high adoption of gaming platforms by younger generations, it is forecasted that by 2023 there will be 3 billion active gamers across the world.

FUTURECAST

Here are some changes I anticipate for the future of eGaming in the metaverse:

>> **Integration of NFTs in eGames:** Games will offer NFT rewards and the ability to purchase NFTs.

>> **Integration of game-streaming services with metaverse platforms:** Some major gaming platforms operate their own metaverse platforms. The future may offer the ability of avatars to go from one game to another seamlessly.

>> **VR-based delivery rather than 2D displays:** A native delivery on VR would mean broadcast equipment and technologies would be optimized for 3D/VR-based display.

>> **Growth of regional markets, such as China, Japan, South Korea, Germany, and others:** Gaming is fast catching up globally.

TOP FIVE GAMING COUNTRIES

Based on current data, here is some future guidance for anyone who is interested in the future of the gaming industry. Whether you're a gamer, a manufacturer, or a gaming company, the industry is rapidly growing across the world. Some of the biggest gaming countries are as follows:

Country	Number of Players
China	685 million
United States	191 million
Japan	75 million
South Korea	33 million
Germany	46 million

In terms of metaverse growth, China and the United States are the two of the biggest regions. With the gaming industry developing in parallel in both these regions, it's expected that the growth of the metaverse will also follow eGaming growth within the metaverse for these regions.

5

The Part of Tens

Put the metaverse to work for your business.

See how popular brands and other businesses apply the metaverse.

Chapter **18**

Ten Ways the Metaverse Can Help Businesses

T hroughout this book, I cover the main ways the metaverse is being used by businesses and individuals. In some chapters, I look ahead to applications of metaverse technology that are being considered and may become common in the future. This chapter describes ten ways organizations can benefit right from the start by incorporating the metaverse into how they conduct (or plan to conduct) business. The chapter is most useful for organizations, businesses, and entrepreneurs big and small, but it offers something of interest for individuals as well.

Gaining First-Mover Advantage

Sometimes success in business is all about being the first one to market. In the business world, *first-mover advantage* is the advantage that a company gains when it's the first to do something. A great example of this is the development and launch of the Apple iPod. In the last two decades, the iPod established Apple as a market leader and exponentially grew Apple's revenue. That subsequently catapulted Apple into the development of the iPhone and beyond.

The metaverse is a great vehicle for gaining first-mover advantage and establishing your business as a leader within a space. Whether you're an accounting firm, a bank, or a government, establishing yourself as the first one in the metaverse could give you a high level of visibility in front of your existing and future customers, paving the way for you to be an industry trailblazer.

Enriching Customer Experience

The success of any business rests with customer connections to the product or service. You may be able to use virtual reality (VR) or augmented reality (AR) to create enhanced customer engagement, especially by leveraging the metaverse as a channel to support product sales. (Turn to Chapters 10 and 11 to find out more about using the metaverse as a business promotion tool.)

As most businesses currently operate, customers encounter the business website, read the copy, perhaps watch a video on the landing page, and interact with a sales rep or chat bot. If all goes well, they sign up, subscribe, or place an order.

Imagine, instead, a customer's experience in which they can learn about your products through do-it-yourself demonstrations or communicate directly with the product support team by interacting with a hologram. Through AR in the metaverse, the customer's experience and interactions become real in the virtual world. Lastly, the metaverse can also function as a channel for customer support and servicing customers and clients post-sale. This could be to connect them with the product owner community or a self-help resource that could provide support. These deepened customer experiences can convert your visitors into customers and your customers into lifelong brand advocates, providing a valuable return on investment (ROI) for your efforts in the metaverse.

Contributing to Successful Product Rollouts

A successful product rollout in the physical world is a race to generate interest, build a customer base, define the brand, and achieve quick sales. A successful rollout in the virtual world needs to be immersive.

From Nike to Coca-Cola and leading fashion brands, innovative companies have started using the metaverse to drive product launch engagement. Did you hear about a beer company launching a metaverse beer with zero beer in it? Yes, it's real. European beer maker Heineken recently took to the metaverse and released what it calls Virtual Heineken Silver (see Figure 18-1).

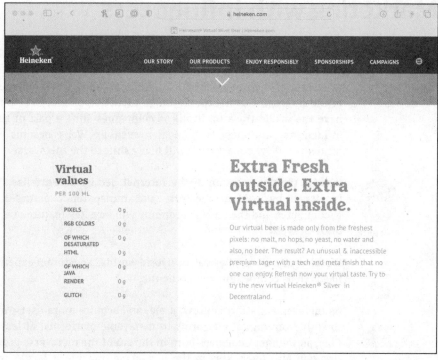

FIGURE 18-1:
Heineken's website describing the new Virtual Heineken Silver.

Source: www.heineken.com/global/en/our-products/virtual-silver

Of course, with a great marketing campaign behind it, the metaverse beer is a good way to get users talking about it and get public relations coverage.

Collecting Data

Presently, data mining in the metaverse is still in its infancy. Although there is some indication that the data-mining tools of today will quickly become obsolete, harnessing data in the metaverse is likely to grow as the data is likely to provide valuable data insight. Data collected in the metaverse will be acquired through multiple modes — for example, user hardware usage data (such as controller movements, eye movements, and head movements) as well as user behavior from within games (to identify user browsing patterns and habits). These data points are key in refining experiences offered to users.

Marketing with Influencers

The rules of marketing are changing regardless of the use of the metaverse. The shift in marketing is led by consumers. Enter *influencers,* those crafty individuals who serve as their own "product placement meets the infomercial" sales channel of the Internet. Cosmetics, clothing, kitchen appliances . . . influencers seem to have the inside track on it all. As companies shift a part of their messaging to influencers, and new technologies such as Web3 become more prominent, influencer-driven marketing will likely shift to the metaverse.

REMEMBER

Web3 is the next version of the Internet, led by decentralized systems. Content is owned by content creators, and transparency across multiple areas of e-commerce and the creator economy will be a key feature of applications developed on Web3.

Whether in virtual, physical, or hybrid worlds, a customer experience with a brand needs to be compelling and authentic.

As metaverse platforms grow, scale, and acquire more users, marketing is likely to shift from digital platforms to metaverse platforms, at least to some extent. Plus, as younger audiences born in the era of the metaverse grow up, their attention will also likely stay in the metaverse, making it fertile ground for product marketing.

TIP

Brands can start small by experimenting with initiatives and engagement and expand their efforts as needs grow. For more on marketing in the metaverse, check out Chapter 11.

Processing Payments and Finance

An important interface with sales transactions in the virtual world is the metaverse as a platform for payment. It will be nearly impossible for companies to successfully launch a product or expect a sale after an immersive experience without a platform to accept payments. With crypto wallets being used as a transaction element for trade and commerce in the metaverse, regulations within markets may end up creating financial stability in the metaverse. Financial stability means less volatility and higher trust, which may push more brands to process higher volumes of e-commerce transactions in the metaverse.

Consider when credit cards were launched back in the day or even when e-commerce was just starting. Transaction volumes were low, and platforms such as PayPal and Zelle emerged as third parties that provided a key integrator feature to facilitate transactions between buyers and sellers. Today online and credit card payments have reached new heights as the industry overall has advanced, instant payments have become common, and more complex technologies such as blockchain are being used in the financial industry.

A similar trend may follow in the metaverse as tokens and crypto payments standardize and get regulated. We may also see full-blown operations of banking-sector operators, such as financial companies, banks, and credit unions, who may opt to choose the metaverse as a medium for customer acquisition and more. (For more about money in the metaverse, check out Chapter 4.)

Testing Hardware

Internet of Things (IoT) products include VR headsets, wearables, and haptic devices that add a new layer of experience to your overall metaverse experience. However, more innovation is needed and new testing grounds are required. As new hardware devices that interface with the metaverse evolve, so will new testing needs and product launch opportunities.

Imagine hardware products being launched exclusively in the metaverse. You can use the metaverse as a testing ground for product launches, whether hardware or software, and test the launch with a unique demographic of clients.

In Chapter 2, I describe a bit how digital twins are used in manufacturing. Digital twin applications are on the rise as different industries create new frontiers. From digital twins of factories to complex nuclear plants, the ability to test systems digitally without putting actual operations at risk is a great time-saver and accelerator. Take the use case of installing a new technology or process in your operations. Being able to see the impact of this on a simulated digital twin is ideal if you want to make any changes or if the response would be disastrous. From a safety pin to a satellite, everything can have a digital twin.

Growing a New Customer Base

In some ways, today, the metaverse is at a similar stage where the Internet was in the early 1990s. There is definitely data gathering and customer data acquisition in place already; however, as with the early Internet, sales channels and growing a customer base are a long way from being fully developed. Future developments in the metaverse will include more focus on native metaverse channels that are used for customer acquisition.

In the future, growing a customer base in the metaverse will be a highly targeted activity where service companies will specialize in metaverse lead generation and customer acquisition.

For brands that want to explore new markets, test new products, or reach out to an entirely new customer base, the metaverse can provide a global base of users, all on a single platform. Think about the metaverse as a tool to build narratives, connect people, build communities and groups, and create think tanks and focus groups.

Increasing Brand Awareness

Throughout this book, I mention dozens of companies that are active in the metaverse, including fashion brands such as Balenciaga, Gucci, Nike, Vans, and many others. More than any other sector, retail brands have taken a good step into the metaverse and continue to do so. Most of these examples share a unique aspect of their participation in the metaverse. Whether these companies create new sales through the metaverse or use it to elevate their brand value, one thing is clear: The metaverse can be used to garner the attention and interest of not just the users in the metaverse, but also people who are just curious about who's innovating and breaking new barriers in the metaverse. As a tool for public relations and to generate new insights about how your brand is being perceived, the metaverse is a new and unique channel.

FUTURECAST

Metaverse platforms present an opportunity to explore the potential of your brand and expand its reach to customers. Perhaps the metaverse will ultimately replace traditional public relations channels. The metaverse may even enable new channels. We'll see what happens as platforms evolve.

Encouraging Employee Engagement

You can make the metaverse a tool for employee engagement. With remote work settings and many organizations changing their work policies, many employers are expected to offer flexible work schedules and relaxed work environments. Additionally, many employees joining the workforce today are likely to be confident with emerging tech, including the metaverse.

Using the metaverse as a tool for employee engagement, bringing employees together virtually, holding employee engagement contests, and providing a space on which they can connect with each other is a great way to start. Some future-focused organizations have already started using the metaverse as a tool for collaboration. One example of this is KPMG, a global consulting giant with operations worldwide. KPMG has jumped into the metaverse and intends to use it as a platform for employee collaboration. KPMG has invested $30 million to enable a collaboration hub and facilitate its employees learning more about the metaverse. Similar efforts are being launched by larger tech companies.

Chapter **19**

Ten Use Cases in the Metaverse

This book is filled with examples of companies creating some form of value in the metaverse. Be it for entertainment or engagement, I offer dozens of examples throughout the book. This chapter summarizes the top-ten use cases that stand out for me and those that I feel are working on something significantly big, value-creating, and growth-focused. These individual examples can also be taken as the best-in-class examples in their industries or sectors.

This chapter shows a variety of use cases — some from hardware, some from gaming, and others from fashion and other industries. The metaverse is a mixed play, meaning many forms of technology will come together to make it a success. The convergence of hardware, software, and physical and nonphysical assets will add individual capabilities to the metaverse and provide users with experiences in personal as well as professional settings.

Microsoft

In the last decade, Microsoft has risen to be one of the most successful technology companies in the world. With its Microsoft Mesh technology, Microsoft has the potential to carve a niche in the metaverse space. Mesh employs *holoportation*, a 3D capture technology that aids in the reconstruction and transmission of high-quality 3D models of people in real-time, and generates customized avatars of users to assist them in establishing a virtual presence on any device.

The company's goal with this service is to make a major virtual reality (VR) statement that will compete with other communication platforms. However, in contrast with traditional videoconferencing systems, Microsoft Mesh enables face-to-face collaboration and shared holographic experiences for parties who are physically separated.

Currently only available in a limited form and only for HoloLens, it has the potential of being adapted by other VR headset manufacturers. This could get big in the metaverse and ease the transition between the metaverse and, say, enterprise communication.

Meta

Arguably, no company is more associated with the metaverse than Meta, which owns Oculus. In fact, Facebook's name change to Meta demonstrates its massive commitment to the metaverse.

Oculus has been a game-changing and highly successful entry into the world of VR. Oculus VR headgear for navigating the metaverse is a system that offers a wide range of reality immersive experiences, such as working out, gaming, and meditating, as well as seeing concerts and traveling the world.

The main competitive market advantage this headgear has over others is that it leads the market as one of the most accessible VR headsets currently available due to its stand-alone functionality, which means it doesn't require a computer. Plus, there are no barriers to enjoying the revolutionary VR world that Oculus provides. This explains why millions of these headsets have been sold.

Oculus is highly interesting because it lowered the bar for access to the metaverse and VR and, with its access to Horizon Worlds, it could be one of the biggest metaverse platforms for years to come.

Gucci

In the world of fashion, Gucci Garden, a virtual garden space on Roblox, is effectively tapping into the metaverse to bring fashion and art closer to millions of people who have become empowered to express themselves in new virtual territories. This is significant for the brand because it marks its entry into the metaverse and builds on the brand's quest to combine the past and the present with telling future stories.

Millions of Gucci fans all over the world can immerse themselves in the rich history of Gucci by traversing through the Gucci shop and shopping with customized avatars.

The Gucci Garden experience is divided into themed rooms, where visitors can immerse themselves in the VR of Alessandro Michele's creative vision, diverse inspirations, and inclusive and audacious philosophy — not to mention share the tour's unique and unrepeatable experience with friends and loved ones.

Surrounded by pink walls enclosing scenery, with an archway through the wall for maximum exploration, each visitor will, according to Roblox, "emerge . . . as one-of-a-kind creations, reflecting the idea of individuals as one among many, yet wholly unique" at the end of the virtual exploration. Other retail and fashion brands are likely to follow Gucci's trailblazing efforts in the metaverse.

Hyundai

Hyundai's Metamobility envisions an interactive and partly virtual future in which a variety of robotic devices interact with humans to provide a wide range of mobility services. The future of these large-scale mobility services is based on automated individual transportation, as well as remote control of robots in "smart" factories.

The underlying philosophy behind this emerging future is to build a bridge between the physical world and new digital realities, leading to a world where space, time, and distance will all become irrelevant. Using robots as physical avatars allow users to complete tasks almost as if they were in the robot's place.

Hyundai has also acquired robot maker Boston Dynamics to accelerate the development of this future in which ordinary people will use robots as physical avatars to move freely between virtual and physical worlds. The COVID-19 pandemic has continued to impede the rapid emergence of this envisioned future, but it's real and dependable. This could get big in the industrial metaverse category.

Walt Disney

The metaverse is set to bring a whole new different experience to the world of entertainment, and Disney is at the forefront of this change. Although the anticipated VR experience in this space has yet to take shape, Disney has already begun making moves to actualize the future in which the physical and virtual worlds are inextricably linked, allowing for limitless storytelling.

As a means of propelling this future, the company has already begun to sell a collection of Disney Golden Moments nonfungible tokens (NFTs) in collaboration with VeVe, as well as purchased a patent for the technology to create a theme park for its users in this virtual space. With the realization of the Disney metaverse, users can expect experiences that combine park, movie, and book experiences. With a massive collection of intellectual property collected over its history, Disney is sitting on a treasure trove of content that can be transformed into metaverse experiences.

Nike

Nike is one of the first major brands to expand into the metaverse, establishing itself as one of the early movers with a strong chance of having its ecosystem triumph.

The sportswear company debuted Nikeland on Roblox in November 2021. Nikeland is a virtual world based on the company's headquarters. On Roblox, it's an open space where anyone can freely outfit their avatar with special Nike products. Roblox, the platform that houses Nikeland, currently allows visitors to play "Tag," "Dodgeball," and "The Floor Is Lava," as well as design mini-games from interactive sports materials.

Visitors to Nikeland can transfer offline movement to online play using accelerometers on their devices, allowing them to experience real-life movement in the digital space. According to Nike, the philosophy underlying this historic move — a creation of a bespoke world with the backdrop of its world headquarters and inside Roblox's immersive 3D space — is to build on its goal of turning sport and play into a lifestyle.

In another development, Nike acquired RTFKT, a start-up that creates one-of-a-kind virtual sneakers and digital artifacts using NFTs, blockchain authentication, and augmented reality (AR), after filing seven trademark applications to help create and sell virtual sneakers and apparel. Nike has been pioneering on the metaverse front and is a great example of a future-focused company.

Epic

Epic's plans to stake a claim in the metaverse are in the works. To that end, the company is heavily investing in growing the popularity of its metaverse platform, Fortnite, as well as developing the Unreal Engine, which provides tools and technologies for creating Fortnite experiences. It hopes to leverage its capabilities in computer graphics, 3D visualization, AR, and VR, all of which are at the heart of the metaverse, as well as its massive user base to test new experiences and develop an appealing metaverse offering.

Although this vision is not yet a reality, the company is taking steps to make the envisioned future a reality sooner. Epic strategically acquired Twinmotion, Cubic Motion, and Hyprsense to strengthen the Unreal Engine, and it acquired Super-Awesome to create safe digital engagement for children under the age of 16.

Plus, through its collaboration with and funding from Sony and the LEGO Group, the company has not only created a future that is already here but has also given itself a significant competitive advantage in this space, expanding into diverse age groups and incorporating a variety of experiences on its metaverse.

Epic is a company to watch due to its track record creating extremely powerful technologies.

Adidas

Adidas has expanded its reach into the metaverse through partnerships with Coinbase and The Sandbox Game. Adidas owns a large plot of land in the metaverse that it intends to fill with exclusive content and experiences. It has also released 30,000 NFTs, the majority of which were reserved for qualified buyers and are now all sold out.

This massive collection of NFTs was created in collaboration with some of the most reputable NFTs personalities, including PUNKS Comic creators, the Bored Ape Yacht Club, and GMoney. As a result, they're genuine and authentic, offering customers a combination of virtual wearables on online platforms and matching physical clothing.

The Sandbox, a blockchain-based gaming world, as well as other platforms, provides platforms for buyers to enjoy these digital items, while physical clothing includes hoodies, tracksuits, and GMoney's signature orange beanie. A purchase of an NFT results in the acquisition of a type of digital deed or proof of ownership that can be bought or sold in the metaverse for buyers and is currently available for resale on OpenSea.

Adidas Originals, the brand's lifestyle label, provides a platform for the launch of Into the Metaverse.

Shopify

With an uncertain future for e-commerce in the emerging metaverse, Shopify envisions a future in which, if people want to engage with them, whether in the physical or digital worlds, they'll be there, ready for them. Simply put, Shopify wants to be future ready. To that end, Shopify is investigating how to combine the digital and physical, employing NFTs to generate buzz around physical products and reward loyal customers. The e-commerce company has already opened an NFT marketplace where customers can buy digital assets in an accessible, open space.

Plus, through its partnership with Poplar Studio, this e-commerce platform now allows its online merchants to launch 3D and AR versions of its products directly on their websites, providing online retailers with experiences that are typically only available in brick-and-mortar stores, allowing customers to better visualize their potential purchases.

Sotheby's

The interaction between high-end art and digital art continues to explode in the art world. Sotheby's is now applying its knowledge and curation to the expanding world of art for the digitally native generation. Bidders can find Sotheby's in Decentraland using a generated personal profile and a unique avatar, navigate through the gallery seeing all necessary information about the available art, and if interested, make bids for and purchase art. Payments are accepted in a variety of cryptocurrencies and fiat currencies (traditional cash).

As of this writing, Sotheby's has sold over $70 million in digital art/NFTs through its proprietary, custom NFT marketplace.

Index

Symbols and Numerics

elementary school education, 205–206

emergency medicine, 210–211

employees

  collaboration between, 176

  encouraging employee engagement, 259

  recruiting talent, 188–189

  team engagement, 191

  training, 149–150, 183–188

  trying out job before accepting, 174–175

  virtual hiring events, 189–190

  virtual job fairs, 190–191

end-user license agreements (EULAs), 49

Engage VR app, 218

enhanced services, providing

  government and municipal services, 147

  overview, 146

Enjin Wallet, 60

enterprise-level businesses, 142

entertainment

  concerts, 23, 120–121, 156, 226, 232–233, 242

  Decentraland, 27

  expert talks, 233

  Horizon Worlds, 23

  master classes, 233

  metaverse studio sessions, 233

  monetizing content, 117–122

  MTV Music Awards, 123

  overview, 113–114

  The Sandbox, 29

  streaming content, 114–117

  think tank events, 233

  thought-leader events, 233

Epic

  EPIC Unreal Engine, 36

  Fortnite, 73, 121, 248, 249

  overview, 265

Epic Games, 36–37, 76, 121

eSports. *See* sports

ethereum gas (ETH gas), 55–57

EULAs (end-user license agreements), 49

events. *See also* global events industry

  monetizing, 229–232

  organizing, 228–229

exclusivity

  gaming, 239

  global events industry, 231–232

exertainment, 216–217

experiential gaming. *See* gaming

experiential learning, 207

F

faith-based metaverse worlds, 227

family doctor visits, 210

field of view, VR headsets, 86

field trips, as teaching tool, 196

financial data. *See also* cryptocurrency

  financial services in metaverse, 148

  securing, 44–46

firefighter training, 196–197

firewall protection, 62

first-mover advantage, 253–254

fitness industry, 11. *See also* health care industry

  brand reinvention, 217

  exertainment, 216–217

  "fitutainment," 216

  hardware, 219–220

  home-based health, 217

  Horizon Worlds, 23

  inclusivity, 217

  martial arts, 218

  nutrition, 217

  overview, 215–216

  personal coaching, 219

  pilates, 217

  seniors, 218–219

  sustainability, 217

  VR headsets and, 85

  wearables, 216

  yoga, 217

  Zumba, 217

"fitutainment," 216

FitXR app, 217

football (American), 246

forever Live mode, 32

Fortnite, 73, 121, 248, 249

Free Guy (movie), 71

Freewallet, 59

fungible tokens, 52–53

G

game controllers
  degree of movement, 99–100
  Meta Quest Touch Pro Controllers, 101
  overview, 98–100
  PlayStation Move, 100–101
  Samsung Gear VR Controller, 100
  SteelSeries Stratus Duo, 101
  tracking system, 99
  Vive Controller, 101
  VR headsets and, 87
gamification, 132
gaming
  attracting younger fans, 237
  augmented reality, 71
  blockchain technology, 74
  chairs, 107
  computers, 97, 106
  console developers, 249
  cryptocurrencies, 75
  developing, 71–72
  Discord, 70
  enhancing experience, 247
  Epic Games, 76
  exclusivity, 239
  finding games, 248
  Fortnite, 73, 121, 248, 249
  future of, 249
  game controllers, 98–101
  game-building, 77–79
  games as teaching tool, 196
  graphic artists, 249
  haptic feedback, 72
  haptic feedback accessories, 108–111
  headsets, 98, 101–105
  Horizon Worlds, 23, 73
  increasing engagement, 236
  IoT, 72, 75
  Meta, 76
  Microsoft, 76
  monetizing, 238–239
  motion simulators, 107–108
  NFT designers, 249
  Niantic, 76
  nonfungible tokens, 75

NVIDIA, 76
  overview, 69–70
  players, 248
  providers, 248
  reaching broader audiences, 236–237
  Roblox, 73, 76
  role of gaming industry in development
    of Metaverse, 8
  The Sandbox, 73
  Second Life, 71–73
  smartphones, 97
  specialty hardware, 249
  Star Atlas, 73
  tools needed for, 74
  top gaming countries, 250
  virtual reality, 71
gaming consoles
  console developers, 249
  overview, 97–98
gardening, 131
Genesis Plaza, Decentraland, 25
GITEX, 227
global events industry
  concerts, 232–233
  creating memorable experiences,
    226–227
  entertainment, 232–233
  expanding in-person events, 227
  faith-based metaverse worlds, 227
  increasing attendance, 226
  monetizing events, 229–232
  organizing events, 228–229
  overview, 225–226
golf, 245
Google Cardboard headset, 92
Google's Starline project, 176
gorilla arm syndrome, 47
government services, 147
Grande, Ariana, 121
graphic artists, 249
graphics processing unit (GPU),
  97, 106
graphics technology, 8
group learning, 200
Gucci Garden, 263
Guetta, David, 121

H

haptic feedback
  accessories, 108–111
  defined, 38, 72, 106
hardware
  computers, 97, 106
  fitness industry, 219–220
  game consoles, 97–98, 249
  game controllers, 98–101
  gaming chairs, 107
  haptic feedback accessories, 108–111
  headsets, 82, 98, 101–105
  motion simulators, 107–108
  securing, 43
  smartphones, 97
  specialty hardware, 249
  testing, 257
Hatch Kids, 203
headsets. *See also* VR headsets
  AR headsets, 104–105
  interpupillary distance, 201
  MR headsets, 105
  Oculus Quest headset, 175
  overview, 101–102
head-up displays (HUDs), 104
health care industry
  3D training, 222
  acupuncture, 212–213
  chiropractic medicine, 211–212
  dentist visits, 211
  digital twins, 221–222
  emergency medicine, 210–211
  family doctor visits, 210
  high entry cost, 223
  interoperability, 223
  mental health services, 212
  osteopathic therapy, 211–212
  pharmacies, 220–221
  physiotherapy, 211–212
  privacy, 222–223
  PTSD treatment, 222
  space travel health care, 222
  surgery, 213–215
  trauma training, 222

Health Insurance Portability and Accountability Act (HIPAA), 223
Heineken, 255
Hero Maker Studios, 79, 114
high school education, 206
hiring employees
  recruiting talent, 188–189
  virtual hiring events, 189–190
  virtual job fairs, 190–191
hobbies and personal interests. *See also* gaming; VR headsets
  baking, 131
  book clubs, 131
  coin collecting, 131
  connecting with other hobbyists, 129–130, 133–135
  enhancing with metaverse, 125–126
  entertainment, 113–122
  expanding knowledge, 129
  finding in metaverse, 12, 127–128
  gamifying, 132
  gardening, 131
  hobby clubs, 130, 134–135
  monetizing, 133
  painting, 131
  poetry writing, 131
  pottery, 131
  professional networking, 132
  singing, 131
  solo hobbies, 131–132
  stamp collecting, 131
hockey, 243
HOLOFIT app, 217
HoloLens 2 headset, 90
HoloLens headset, 81, 85, 170, 175, 185
holoportation, 262
home-based health, 217
Horizon Worlds, 14, 73, 79
  entertainment, 23
  for gaming, 23
  health and fitness, 23
  live entertainment, 121
  overview, 22
  as social network, 23
hot wallets, 45
HP Reverb G2 headset, 89–90
HR (human resources) professionals, 178–179

HUDs (head-up displays), 104
Hulu, 115
human resources (HR) professionals, 178–179
hyper-modal haptics, 109
Hyundai, 263

I

Illuvium, 14
ILO (initial land offering), Somnium Space, 32
imagination, VR headsets and, 83
immersive learning, 207
immersive storytelling and role-playing, 196
immersive virtual reality (IVR), 83
IMUs (inertial measurement units), Teslasuit, 109
industry in the metaverse. *See also* education and learning; gaming
  fitness, 215–220
  global events industry, 225–233
  health care, 210–215, 220–223
  sports, 240–246
inertial measurement units (IMUs), Teslasuit, 109
influencers, 120, 256
in-game apps, 154
initial land offering (ILO), Somnium Space, 32
inside-out tracking, VR headsets, 87
instructor led employee training, 185
interactive employee training, 184
interactive workshops, 185
Internet
  firewall protection, 42
  guest Wi-Fi access, 43
  password security, 42–43
  router security, 42
  securing, 42–43
  Web 2.0, 115
  Web 3.0, 115, 256
Internet of Things (IoT) devices, 72, 75, 257
interoperability, health care industry, 223
IVR (immersive virtual reality), 83

J

Jeelani, Owase, 215
job interviews, 189
job roles

design, 180
HR professionals, 178–179
marketing, 180
metaverse as management tool, 180–181
operations teams, 179
sales professionals, 179

K

Kalt, Daniel, 182
Kanial, Kiana, 52, 57
KARA Smart Fitness Mirror, 220
kindergarten, 205
KOR-FX gaming vest, 110
KPMG, 140, 146, 191, 259

L

L&D (learning and development) industry, 186–188, 207
La Liga team, 246
land parcels
  Bloktopia, 35
  Decentraland, 25–26
  podcasting and, 122
  Somnium Space, 32
Laurence, Tiana, 54
LCD (liquid-crystal display) panels, 86
League of Legends, 248
learning and development (L&D) industry, 186–188, 207
learning environment
  designing, 198–199
  group learning, 200
  learning design team, 198
  Masterclass, 197
learning management systems, 202
Ledger crypto wallet, 59
Lenovo ThinkReality A3 Smart Glasses, 90–91
liquid-crystal display (LCD) panels, 86
Liteboxer VR app, 217
live events, 120–121, 156, 215, 217
lunch and learn training, 185

M

Magic Leap 1 headset, 91
Major League Baseball (MLB), 242

About the Author

Futurist Ian Khan is a global authority on the metaverse, Web 3.0, blockchain, and emerging technologies. He is a globally recognized emerging technology educator and an instructor of metaverse-related courses on LinkedIn Learning (www.linkedin.com/learning/instructors/ian-khan). Ian is also a contributor to McGraw-Hill, *Forbes, Entrepreneur* magazine, Business.com, and other highly recognized media outlets. CNN, Bloomberg, Fast Company, Fox, ABC News, and multiple global media regularly feature him as a guest.

Ian speaks across industries including banking, manufacturing, professional services, retail, health care, transportation, and others, on topics including the metaverse, the future of work, blockchain, Bitcoin and other cryptocurrencies, artificial intelligence, and future readiness. He is also the creator of the Future Readiness Score, helping organizations become disruptive-proof through a data-point-based measurable approach to future readiness.

Dedication

To Sabeen, my wife, for constantly supporting me in my craziest ideas. To my children, Eliyaan and Aira, for being the light of my eyes and inspiring me to be the best I can ever be.

Author's Acknowledgments

To God, who made us all as one and gave us the capacity to do incredible things.

To my parents, who always stood by me and supported me in every way they could. Thank you for an incredible upbringing and an amazing childhood.

To my family, who bring the best out of me.

Publisher's Acknowledgments

Executive Editor: Steven Hayes
Development Editor: Elizabeth Kuball
Copy Editor: Elizabeth Kuball
Technical Editor: Kyle Allison

Production Editor: Saikarthick Kumarasamy
Cover Image: © Sergey Nivens/Shutterstock
Special Help: Colleen Diamond